TO

DR. JAMES BURNES, F.R.S.

KNIGHT OF THE ROYAL HANOVERIAN GUELPHIC ORDER,

THIS NARRATIVE

Is Inscribed,

WITH EVERY SENTIMENT OF ESTEEM AND REGARD,

BY HIS AFFECTIONATE FRIEND,

THE AUTHOR.

The Wild Sports of Southern Africa: Being the Narrative of an Expedition from the Cape of Good Hope, Through the Territories of the Chief Moselekatse, to the Tropic of Capricon

Sir William Cornwallis Harris

WILD SPORTS

OF

SOUTHERN AFRICA.

THE

WILD SPORTS

OF

SOUTHERN AFRICA;

BEING THE

Narrative of an Expedition

FROM

THE CAPE OF GOOD HOPE,

THROUGH THE TERRITORIES OF THE CHIEF MOSELEKATSE,

TO THE

TROPIC OF CAPRICORN,

BY

CAPTAIN WILLIAM CORNWALLIS HARRIS,

Of the H.E.I. Company's Engineers on the Bombay Establishment.

LONDON:

JOHN MURRAY, ALBEMARLE STREET.

MDCCCXXXIX.

" Afar in the Desert I love to ride,
With the silent Bush-boy alone by my side :
Away—away from the dwellings of men,
By the Antelope's haunt, and the Buffalo's glen :
By valleys remote, where the Ourebi plays ;
Where the Gnoo, the Sassayby, and Hartebeest graze ;
And the Eland and Gemsbok unhunted recline :
By the skirts of grey forests o'erhung with wild vine ;
Where the Elephant browses at peace in his wood ;
And the River-horse gambols unscared in the flood ;
And the mighty Rhinoceros wallows at will,
In the pool where the Wild Ass is drinking his fill ;
Where the Zebra wantonly tosses his mane,
As he scours with his troop o'er the desolate plain ;
And the stately Koodoo exultingly bounds,
Undisturbed by the bay of the hunter's hounds ;
Where the timorous Quagga's wild whistling neigh,
Is heard by the fountain at fall of day ;
And the fleet-footed Ostrich over the waste
Speeds like a horseman who travels in haste ;
Hieing away to the home of her rest,
Where she and her mate have scooped their nest,
Far hid from the pitiless plunderer's view,
In the pathless wilds of the parched Karroo.''

PRINGLE.

CONTENTS.

CONTENTS.

List of Plates.

PROPOSAL

FROM

CAPTAIN W. C. HARRIS,

TO THE

Geographical Society of Bombay.

————————

Belgaum, August 1st, 1838.

SIR,—I do myself the honour of requesting that you will lay before the Geographical Society of Bombay the accompanying Narrative of my recent expedition into the interior of Southern Africa; I have already had the pleasure of directing a copy of it to be forwarded to the Royal Geographical Society of London.

My journey from the Cape Colony through the territories of the chief Moselekatse to the Tropic in 29° east longitude, and my subsequent return across the head of the Vaal River by an unexplored route, through the scene of that prince's hostilities against the emigrant farmers, to the colony, being distinctly

traced on my map, a copy of which you are aware
I had also the honour of forwarding to the Secretary
of the Royal Geographical Society from Cape Town
in October last, it would be a needless trespass on
the Bombay Society's time were I here to enlarge
on the subject; I shall therefore simply state that
the map includes a section of Southern Africa,
hitherto either imperfectly described or entirely unknown, and was compiled during my expedition
from personal observation, and from authentic information afforded by missionaries and intelligent
traders, upon whose accuracy I could rely.

I beg, however, particularly to solicit the attention of the Society, to the fact of my having penetrated to a spot which was described as being not
more than six weeks' or two months' journey from
that great Inland Lake, the actual existence of
which, between the Equator and the Tropic of
Capricorn, was first satisfactorily established by Dr.
Smith's expedition in 1835—and that every circumstance conspiring to favour the successful con-
tinuation of my journey, I was only deterred from
making the attempt to reach that remarkable point

in the desert, towards which geographical attention has been so long directed, by the fear of exceeding the limits of my furlough from India.

For reasons of his own, which will readily be
understood from a perusal of my narrative, it will
be seen that Moselekatse was particularly anxious
that I should proceed to the northward, instead of
returning by the Vaal River; and to that end volunteered me every assistance. My oxen were in the
finest condition, and the recent heavy rains having
filled the pools in the desert upon which my supply
of water must entirely have depended, it was with
no common feelings of disappointment and regret
that I found myself compelled to retrace my steps
at a moment when a prize of such value was apparently within my grasp.

Feeling an irresistible desire to extend my acquaintance with Africa, and still further to assist
in filling up the chasm which is yet to be supplied
in her geography, and having already, upon my
private means, without any previous experience in
African travelling, and at a most unfavourable conjuncture, safely accomplished a long and perilous

journey among savage tribes, I now venture to make, through the Bombay Society, an offer of my services to the Royal Geographical Society; and being fully confident that unrestricted by time, with a due regard to the seasons, aided by the knowledge I have already acquired, I should experience little difficulty in penetratiug to the Lake in question, I beg to volunteer to make the attempt, and earnestly to solicit the support and recommendation of the Society here, to which I have the honour to belong, in favour of the object which I have in view. Coming from the Royal Geographical Society, there can, I think, be but little doubt that an application for my services for such a purpose would be met by the Honourable the Court of Directors with their accustomed and well-known liberality as a public body, and with a spirit not likely to prove injurious to my personal interests.

In conclusion, allow me to say that I am ready to proceed upon this expedition at any time that permission shall be obtained, but as it is highly advisable, if not indispensable, that a second officer should be of the party, and as there would obviously be little or no prospect of immediately finding at the Cape one combining the inclination and necessary qualifications, I beg to submit that in the event of my offer being favourably received, the Society should recommend permission for a similar purpose to be granted to Lieut. George Fulljames, of this Establishment—an officer every way qualified for the undertaking, equally zealous and enthusiastic in the cause with myself—who has volunteered, and is ready to accompany me.

I have the honour to be,

Sir,

Your most obedient Servant,

(Signed) W. C. HARRIS,

Captain Engineers.

To *Dr. James Burnes, K.H., F.R.S.,*

&c. &c.

INTRODUCTION.

FROM my boyhood upwards, I have been taxed by the facetious with *shooting madness,* and truly a most delightful mania I have ever found it. My first essay in practical gunnery was made at the early age of six, by the discharge of an enormous blunderbuss, known to the inmates of my paternal mansion by the familiar soubriquet of " *Betsey.*" A flock of sparrows perched upon the corner of a neighbour's pigstye, were the only sufferers; but information was maliciously laid against me, and I underwent severe corporal chastisement. About a year afterwards I took ample revenge upon my ill-natured neighbour, by *pinking* his ducks and geese with a cross-bow of my own construction; but my catapult was unfortunately discovered, seized, and confiscated. I next clubbed my Christmas capital with that of two sporting confederates, and raised a sufficient joint stock to purchase a condemned musket, with which, during the holiday vacation, we shot, and *tyed*. But the partnership proving unsatisfactory, it was soon dissolved by mutual consent, and I found myself sole and undisputed *Master of the Ordnance*. From this eventful and dignified epoch in my life, I date my rapid improvement in the noble science of projectiles.

After this sketch of my puerile biography, it is scarcely necessary to inform the reader that I was considered by my partial friends to be fitting food for shot and powder. Accordingly I was entered at the Military College, where my worthy superiors having pronounced me competent for a commission in the Engineers, I found myself at the early age of sixteen, an officer of that distinguished Corps in Western India; one of the not least valued of my distinctions being the possession of a rifle, before the deadly grooves of which a kite had but little chance at one hundred and fifty yards. Armed with this weapon, I had ample opportunities of indulging in my favourite pursuits, and may safely affirm, that during many years I enjoyed ball-practice in perfection.

But whilst silently stealing on the recent tracks of the "antlered monarch of the waste," or perseveringly stalking a stately buck—whilst urging my elephant to his utmost speed in pursuit of a retreating tiger, or contemplating with delight the grizzly figure of a prostrate lion—how frequently did my thoughts wander to the wilds of Africa, the tales of sport connected with which had ofttimes reached my ears, and how impatiently did I long to make the acquaintance of her motley group of four-footed denizens. As a boy, well do I remember copying and re-copying Bewick's eccentric figure of the gnoo, when I could barely hold a pencil; and often in my dreams, did I see, now at the extremity of a long vista of years, that intervened betwixt me and my furlough, the slender and swan-like neck of the stately giraffe, bowing distantly to our better acquaintance; Behemoth, with his square and mirth-exciting snout protruded from the yellow waters of a vast river, acting the part of master of the ceremonies; whilst a host of rhinoceroses, supported by gigantic elephants, eccentrically horned antelopes, and other fascinating strangers, awaited their turn of presentation with evident impatience.

With such strong impressions, it will easily be believed that I scarcely regretted the sentence of a Bombay Medical Board, transporting me for two years to the Cape of Good Hope; and as this was accompanied with a welcome recommendation to travel, I made preparations, before quitting India, to penetrate into the interior of Africa. It would be injustice to myself, however, to leave an impression that sport was my only object—for both from education and taste, I possessed an ardent desire to contribute my mite to the Geography and Natural History of the countries I was about to explore.

At the period of my arrival at the Cape of Good Hope, public attention was much excited by an event which has probably no parallel in our Colonial history. I allude to the emigration of a large body of Dutch farmers, who voluntarily forsook the British protection and territory, to effect an establishment in the wilderness, where it was believed—as indeed the result fully proved—they would encounter the severest hardship; and it was no small additional spur to my spirit of enterprise, that I might trace the steps of these wanderers, and, without mingling in politics, investigate, on the spot, the origin of so remarkable an expatriation. The map that accompanies this volume, for the outlines of which I am indebted to Arrowsmith's Atlas, published in 1834, is principally illustrative of the history of this singular event. Many interesting geographical chasms, however, have also been filled up, and numerous additions made, either from personal observations, or from materials obligingly furnished by missionaries and intelligent traders, upon whose correctness I could rely. Nothing has been inserted upon vague report; and although it will be remarked that my inconvenient mode of travelling would not admit of my making a strictly scientific survey, I trust that I have been enabled to embody information of interest and importance, in a manner sufficiently accurate to answer the object in view.

My passion for *venerie* had long afforded me opportunities of discovering that the delineations given in popular books of Natural History, of many of the larger quadrupeds, were far from being correct; and I had, during my service in India, devoted a portion of my leisure to making more accurate portraits of them with appropriate scenery. A wide field for the gratification of this taste lay before me in Africa, of which I did not fail to avail myself, nor do I despair of being enabled shortly to lay before the public, the result of my labours in this department.

These pages were originally written for the perusal of some of my brother officers in India, with whom I have oft stalked the forest, and scoured the plain; and it is to them chiefly that I still present them, trusting that in the scenes depicted and described, they will recognize their friend and brother huntsman, and participate with him in the emotions which the overpowering excitement of African wild sports naturally produced in his breast. I knew them to be persons equally attached to the pleasures of the chase with myself, but generally unacquainted with African story, which will account for the occasional introduction of information derived from works already published. My journal having, however, casually fallen into the hands of others, not sportsmen, whose opinions I respect; and to whom it afforded gratification, I have ventured to submit it to the public, being assured that my habits of life, and occupation in the details of military duty, will afford a ready excuse for the imperfections it contains, more particularly when I add that it has passed through the press without my personal corrections, and at a distance of some hundred miles from the cantonment in which I am quartered.

W. C. HARRIS.

Be'gaum, 15th July, 1838.

POSTSCRIPT.

AUGUST 1st, 1838.—Recent files of the Graham's Town Journal, which have been received in India since the following pages were printed, contain a tragic sequel to the History of the Border Colonists. It appears that in February last, an advanced party of the emigrants, led by Retief, having negociated a formal treaty with Dingaan, had been suffered to pass unmolested through the territories of that chieftain, to Port Natal, in the neighbourhood of which they had proposed 'to establish themselves. Being lulled into perfect security by the friendly reception they had experienced, many families imprudently detached themselves from the main body, and were actively engaged in the division of the land; when, on the fifth day after their separation, they were treacherously attacked by the crafty savage, and man, woman and child, indiscriminately butchered. It is confidently reported that Retief, together with two hundred and seventy souls, had thus miserably perished; and the intelligence of the dreadful catastrophe having been conveyed to Maritz, he was exerting himself to obtain reinforcements from among the emigrants who were still on the Reit and Modder rivers, with the design of taking summary vengeance on the despot, and succouring the remnant of Retief's unfortunate party; but so great had been the panic created, that his endeavours had hitherto proved unsuccessful; and the escape of the survivors from their hampered position among hostile tribes, and natural barriers, being next to impossible, as a glance at the map will show, it is too probable that accounts will shortly be received of still further massacres.

In the mean time, our Colonial authorities were using their utmost exertions to check further emigration, as will appear from the following extract of a proclamation by the Governor, dated Cape Town, the 26th April last :—" His Excellency earnestly exhorts the Civil Commissioners, and all

Public Functionaries throughout the Colony, as well as all ministers of religion, and other persons of sound views, who cannot but foresee the inevitable result of the prevailing mania of emigration, to endeavour by every means in their power, to dissuade intending emigrants from the prosecution of plans which cannot fail, sooner or later, to involve themselves, and their families who are prepared to accompany them, in certain and irretrievable ruin."

W. C. H.

EXPEDITION

INTO

SOUTHERN AFRICA.

CHAPTER I.

VOYAGE FROM INDIA TO THE CAPE OF GOOD HOPE, AND THENCE TO ALGOA BAY.

On the 16th March, 1836, I sailed from Bombay in a large Indiaman, advertised to be a fast sailer, fitted up expressly for passengers. Amongst many others who, like myself, had been attracted by this inviting announcement to enter upon a voyage to the Cape of Good Hope, was William Richardson, Esq. of the Bombay Civil Service, a gentleman whose acquaintance I had never before had the pleasure of cultivating, but who had long been known to me by repute as a devoted sportsman. To him I communicated my intention of penetrating as far into the interior of Africa as my limited leave would permit, and he immediately agreed to accompany me, embarking from that moment heart, hand, and purse, in the plan I had projected. The usual duration of the voyage is six weeks, but in our case it was protracted to eleven, nor did we reach Simon's Bay until the 31st May.

B

The first glimpse of the shores of Africa awakened
in my bosom the strongest emotions. I already saw
realized those fairy dreams which had haunted my
imagination, and felt within my grasp the substance
of those shadows which had long strewed my path.
On arriving at Cape Town, I was so fortunate as to
meet with Dr. Andrew Smith, the well-known ta-
lented leader of the scientific expedition which had
just returned from the interior, who afforded me information of the highest value, and gave me accounts
of what I should see in the way of sport, which determined me to lose no time in taking the field. A
few days sufficed to complete our arrangements and
purchases. The former were confined to obtaining
passports, visiting the children of missionaries whom
we expected to meet, and engaging a servant, whose
name will frequently appear, in lieu of a Mahomedan
whom I had brought from India, and who, having
already seen enough of the Cape of Good Hope, preferred returning to eat his curry with true believers,
to undergoing contamination amongst accursed Kafirs or infidels. Our purchases comprised every
article that we fancied could be of service to us in
a country where few of the necessaries and none of
the luxuries of life can be obtained, in which no cir-
culating medium exists, and where even mercantile
transactions are conducted exclusively by barter.
Beads, buttons, brass wire, common trinkets, cheap
gewgaws, and ornaments of the baser metals, formed
no inconsiderable items of our expenditure, not forgetting an abundant supply of snuff and tobacco. I

had brought with me from India pots, kettles, and camp furniture, together with my tent, and an ample stock of gunpowder ; and a Parsee servant, named Nesserwanjee Motabhoy, who had accompanied my friend Richardson, declared his determination of following our fortunes.

By Dr. Smith's kind advice, we ordered from a tailor in Cape Town, as a present, amongst others, to the redoubted Chief Moselekatse, called by some *Umsiligas,* whom we proposed to visit, a great coat, in itself so perfectly unique that I may be excused for describing it. Of dimensions suited to the figure of a portly gentleman, pointed out by the Doctor, as resembling the Chief, it was composed of drab *duffel,* a coarse shaggy cloth commonly worn by the colonists, surmounted by six capes, and provided with huge bone buttons, and a ponderous brazen clasp in the shape of a crest, the whole being lined and fancifully trimmed with scarlet shalloon in a manner calculated to captivate the taste, and propitiate the esteem, of the most despotic and capricious of savages.

With this curious investment we embarked on the 2nd July in a small schooner bound for Algoa Bay, one of our fellow-passengers from India accompanying us to the pier, unable to persuade himself, until the boat had fairly pushed off, that we really intended to venture upon a second voyage in such a craft so immediately after the troubles we had undergone. In addition to a mate, a cook, and a Mozambique negro, dignified with the appellation of steward, our crew consisted of three men and a boy; our fellow-passengers being two adventurers, who occupied the berth opposite to our own in the only cabin, and a tailor, with his wife and nine daughters, some marriageable, others at the breast. This unfortunate family, every member of which was sea-sick during the whole voyage, located themselves in the steerage, an apartment about eight feet square, ventilated only by the hatchway. The passage up the coast at that season seldom occupies more than three days, but the fates decreeing that our progress should still be opposed, adverse winds had taken the place of the north-wester, which had been blowing without intermission during the preceding six weeks, and which, had it but continued a day longer, would have wafted us to our destination.

The little vessel was usually gunwale under. Stormy seas breaking over her, obliged the tailor to seal up his family hermetically; heavy lurches during the night ejected us from our narrow precincts, and more than once brought my companion, who slept in a shelf above me, and myself, into awkward and violent collision; whilst the rolling during the day repeatedly swept the table, and deposited the viands in our laps. Being the whole time within sight of land, no observations were taken, and on the afternoon of the eighth day we entered St. Francis' Bay, in mistake for that of Algoa, not discovering our error until we were about to let go the anchor. The opinions on the subject were various and conflicting. The tailor, who had

made the voyage before, courageously ascended the
mast-head, in spite of the remonstrances of his love-
sick spouse, to make an attempt at recognition; and
regaining the deck gravely asserted that we were in
Plettemberg's Bay, nearly two degrees to the westward.   Doubts being entertained of the soundness
of his opinion we were consulted.   The chart was
produced, and being satisfied that we were close to
Cape Recif, a dangerous reef of rocks, we advised
the ship to be hove to; but sail having been again
made during the night we contrived to weather the
point, and having narrowly escaped foundering on
the Bird Islands floundered by good fortune into
the harbour of Port Elizabeth.

CHAPTER II.

JOURNEY FROM PORT ELIZABETH TO GRAHAM'S TOWN.

ALGOA Bay is exceedingly open and exposed, and the anchorage very insecure. During high winds ships not unfrequently go on shore, a tremendous surf often rendering it dangerous, and at times even impossible, for boats to land. We were fortunate in being able to prevail on the Port Captain to take us ashore in his barge, a favour which our uncouth habiliments rendered him somewhat cautious in vouchsafing. The town of Port Elizabeth, though rapidly increasing, does not consist of above one hundred and fifty houses. It is built along the sea shore on the least eligible site that could have been selected. The soil in the neighbourhood is a sandy loam, producing fine crops of wheat and barley without irrigation, its contiguity to the sea affording sufficient moisture.

We tarried a week at Mrs. Scorey's fashionable hotel, and were actively engaged in an attempt to purchase horses, which we understood were to be obtained in the adjoining districts in considerable numbers, and of an excellent quality. It was with inconceivable difficulty, however, that we at length succeeded in procuring two miserable quadrupeds, that appeared to have scarcely sufficient stamina to carry us to Graham's Town. The recent Kafir war having trebled the price of every thing, and of live stock in particular, the demands upon us were exorbitant. With the assistance of Colonel Tripp, the Commanding Officer at Algoa, from whom we experienced great kindness and hospitality, we also became the proprietors of a comfortable travelling waggon, seventeen feet in length, and a span or team of twelve tough little *Faderland* oxen. The former owner, an honest Yorkshireman, named Matthews, whom I specially recommend to all persons requiring a similar conveyance, was with difficulty induced to part with it, and after twelve months' experience of its comforts, we had no hesitation in pronouncing it to be a cheap and valuable purchase.

With this vehicle, driven by a drunken Hottentot, we took the road to Graham's Town under convoy of Joe Butler, a merry Irishman, of whom we had hired a second waggon for the conveyance of our wares. The activity and skill displayed by Joe in the guidance of his straggling team of oxen, and the unerring dexterity with which he wielded his long and formidable whip, did not fail to excite in us the same astonishment that has been expressed by every traveller in South Africa. Richard, my new valet, voluntarily assumed the office of cook, conceiving himself also, in virtue of the experience he had acquired during a trip to Litakoo, a few years before, with a party of Indian gentlemen, specially charged with our safety. On this occasion, however, he had strangely forgotten to lay in supplies for the road, and we fared badly in consequence.

I do not profess to write a *journal*, and may therefore spare my reader the annoyance of perusing on every page those uninteresting details connected with the interior economy of a *cafila*, which are doubtless too often the cause of a volume being thrown aside in disgust. Once for all let me state that we usually rose with the dawn, breakfasted at nine or ten, or as soon as water could be obtained, and after halting an hour for that meal, continued our pilgrimage until a favourable spot presented itself for the nocturnal bivouack. Whilst the cattle were turned out to graze for a couple of hours, joyous fires sent forth their cheering influence in various parts of our gipsy camp; and when supplies were to be had, sundry cooks were presently discharging the important functions of their office. Pots, kettles, and gridirons, were in universal demand, and after washing down a meal comprising nothing beyond plain baked, fried, or boiled, with libations of tea or coffee—the *second edition* of which became the acknowledged perquisite of the followers—every one betook himself to sleep as best he might, either in, below, or about the waggons; the scramble for places usually involving a severe hustling and kicking match, if it did not end, as was too frequently the case, in a battle-royal.

In the course of the journey few other incidents occurred worth mentioning. With the assistance

of Butler's team, making in all twenty-four oxen,
we ascended the Zwartcop mountain by a steep and
difficult acclivity during the first night, and encamped near an extensive grove of aloe-trees in full
blossom.   Thence, a rugged and circuitous track of
about one hundred miles in length constituted the
road, the scenery comprising a mixture of barren,
unprofitable valleys, and stony, uninteresting hills,
varied occasionally by deserted farms, where depo-
pulation had stayed the hand of the husbandman,
and the blackened walls of roofless cottages which
had been sacked by the Kafirs during their late
irruption.

Throughout this miserable country, which had
been described to us as abounding with game of
every description, our diligent researches were once
repaid by a glimpse, on the distant horizon, of
three ostriches, and about a score of spring-bucks.
This event occurred at a place called Quagga's Flat,
where we halted a day, and were treated with hospitality by three English settlers, brothers named
Pullen.   Occasionally, too, the light and graceful
rhee-buck was to be seen bounding over the hill-
tops, or up their sides; stopping at intervals, stamping with his slight fore-foot, and sending down the
breeze his not-to-be-mistaken whistle, as he gazed
at the waggons winding beneath him.   Besides
gin-shops, there are two inns on the road; the first
at Sunday River, the second at Bushman's Hill;
but at neither of these could we procure bread or
forage, and the country not producing a single blade

of grass, our cattle daily presented more finished
specimens of anatomy. Old Pollard, the loquacious
landlord of the last-mentioned inn, endeavoured by
his wit to supply the want of cheer, gravely assuring
us that had we employed him we might have obtained horses, waggons, and oxen, at a tenth of the
price. This worthy Boniface's daughter here joined
our party, proceeding to Graham's Town on a
matrimonial expedition, or, in other words, to be
present, agreeably to colonial custom, when her
marriage banns were proclaimed in church.

Whilst descending a steep hill by night, one of
the oxen contrived to strangle himself—a circumstance only remarkable from the great sensation
produced by the Parsee's steady refusal to partake
of the flesh. We often overheard our followers
afterwards talking of the cow-worshipper, who was
not allowed to eat beef.*   It rained repeatedly and
heavily during our journey, the roads in an instant
becoming so slippery that it was impossible to proceed a single step until the water had run off. At
a place called Assegai Bush, the ground in the
morning was white with hoar frost ; and all the
brooks were frozen over, a sight we had not witnessed for years.   It was piercingly cold, and even
at 7 A.M. the thermometer stood at 34°. When

---

* The well-known objection on the part of the Parsees, or fire-
worshippers of India, to eating beef, is believed to have arisen
from a compact formed with the Hindoos on their first arrival.
A respect for Mahommedan prejudices is understood to influence
them equally against partaking of the unclean beast.

within a few miles of Graham's Town, which we reached on the seventh day, the baggage-waggon was accidentally upset in a deep hole by the road-side, and the upper works completely broken, although little injury occurred to the contents, beyond the destruction of our chairs and crockery.

Graham's Town is situated at the source of the Cowie River, at a distance of six hundred and fifty miles from Cape Town, and thirty from the nearest point of the coast. It is well built, and contains nearly seven hundred houses, with about three thousand inhabitants, principally English. Here we made further purchases, and with difficulty obtained two additional horses, residing four days at Parke's excellent hotel. We also made a valuable friend in the person of Captain Stanford, of the 27th Foot, who introduced us to two intelligent men, David Hume and Robert Scoon, both of whom had performed several journeys into the interior, for the purpose of trading in ivory, and who afforded us much valuable information. Hume provided us with a new driver, a pensioned private of the Cape Rifle Corps, minus a right eye and a fore-finger, proud of his ancestry as a Hottentot, and glorying in the name of Andries Africander. This highly favoured individual had already made no less than five trips with Hume and others into Moselekatze's country, and besides being well acquainted with that Chief, possessed a fair smattering of the English and Sichuana languages. He was, moreover, according to his own account, a crack shot, an intrepid elephant hunter, and a finished waggon-driver; thus professing to combine, beneath a mutilated and unprepossessing exterior, every qualification that could be required in a servant by men in our situation. Had but the virtues of this man kept pace with the accomplishments to which he laid claim, he would indeed have been a valuable acquisition: but unfortunately the result proved that he had not a single redeeming quality that we could discover. A coward, a mutineer, and an inveterate liar, it will be seen that Andries caused more mischief and trouble to us by his pernicious example and rebellious conduct when beyond the reach of the law, than can be well conceived by those who have never had the misfortune to be exposed to the machinations of so dangerous a ruffian.

Wherever we were likely to obtain recruits to join our expedition, we hoisted our standard, in the hope and expectation that numbers would flock around it. But whilst some had married wives, and others had purchased farms, we saw too plainly written in the countenances of all, that they felt convinced of the impossibility of two poor Indian gentlemen, who had been only three weeks in the colony, achieving, alone and unassisted, amongst savage nations in South Africa, a long and perilous journey, which had never been undertaken except by a few persons whose experience of the country might be traced back almost to their cradles, and even by them had been accomplished with great difficulty and hazard.

ANDRIES AFRICANDER, A MULATTO HOTTENTOT.

CHAPTER III.

JOURNEY FROM GRAHAM'S TOWN TO GRAAFF REINET.

FOR the moderate remuneration of one hundred Rix dollars, equal to about seven pounds sterling, Mr. Pollard, junior, the innkeeper's son, volunteered to accompany us with his waggon as far as Somerset, a small town about half way to Graaff Reinet, where his maternal uncle resided; but by dint of attending the market every morning we contrived, on the 26th of the month, to obtain a return vehicle for one-fourth of the sum. When we had proceeded about a mile, one of the lately purchased horses deserted, and I did not succeed in re-capturing him until he had re-entered Graham's Town. After travelling ten miles, our waggon having been carelessly driven by Andries, became entangled in a wiry unyielding bush, and could not be extricated without the assistance of hatchets. John Strydom, the fat good-natured proprietor of the waggon that we had hired, took advantage of this delay to ride back upon a horse that he borrowed from us, in order to recover a cash receipt of some importance, which he fancied he had dropped, and returned about the middle of the night, having completely knocked up the steed. What added to our vexation

was, that he found the missing document in his
waistcoat pocket.   The leader of our team having
stolen a horse during our sojourn at Graham's
Town, had been incarcerated, and our difficulties
had not been a little multiplied by the impossibility
of finding a substitute.   Fortunately, however, in
the course of the second day's journey, a Hottentot,
whom we found sunning himself by the way-side,
consented to enter our service in the vacant situation.

The country was still of the same barren, uninteresting character as that already described, but
generally more level, less abundantly watered, and
more thickly covered with brushwood and succulent
dwarf trees, called by the colonists speck-boom.
We travelled at the rate of thirty miles a day, twice
passing the night without water for the oxen—saw
several small herds of spring-bucks, of which beautiful little antelope I killed three—and arrived late
on the evening of the 29th at the home-sick Strydom's
cottage, on Mynheer de Klerck's farm, where his
doating young *vrouw* received him with overflowing
eyes and open arms.   On the journey we had
picked up a disconsolate wheelwright, whom we
overtook plodding his weary way along the road,
with a green veil over his face, and a saddle, bridle,
and bundle, on his head; his horse having most
unceremoniously abandoned him under cover of the
night, an event by no means uncommon in the
annals of South African travelling, and one to
which our dismounted equestrian was so well accustomed, that he had lost no time in precarious

search, but had set out forthwith in the pedestrian order I have described, well convinced that if his truant horse were not already at home, he would shortly return thither.

John Strydom having messed with us on the road, his good *vrouw* insisted in return on entertaining us at supper. Mynheer de Klerck, and several of the members of his family, visited our host after the repast was over, and were very slow in taking the hint conveyed by his violent yawnings, that he was anxious to retire to rest. We slept in the waggon, as usual, and were amused during the greater part of the night by the drunken merriment and boisterous singing of a lame Irish cobbler, who was " keeping it up" in a roofless mud outhouse, with two Hottentot " boys," neither of whom was under fifty years of age. The cobbler apologized next morning for not inviting us to the wassail, on the score that we were *gentlemen*, adding that not being at the time altogether " compos mentis," he hoped we would excuse his apparent want of politeness.

We halted one day, in order to enjoy the diversion of wild Guinea-fowl shooting on De Klerck's farm, where we found these birds in abundance, lying in coveys amongst the long grass and under-growth. When flushed, they rose whirring like pheasants high above the tops of the trees. On the 31st we continued our journey about five miles, to Somerset, at which we hoped to obtain another waggon; the uxorious John Strydom having been proof against the most tempting bribes offered to induce him to transport our baggage beyond it. The paltry little town of Somerset consists only of about two dozen English houses, and stands in a swamp at the western base of a mountainous range called the Zuur-berg, being completely environed on three sides by the Little Fish River, in attempting to cross which treacherous stream, my horse was suddenly engulphed in a quicksand, and nearly drowned before I could extricate him.

My recollections of Somerset, a place through which I have twice passed, are, I confess, far from pleasing. After I had thrown off my wet garments, we prosecuted our search for a vehicle, and literally visited in succession every house in the village, taking Jackson the Tinman first in order, to whom we had brought a strong letter of introduction from the crippled cobbler, but who, nevertheless, received us with marked contumely, turning us from his door with dirt upon our beards, as our Persian friends in India would say. The proprietors of no less than nine out of the twenty-four mansions, were surnamed Smith, an appellation by no means less common in the Cape Colony than in other parts of the British dominions. But although all the Messrs. Smith had waggons, not one of them could be induced to accede to our request. One of the several John Smiths, a straight-haired methodistical little man, was sitting down to dinner with Mrs. Smith and the children, when we called to pay our respects, and, bowing to the ground, ventured to seat ourselves on a vacant sofa; but though the young Smiths stared abundantly at us, neither the master nor mistress even condescended to look at us, the lady after a time informing us, whilst she shovelled down the pease and gravy with her knife, that she could not think of allowing her poor dear oxen to go another journey so immediately after their return from the country.

In the course of our perambulations through the town, we stumbled upon a waggon discharging a cargo of oranges, which was to return the very next day to within a few miles of Graaff Reinet; yet, strange to say, the bull-headed proprietor, after taking an hour to consider of our offer, preferred returning empty to receiving our freight and fifty Rix dollars. In the end, being utterly discomfited, we had no alternative but to avail ourselves of an offer obligingly made by a Mr. Thomas Butler, to deposit our effects in his warehouse; and having strictly enjoined him to forward them to us by the first opportunity, we crossed the Little Fish River a second time, and, shaking the dust from off our feet, departed from Somerset.

The following morning, according to arrangements previously made, Mr. John Campbell, a kind and obliging friend whom we had met at Graham's Town, and to whom we had been introduced by Colonel Tripp, overtook us, and shared our gipsy breakfast on his way to Graaff Reinet. The road over Bruintjes Hoogte, comprises a succession of formidable acclivities and perilous descents, and we were frequently obliged to lock both hind-wheels at the same time, the path skirting the very brink of yawning chasms several hundred feet in perpendicular depth, over some of which the clumsiness of Andries, more than once, nearly precipitated us.

It was pitch-dark before we had cleared this mountain barrier, and the oxen being greatly in want of water, I groped my way in advance, directed by a light, to the dirty cottage of a neighbouring boor, and with some difficulty obtained unwilling permission from the owner, who gloried in the virtuous appellation of Erasmus, to unyoke on his farm.   Here a trial of temper awaited us, that immeasurably eclipsed all that we had been destined hitherto to experience.   A strong disagreeable wind was blowing, which, added to the impossibility of obtaining on the spot more than barely sufficient fire-wood to boil the water in the kettle, caused every one to retire early to bed ; and the oxen having literally tasted nothing since leaving De Clerck's, were left at liberty to graze upon the farm during the night, instead of being secured, as usual, to the wheels of the waggon.   On our awakening the next morning they were nowhere to be found, and the stony character of the country, in every part clothed with a high thicket of speck-boom, added to the violent wind that had blown during the night, and effaced the trail, rendered utterly fruitless our diligent search for them during the whole day.

A combination of circumstances led us to suspect that Erasmus was concerned in the abstraction of our cattle, with the design of extorting a reward for their restitution. He had been seen lurking about the waggon with some of his associates the preceding evening, and now, far from rendering us any assistance towards their recovery, turned a deaf ear to our application, and studiously absented himself from the house. The sequel proved that our suspicions of his dishonesty were not unfounded. The promise of a reward induced him, on the 3rd August, to return four of the oxen, but as these were insufficient to draw the waggon, we proposed that he should furnish us on hire with a team of his own. To this he at first consented, but altered his mind upon some frivolous pretext, even before the operation of yoking was completed. Our own provisions, on which we entirely depended, were by this time exhausted, and I considered myself fortunate in killing two spring-bucks.

On the third day, the accidental and opportune arrival of a field cornet named Cornelius, a centurion having soldiers under him, gave a favourable turn to our affairs, at the very moment that I had resolved to ride on to Graaff Reinet for magisterial assistance. We stated our case to this worthy individual, who forthwith accompanied us to the nest of thieves amongst whom we had fallen, and having threatened them with legal retribution, sent to our aid two of his own servants, who succeeded on the following day in recovering the twelfth ox, the other seven having been in the mean time cunningly restored by Erasmus, whose finished villany we could not help admiring, however much we had suffered

by it.   Leaving him to the tender mercies of the
field cornet, who prohibited us from paying any
reward, we pursued our journey on the morning of
the 5th.   Before dismissing Erasmus from these
pages, I may add that on our way back through
the colony, about twelve months afterwards, we were
forced by heavy rain, I need scarcely say contrary
to our wishes, again to halt at his farm.   The hand
of fate had fallen heavily upon him and his race;
the house was deserted and its inmates extinct—a
small group of graves before the door being all that
remained, instead of a numerous and well-favoured
family.

As we advanced, the country became more open
and practicable, and was covered with large herds
of elegant spring-bucks, bounding playfully across
the road.   Whilst vainly pursuing some of these
antelopes, a favourite dog belonging to my companion
ruptured a blood-vessel, and died shortly after.   On
the 6th we rode on at noon in advance of the waggon,
but darkness overtaking us, we had great difficulty
in finding our way.   Crossing the Sunday River
three several times, we at length arrived at Graaff
Reinet, having ridden six-and-thirty miles, and thus
completed a total of two hundred miles from Graham's Town.

CHAPTER IV.

GRAAFF REINET—AND FINAL PREPARATIONS FOR OUR JOURNEY INTO THE INTERIOR.

THE picturesque little Dutch village of Graaff Reinet, with its adjoining gardens and fields, is nearly surrounded by the Sunday River, which takes its source in the Sneuwbergen, a lofty range of mountains immediately to the north, and flowing through the districts of Camdeboo and Uitenhage, falls into the sea at Algoa Bay. The village is sheltered on each side by high conical mountains decorated with perpetual verdure, which is derived from the abundance of speck-boom that covers their rocky declivities. The serpentine banks of the river are lined with willows and acacias—many of these latter are overgrown with mistletoe, and both with evergreen creepers, which climbing to the very topmost branches fall gracefully in festoons, adorned with a profusion of fragrant white flowers, not unfrequently concealing the tree upon which they have entwined themselves.

The district of Graaff Reinet was formed in 1786 under the administration of Governor Van-der Graaff, whose name it received with the adjunct of that of his lady. Nothing can exceed the neatness of the quaint little Dutch houses; and whilst the salubrity of the climate has no rival in Southern Africa, the

produce of the gardens and vineyards may vie with
those of Europe.   Fruits and vegetables of all kinds
grow here in abundance and perfection.   I have before said that we entered the village after dark ; on
looking out of the window in the morning, we saw
the street carpeted with snow, while garden hedges
of quince, and a row of lemon-trees on either side,
bending beneath a load of ripe fruit, formed deco-
rations as beautiful in themselves as they were novel
to an Indian eye.

We considered Graaff Reinet to be the starting
point or base of our operations.   Our object now
was to sweep-rapidly over a great extent of country,
in order to reach the most distant point that our
time and the duration of our supplies would permit
us to visit.   This method of proceeding not only
greatly increased the probability of romantic peril,
adventure, and discovery, but also enhanced our
prospect of sport.   We therefore resolved to reach
Kuruman, or New Litakoo, a missionary station of
importance, four hundred miles to the northward,
with all practicable expedition, and to proceed thence
to the country of Moselekatse, king of the Abaka
Zooloos, or Matabili, a powerful and despotic monarch, whose dominions were known to abound
with game, and possessed the additional advantage
of having been little traversed by our countrymen.
Arriving there, time and circumstances would enable
us to form a further programme of our proceedings;
but I determined at all events to extend my researches to the tropic of Capricorn, and even if

possible also to visit the Great Lake, which is reported to exist considerably beyond it in the interior —finally forcing my way back to the colony by the hitherto unexplored route of the Likwa or Vaal River, which, though the most direct, had hitherto, in consequence of Moselekatse's interdiction, remained unexplored by Europeans, and which I intended to survey. I need scarcely say that at this time the result of Dr. Smith's recent inquiries had not been made public, and even while I now write, his work has not reached India.

At the time of our arrival at Graaff Reinet, the rage for emigration beyond the boundary was rapidly spreading, and waggons being consequently at a high premium, we had no little difficulty in obtaining a second one for our journey. This will appear strange to those who know that in the Cape Colony five out of every six tradesmen are wheelwrights or waggon-builders; but Gertz Maritz, the principal waggon-maker at Graaff Reinet, a wealthy and discontented man, who, it will be seen, afterwards took a prominent part in the proceedings of his expatriated countrymen—being about to emigrate, had not only purchased as many as he could obtain, but was also busily engaged in manufacturing for himself.

To our surprise, we found that the various wares we had obtained at Cape Town, and which we had unfortunately been obliged to relinquish at Somerset, could easily have been procured at Graaff Reinet. Unwilling, however, to incur fresh expense, or to be delayed beyond the 1st September, the day we had

fixed for our departure, we despatched a cart to
Somerset with instructions to Mr. Butler to forward
the articles under his charge; and were not a little
mortified to find that during our short absence they
had been devoured, as he asserted, by the rats and
other vermin, and were consequently not forthcoming.
So that in the end we were not only saddled with
the extra charge for the cart, but also obliged to
make further disbursements for a fresh supply.

The agent we employed here was Mr. John Bur-
net Biddulph, a trader who had some years before
visited Sobiqua, king of the Wangkets, and whose
name, in conjunction with that of Mr. Bain, will be
found referred to in Arrowsmith's map of South
Africa. Knowing exactly what we required, he succeeded in obtaining for us from one *Naudé*, a capital
waggon with thirty draught oxen; and we had in
the mean time completed our stud of horses to twelve
of all sorts and sizes, conceiving that these would
suffice, though in this supposition we were greatly
mistaken.

Our waggon, fitted up with water-casks, tar-
buckets, side-chests, beds, pockets, and other ap-
purtenances for the long journey before us, during
which it was to be our only abode, might now not
inaptly be compared to a ship proceeding to sea.
Besides ourselves and our personal conveniences, it
contained, with the addition of a barrel of gunpowder and the commodities for barter already enume-
rated, six sacks of flour, two bags of rice, and two
of sugar, with chests of tea and bales of coffee.

The baggage-waggon carried tent, camp-stools, table, and cooking utensils; hams, tongues, and cheeses in profusion; salt and dried fish, biscuits, wax candles, soap, and oilman's stores, or in other words, sauces and pickles. The luxury of beer, so palatable to an Anglo-Indian, we were compelled to dispense with in consequence of its bulk; but we provided ourselves instead with a few dozens of brandy, and a small barrel of inferior spirits for the use of the followers. Crevices and empty spaces were filled up with spades, pickaxes, hatchets, sickles, and joiner's tools, together with nails, screws, spare bolts, and linchpins; and as if all these were not weight sufficient, no less than eighteen thousand leaden bullets, duly prepared—to say nothing of a large additional supply of that precious metal in pigs, to be converted into instruments of destruction as occasion required—were added to our stock.

At Graaff Reinet we engaged six additional Hottentots under a formal contract of service for six months, executed in presence of the Clerk of the Peace. As these were our only associates for many months, and will occasionally appear in prominent relief, I may be here excused consigning them to print, under the appellations of Piet-van-Roy, a man of mixed breed, Cobus Jacobus, John April, Claas September, Frederick Dangler, and Ethaldur Wildman. Nearly all of these being *tronk volk*, or in other words, discharged criminals, no agreement less binding than the one we had made would have answered our purpose. But

c

scarcely a day had elapsed before we had reason
to regret our part in the contract, for perpetual
drunkenness and debauchery found their way into
our peaceful family, and while our cattle were left
to stray in the fields, their keepers were generally
reposing in a happy state of oblivion by the road-
side. The result was, that two of our oxen died,
and most of the others lost their condition. The
characters of these baboon-faced gentlemen, however, as they became gradually developed to their
masters, will be sufficiently unfolded in the course
of these pages.

Before quitting Graaff Reinet we obtained from
Mr. Ryneveldt, His Majesty's Civil Commissioner,
a further passport, claiming protection for us in the
wards of the different field cornets on our route;
together with introductory letters to Captains Waterboer and Cornelius Kok, two Griqua chieftains
in alliance with the colonial Government. Without
such an official authority, we could not have ventured
to carry across the frontier so large a supply of ammunition, the policy of Government rendering the
transit of gunpowder into the territories of the native
princes altogether contraband.

Our party now amounted in all to eleven. As a
body of men intended to resist a hostile tribe this
number was very insufficient; but with due prudence
and courage, we felt confident of repelling any predatory attack, and with the advantage of fire-arms
of withstanding even a multitude of such opponents
as those by whom we were likely to be assailed.

CHAPTER V.

FROM GRAAFF REINET, BY THE SNOWY MOUN-TAINS, TO THE BORDERS OF THE COLONY.

EVERY preparation for our final departure was completed on the 1st September; but that day, so auspicious to sportsmen in Europe, "looked lowering upon us,"—dawning with a tremendous deluge of rain, which continued until after noon, and afforded the Hottentots more than sufficient leisure to indulge in their vicious propensities. In accordance with advice that we had received, but the futility of which we were not long in discovering, they had each been furnished with a musket, as a defence against the wild beasts and savages; and it will be seen hereafter, that whilst their pusillanimity prevented their turning these weapons to our advantage, they employed them but too successfully in scaring the game from our encampments. On the present occasion our astonishment may be conceived, when on preparing to start in the evening, one-half of the muskets were found to be already in pawn, and the proceeds squandered in the gin-shop. As a consequence, most of the Hottentots themselves were discovered to be in such a brutal state of inebriety, that we were obliged—after various ineffectual attempts to rouse them, on our own part and that of

C 2

their more sober brethren, who banged them without mercy—to transfer them like pigs into the
waggons which they had been hired to drive.

In this comfortable condition we commenced our
march—but had scarcely passed the outskirts of the
village when the rain descended in torrents, and left
us no alternative but to return : in doing which, one
of the less intoxicated Hottentots civilly carried off
the corner of a house, by propelling the heavily
laden vehicle against it. Dreading further mishaps,
and satisfied that no dependence could be placed
upon our followers, if once allowed to recover their
sobriety and liberty, we finally quitted Graaff
Reinet at six P. M. and by ten o'clock had formed
our camp ten miles off.

The morning's dawn did not find the Hottentots
much gratified at their transportation into the desert,
coupled as it was with the prospect of a long and
tedious separation from gin and bitters ; and to add
to their distress, we insisted also that they should
part from their *vrouws*, or wives, before crossing the
Snowy Mountains. As we ascended the acclivitous
road leading over Sir Lowry Cole's pass into that
range, the farewells were abundantly affecting.
John April's interesting spouse in particular, a
negress possessing all the Hottentot peculiarities
fully developed, clung round the neck of her " dear
man" and half smothered him with kisses.

Before we had proceeded many miles, we were
met by a Hottentot riding post to Graaff Reinet for
medical assistance ; his master, a young Dutch

boor, having been fearfully clawed in a clumsy attempt to destroy a leopard. Soon after, a courier overtook our cavalcade, having been hired, at an expense of *four* Rix dollars, to gallop after us to recover a debt of *five*, which, in the hurry of departure, we had neglected to settle—an ominous proof that the good people of Graaff Reinet had little expectation of seeing us again. Our friend Mr. Campbell, together with Mr. Lloyd, His Majesty's Special Justice, and several other gentlemen, joined our party in the evening, and remained with us until the following day.

As we advanced through the elevated region of Sneuwberg Proper, the vegetation became visibly more abundant, and the air sensibly colder. That greatest of all rarities in South Africa, a real turf or sod, was to be seen interspersed with mat rushes. Around, nothing presented itself in the landscape but rocky mountains, of which the summits were enveloped in mist and snow: the unsettled state of the weather heightening in no small degree the sublimity and frowning grandeur of the scene. Peak towering above peak, the lofty and broken mountains appeared to crowd in one upon the other —the Spitscop, a remarkable and pre-eminently lofty crag, soaring above the whole: whilst the rude and bold features of nature were for miles unmingled with any trace of human works, beyond the beaten track that we were following along steep acclivities. But for this, and an occasional wreath of smoke, ascending from the bosom of some sunken valley, no one could have supposed that the abode of man was to be found in a region, apparently so deserted and inhospitable.

A chilly mist overtaking us, we resolved to halt for the night at a kraal* of Fingoes or tame Kafirs, where barely a sufficient quantity of fuel, from a shrub called the rhinoceros bush, could be obtained for culinary purposes. Although still within the Cape Colony, our tobacco proved of use in the purchase of goats' milk; and I may here remark that this precious weed, which may be denominated the current coin of the realm, is carried about in Africa twisted in long thin ropes, which are coiled up in rolls. A roll is considered a splendid oblation to a prince, and an inch a handsome present to a commoner; it is in fact a universal favourite, and, meted out by the span in traffic, will purchase whatever this most benighted of countries can produce, when almost every other commodity is rejected with disdain.

The following day, after passing the residence of Piet Van-der Merwe, yclept Dickwang, or double-chin,—a soubriquet with which a large wen on the throat has saddled him, as a distinction from his neighbours of the same name—we cleared the Sneuwbergen, and arrived at a deserted farm, named

* Notwithstanding that it has been the habit to employ the terms *Kraal, Caross,* and *Assegai,* as respectively indicating a native village or cattlefold, a skin cloak, and a dart or spear—not one of them have any signification in the native languages, but are supposed to be a corruption of Dutch and Hottentot.

Dassies-fontein.   Here we were struck with the sight of an old Kafir smoking dacca, or the narcotic wild hemp, in which the natives greatly delight. Seated at the door of a miserable hovel, a squalid picture of poverty, the decrepit wretch was inhaling the pernicious drug through water from a bullock's horn.   Volumes of smoke were forced into his stomach by draughts of water, and the result was a violent fit of coughing, attended by raving delirium. We actually saw him throw off his slender apparel, and rush forth into the plain like a wild beast or a maniac from Bedlam.

At noon on the 5th the thermometer stood at 32°, the snow falling in quantities during the whole of the day.   We however travelled twenty-five miles, and reached Vogel Valley, where, the following morning, the whole of the brooks were frozen over with ice a quarter of an inch thick, and the manes of the horses, and the herbage around, were decorated with icicles.   The glass at 7 A.M. had sunk to 18°, yet the cold to the feeling was neither intense nor disagreeable.   Here, for the first time, we saw large troops of those eccentric animals the Gnoos,* three of which we killed, having hemmed a herd into a valley, and obliged them to run the gauntlet.

Of all quadrupeds, the gnoo is probably the most awkward and grotesque. Nature doubtless formed him in one of her freaks, and it is scarcely

* *Catoblepas Gnoo.*   Delineation in Captain Harris's African Views. *Vide* Appendix.

possible to contemplate his ungainly figure without laughter. Wheeling and prancing in every direction, his shaggy and bearded head arched between his slender and muscular legs, and his long white tail streaming in the wind, this ever-wary animal has at once a ferocious and ludicrous appearance. Suddenly stopping, showing an imposing front, and tossing his head in mock defiance, his wild red sinister eyes flash fire, and his snort, resembling the roar of a lion, is repeated with energy and effect. Then lashing his sides with his floating tail, he plunges, bounds, kicks up his heels with a fantastic flourish, and in a moment is off at speed, making the dust fly behind him as he sweeps across the plain.

On the 7th we reached Boks-fontein, where, during the night, two of the horses absconded. Having been bred in the neighbouring district, called New Hantam, to the grass of which cattle are much attached, it was surmised that they had strayed thither: and whilst Piet and Andries were despatched in pursuit of them, we continued our journey to the Seven Fountains. Here the face of the country was literally white with spring-bucks,* myriads of which covered the plains, affording us a welcome supply of food. When hunted, these elegant creatures take extraordinary bounds, rising with curved backs high into the air, as if about to take flight: and they invariably clear a road or beaten track in this manner, as if their natural dis-

* *Gazella Euchore.* Delineated in the African Views.

position to regard man as an enemy, induced them to mistrust even the ground upon which he had trod.

The *trek bokken,* as the occasional immigration to the abodes of civilization of countless swarms of these antelopes is called by the colonists, may be reckoned amongst the most extraordinary examples of the fecundity of animal life.   To offer any estimate of their numbers would be impossible: pouring down like locusts from the endless plains of the interior, whence they have been driven by protracted drought, lions have been seen stalking in the middle of their compressed phalanx, and flocks of sheep have not unfrequently been carried away with the torrent.   Cultivated fields which in the evening appeared proud of their promising verdure, are, in the course of a single night, reaped level with the ground, and the despoiled grazier is constrained to seek pasture for his flocks elsewhere, until the bountiful thunder-clouds restore vegetation to the burnt-up country.   Then the unwelcome visitors instinctively retreat to their secluded abodes, to renew their attacks when necessity shall again compel them.

Two of our oxen having become exhausted, we presented them to Frederick Mark Graaff, an itinerant pedagogue and masonic brother, whom we here met, and from whom in return we received a handsome and powerful dog. At Vendussie Kuilen, a waterless station, at which we encamped the next day, Piet returned, not only unsuccessful, but hav-

C 5

ing completely broken down, and so deeply galled
the back of one of the best horses, that he was
utterly useless during the rest of the trip.   Andries
still remained to carry on the search for those that
had strayed.

Three tedious marches through an arid level
country, quite denuded of herbage, and nearly destitute of water, brought us across an extensive tract,
impregnated with salt, to the residence of the frontier Field Commandant, whose domains are situated
on the extreme border of the Colony, and are
bounded by the Nu Gareep (one of the two principal branches of the Great Orange River), where
we encamped to enjoy the luxury of bathing, and
having our linen washed.   This day, three more of
our oxen dropped down on the road, and being
unable, from fatigue and want of sustenance, to
advance another step, we had no alternative but to
leave them a prey to the wild beasts.   A forlorn
traveller, whom we overtook, might have shared the
same fate had we not succoured him, for his horses,
agreeably to colonial usage, had absconded, leaving
him to pursue his journey on foot.   In return for
our opportune hospitality, Mynheer afforded us a
fund of diversion by his uncouth and futile attempts
to convey boiled rice into the cavity of his mouth
through the unwonted agency of a silver fork.

We were at first rather coolly welcomed by the
Field Commandant, to whom we presented the
Government letter.   He received it with great res-
pect, and putting on his spectacles, laboured hard

to decipher its contents ; but after halting at every
word of more than two syllables—taking his leisure
to comprehend the meaning of each sentence—
overrunning the stops, and making a pause to re-
consider them—he consigned it to his wife, who,
although scarcely a better scholar than himself, reported so favourably of its purport, that the worthy
Warden of the Marches at once invited us to join
his evening meal.   In the course of conversation,
we found that Mynheer, although ignorant of all
languages except Dutch, claimed a Scottish extrac-
tion.   His board was graced by many sturdy scions
of his stock, the younger of whom adhered to the
primitive custom of standing behind and attending
on their parents and guests.   Before supper commenced, a slave made a circuit of the room with a
tub filled with water, offering it to us, and to the
members of the family, who each, according to
seniority, washed their feet therein—a custom not
very congenial to our tastes, and with which we declined to comply—considering that the same water
served for all, and that the operation was followed
by a general appropriation of the table-cloth instead
of a towel.   After a long grace—repeated, or rather
sung, with the most puritanical countenance and
tone by one of the young men, who occupied an
elevated position behind his father's chair—the
Field Commandant gave the order for the onslaught,
and commenced his revel with an earnest.   A scene
of conglomeration and tobacco smoke ensued, from
which we were unceremoniously dismissed at 9

o'clock, by an intimation from our landlord that he
was about to proceed to bed.

After great solicitation on the following day, the
Commandant consented to dispose of one hundred
of his wether sheep to us, but in the end did not
supply us with more than sixty. These we purchased from him at three Rix dollars per head, and
being on the opposite side of the river, their transit
across the stream gave us the greatest trouble and
annoyance. No less than thirteen persons were
engaged in the attempt to bring them over, but it
was not until one of Mynheer's sons had brought a
large black goat, which headed the flock, and
strange to say took the water like a Newfoundland
dog, that we got them transported. On inquiry we
found that the old goat was a Palinurus frequently
employed for the purpose. I may here remark, that
although the Merino sheep has been introduced, the
Cape colonists continue to be attached to the African
breed, the large tails of which, composed of solid fat
which literally trails on the ground, producing a
luxury that is essential to the comfort and enjoyment of every South African settler.

CHAPTER VI.

FROM THE BOUNDARY OF THE COLONY, ACROSS THE GREAT ORANGE RIVER, TO KURUMAN.

WE had now fairly quitted civilization, and were entering upon a sterile inhospitable region, sparingly inhabited by Bushmen—the remnant of Hottentot hordes, and the wild aborigines of the country —who, gradually receding before the encroachments of the European colonists, have long since sought refuge in the pathless desert. Unblessed amongst the nations of the earth, the hand of these wandering outcasts is against every man, and every man's hand is against them. Existing precariously from day to day—heedless of futurity, and forgetful of the past,—without either laws, arts, or religion— only a faint glimmering ray of instinct guides their benighted path. Depending for subsistence upon the produce of the chase, or the spontaneous gifts of nature, they share the wilderness with beasts of prey, and are but one grade higher in the scale of existence.

From this point until we reached Kuruman, a distance of two hundred miles, the number of our oxen became daily diminished by the effects of a drought which had prevailed, and which had so completely removed every vestige of vegetation, that

they were frequently compelled to pass two days
without tasting food or water. Extensive—to the
eye boundless—plains of arid land, with neither
eminence nor hollow, were on all sides expanded
to the view: of these the prevailing colour was
brownish yellow, variegated with a few black and
sickly shrubs. Scarcely an object met the straining eye but an ostrich sometimes striding in the
blank horizon, or a solitary vulture soaring in the
sky. Over the wide desolation of the stony waste
not a tree could be discerned, and the only impression on the mind was—that of utter and hopeless
sterility. Occasionally, however, as we advanced,
the sameness of the scene was varied by a wide-
stretching surge-like undulation. Our caravan was
then the only object in the landscape upon which
the eye could repose. Waggon after waggon slowly
rising to view, the van was to be seen advancing
over the swell, whilst the cattle and sheep were yet
hidden from the sight. The world before us was
still nought but barren earth and burning sky—
hill following hill, and hollow succeeding hollow,
with the same unvarying regularity as the billows
of the ocean. Not a green herb enticed the vision,
not a bird winged through the air : the loud cracking of a whip rolling in suppressed echo along the
sun-baked ground alone disturbed the silence of the
sultry atmosphere, which gave to the azure vault
of heaven the semblance of an unnatural elevation
from the globe.

Whilst the days were oppressively hot, and the

sky unveiled by a cloud, the nights were piercingly cold——our feelings during the latter indicating as well as the thermometer, that the temperature was near the freezing point : and to add to our discomfort, fuel was rarely procurable.   In the morning, the ground was sometimes covered with hoar frost : but the absence either of vapour or cloud to diminish the heat of the sun, soon dispelled the appearance, and rendered visible the nakedness of the land. Mirage in these regions, flickering in the distance, presents to the thirsty traveller an illusion as tempting as tantalizing.   Blue and delusive lakes, of which the surface seems agitated by a ripple, recede as he advances — and ultimately disappearing, " leave not a wreck behind."

But the monotony of this wearisome journey was not always unbroken by events. We halted the first day on the borders of what appeared to be a body of water many miles in circumference——an oasis in the desert, towards which, after a sultry march of twenty miles, lured by the appearance of several waggons on its brink, both man and beast rushed with impetuosity. We soon perceived, to our disappointment, that we had been deceived by a saline deposit of immense extent, at which a party of Boors were engaged in obtaining salt for the use of the colonists : but it was long before the broken-hearted oxen discovered that what they had understood to be water, was a mere mineral efflorescence in the desert.

The fourth day brought us to the magnificent

Orange River—the only stream within many hundred miles that is entitled to the appellation. Emerging from this desolation and sterility, the first glimpse that we obtained of it realized those ideas of elegant and classic scenery which exists in the minds of poets. The alluring fancies of a fairy fiction, or the fascinating imagery of a romance, were here brought into actual existence. The waters of this majestic river, three hundred yards in breadth, flowing in one unbroken expanse, resembled a smooth translucent lake; and as its gentle waves glided past on their way to join the restless ocean, bearing on their limpid bosom as in a polished mirror, the image of their wood-clothed borders, they seemed to kiss the shore before bidding it farewell. Drooping willows, clad in their vest of vernal freshness, leaned over the bank—and dipping their slender branches into the tide, which glistened with the last rays of the setting sun—seemed fain to follow: whilst at intervals, the wrecks of stately trees that had been torn from their roots by the violence of the torrent during some vast inundation, of which the traces on the shore gave evidence—reared their dilapidated heads in token of the then resistless fury of that flood, which now appeared so smooth and tranquil. To those who may conceive this description overcharged I will only remark, that the sight of water after days in the desert, is probably one of the most delightful sensations that a human being can experience.

Our transit across the Orange River was highly amusing. In consequence of the depth of water, we were obliged to make an elevated platform within the waggons, on which to place our baggage. The double line of oxen stoutly stemming the current, the frantic gestures of the drivers, and the singular appearance of the followers, now wading, now swimming, laden with the lighter baggage, and urging on the loose horses and sheep, altogether presented a picture which I shall not readily forget.

Before reaching Campbellsdorp, a missionary station, we observed a large party of Corrannas engaged in an attempt to run down an ostrich on foot —a prodigy of speed which these people sometimes achieve. Their prevailing dress is a cloak and cap of leather, bedaubed, in common with their own skins, with an unguent of grease and red ochre; but the exhortations of the missionaries have, in some instances, caused this primitive garb to be supplanted by leathern jackets and trowsers of European fashion. At Campbellsdorp we were kindly received by Mr. Bartlet the missionary, but were disappointed at learning that the Chief Waterboer was not at Griquastaad. Captain Cornelius Kok was also absent, but his *locum tenens* being desirous of purchasing finery for his wife, obliged us with three fat oxen in return for a glaring stamped table-cloth, to which we added a pound of tea. Mr. Bartlet considered himself well repaid for a sturdy ox by a small canister of gunpowder.

When near Daniels-kuil—a kraal of Griquas, or

mulatto Hottentots, we met their Chief, Captain
Dowd, whose mouth watered at the appearance of
our waggons, and who requested particularly that
we would not transact any business with his people
until the morrow.   This man is remarkable as being
one of the only two Griquas who escaped the general
massacre of their army by Moselekatse's warriors
in 1831, the particulars of which we obtained from
himself.   From him also we received five fresh oxen,
in lieu of our six lame ones and a cast-off surtout
coat of Richardson's, which he immediately donned
with great exultation.

At Kramers-fontein next day, a horrible spectacle presented itself to us in the form of an
emaciated old Bushwoman, who had come down
from her kraal, five miles distant, to fill two ostrich
egg-shells with water.   "Grim misery had worn
her to the bones," and it is no exaggeration to say
that her attenuated form appeared a skeleton covered
with a wet cloth.   Those rounded proportions which
are given to the human form divine, had no existence in her.   Her skin resembled wrinkled leather,
and I can compare her legs and arms to nothing
but straightened sticks, knobbed at the joints.   Her
body was actually crawling with vermin, with which
she was constantly feeding a little half-inanimate
miniature of herself in arms.

> ————"Withered and wild in her attire,
> She looked not like a habitant of earth,
> And yet was on it."

We were glad to bribe her to depart by a present

of tobacco, and the wretched creature's countenance evinced thankfulness at our liberality.

The pigmy race of which this woman was a characteristic specimen, usually reside in holes and crannies of rocks, and sometimes in wretched huts incapable of protecting them from the inclemency of the seasons. These, their constant fear of discovery induces them to erect in secluded spots at a great distance from water: a precaution to which they are further prompted by a desire to leave the pools open for wild animals, which they occasionally shoot from an ambush with poisoned arrows, and devour on the spot. They possess neither flock nor herds—are unacquainted with agriculture—and the most wealthy can boast of no property beyond his weapons and his starving dog. With no cares beyond the present moment, they live almost entirely upon bulbous roots, locusts, reptiles, and the larvæ of ants, with the habitations of which latter the country is in many places thickly strewed. Not a trace of their hovels could be seen from the road, and a traveller might even pass through their country without seeing a human being, or suspecting that it was inhabited. Such is their general distrust of visiters, that the males would never willingly approach us, evincing great trepidation when forced to do so—no object being more unwelcome to their sight than a troop of horsemen on the plain.

The stature of both sexes is invariably below five feet. The males are usually meagre, bow-legged, and ill made: yet they display a singular ease of

motion and flexibility of joint. The rapidity with
which they drive off a herd of cattle is perfectly
astonishing. Their complexion is sallow brown,
darkened by dirt and grease: their only dress a
piece of leather round the waist, and their sole
defence a diminutive bow, with poisoned arrows,
rather resembling children's toys than mortal weapons.

The women, who were much less shy, and who
never failed to follow the tracks of our waggons
when they happened to come upon them, with the
hope of obtaining tobacco in exchange for ostrich
eggs, are of small and delicate proportions, with
hands and feet of truly Lilliputian dimensions.
Their foot-prints reminded us of Gulliver's adventures, and are not larger than those of a child.
When young they have a pleasing expression of
countenance, which they take care to render as
captivating as possible by bedaubing their flat noses
and prominent cheek-bones with a mixture of red
ochre and fat. The toilets of many were made
with scrupulous attention, the effect of the paint
being enhanced by necklaces composed of the fresh
entrails of wild beasts—a few cowry shells, old
bones and buttons, being also interwoven with their
matted hair; but the life they lead, their frequent
long abstinence, and constant exposure to the wind
and glare of light in a dry open country, soon
inducing the habit of keeping their naturally small
eyes more than half closed, their comeliness is very
ephemeral, and never extends beyond youth. The

females possess much greater volubility and anima-
tion of gesture than the men—but the sounds they
utter are a succession of claps of the tongue produced by forcing that unruly member against different parts of the teeth and palate: and whilst the
enunciation is thus rendered troublesome and full
of impediment, it resembles rather the chattering
of monkeys than the language of human beings.

At Koning, on the 25th, we had the unexpected
pleasure of meeting Captain Sutton of the 75th
Foot—a mighty Nimrod, and a man after my own
heart,—who was returning to the Colony from a
successful expedition against the elephants. Together with a seasonable addition to our stud, and
soul-stirring accounts of what he had seen, we
obtained from this gentleman the first unwelcome
intelligence that Moselekatse was embroiled with
the emigrant farmers.

The following day we entered Kuruman, or New
Litakoo, a lovely spot in the waste by which it is
completely environed. In this speck of civilization,
seeming as though it had been accidentally dropped
into the very heart of the wide wilderness, we received
a very cordial welcome from a missionary of the
London Society—the Rev. Mr. Moffat,—whose
children, amongst others, we had visited in Cape
Town. To this excellent Clergyman, who, together
with his amiable lady, has devoted his life to the
cause of Christianity, we were indebted, during our
stay at Kuruman, for hospitality and kindness
which we shall never be enabled to repay.

CHAPTER VII.

FROM KURUMAN TO LITTLE CHOOI.

TWENTY days had now elapsed without any tidings of Andries, when at last that worthy follower of our fortunes was seen approaching in equestrian order. Whilst, however, he had undoubtedly brought back the horses, he had contrived to render them unserviceable for some weeks by galling their backs : and had besides sacrificed the mare upon which he had set forth on his quest.   Had the accounts that he gave of the privations he suffered on the road, and of his personal combats with surly Boors, who had opposed themselves to the fulfilment of his mission, been correct, his claims to our everlasting gratitude might have been acknowledged; but, unfortunately for him, we subsequently discovered that they had no foundation in truth; and on the contrary, that having speedily recovered the fugitives, he had embraced the opportunity of surreptitiously paying a visit to his mother, and some of his cronies who resided at a distance.

Mr. Moffat confirmed the reports that we had heard from Captain Sutton respecting the attacks made upon the emigrant farmers by Moselekatse, of whose history it will be expected that I should here offer a brief outline.   He is the despotic ruler

of a powerful tribe called Abaka Zooloo, or Matabili.
His father was a chieftain, whose territories lay at
some distance to the north-eastward of Natal, but
being attacked and totally defeated by a neighbouring tribe, he took refuge with Chaka, the Zooloo
tyrant, (predecessor of Dingaan,) with whom he
remained till his death in a servile state, resembling
that of the Fingoes amongst the Kafirs. Moselekatse, however, succeeded in gaining the favour and
confidence of Chaka, and in process of time was
intrusted with the command of an important military
post, and the charge of a large number of cattle.
Seizing his opportunity he revolted, and fled with
his people and the booty towards the north-west,
eating up in his progress the several tribes which
then occupied that country, and soon becoming so
exceedingly formidable, that his very name inspired
terror through a vast region. Having completely
subjugated or destroyed every tribe from whose
opposition he had anything to dread, he ultimately
selected the country near the sources of the Molopo
and Moriqua Rivers for his permanent residence,
where he now reigns, the terror of the surrounding
nations.

Bidding adieu to the worthy missionary, we resumed our journey on the 29th of September,
towards Mosega, the capital of Moselekatse, distant
about two hundred miles in a north-easterly direction. As we were now entering upon a country
hitherto little explored, and, as far as I know, only
partially described by Mr. Campbell on his journey

towards Kurrechaine, I shall be excused being a
little more minute in my descriptions.

The road from Kuruman to our intended halting
ground was so circuitous that we despatched the
waggons in advance, and rejoined them by a more
direct route accompanied by Andries, who, after
all his achievements, was not a little mortified at
perceiving that the sorriest horse of all had been
reserved for him.   Naturally of an unassuming disposition, he humbly conceived himself entitled to
the best : and thus disappointed, unhesitatingly
declared his inability to show the way, which nevertheless to his disgust we contrived to find for ourselves.   The presentation of an old waistcoat in the
evening, however, had the effect of soothing his
feelings.

The next morning, a messenger arrived with
letters for us from Mr. Moffat to the missionaries
at Motito and Mosega.   A Bechuana gentleman
of quality, to whom we had been introduced at
Kuruman, came at the same time with his two
daughters, having conceived a desire to join our
mess as far as Motito.   We had received a bad
character of this personage, but as far as our experience of him went, he was very orderly, and
afforded a fund of entertainment by his ridiculous
attempts to colloquise in Dutch.   His skin was
blacker than a boot, and in texture resembled a
rhinoceros hide : yet he studiously interposed a
parasol, composed of ostrich plumes, betwixt the sun
and his nobility, leaving his little daughters to

bestride a pack-bullock, and their complexions to take care of themselves.

Our march was a very hot one, across measureless plains, vaulted over by a sea of pure and spotless azure, and bounded only by the distant horizon: the fading blue summits of the Kamhanni Mountains near the Kuruman, very slightly breaking the evenness of the line from which we were receding. The soil consisted chiefly of red sand, abounding at intervals with long coarse grass, which being dry, gave to the plains the delusive appearance of ripe corn-fields. Fourteen miles brought us to the Matluarin—a periodical river, with a few detached pools of hardly drinkable water—where bulrushes, and a scanty turf, afforded barely sufficient pasture for the oxen.

We had hitherto failed in our endeavours to obtain an interpreter to accompany us—the only available person in that capacity being a Bechuana residing at Motito, against whom we had been particularly warned by Captain Sutton as a mischief-maker; but in default of a better, we had resolved, by the advice of Mr. Moffat, to entertain this man. It unfortunately so happened, however, that he passed through our camp during the night on his way to Litakoo (whither he had been despatched by Mahura, chief of that place), a circumstance which the Hottentots carefully *concealed,* from motives of their own, until he was far distant.

The weather was piercingly cold when we resumed our journey in the morning. Our people had

D

for once taken the precaution of filling the casks,
and we were thus enabled to obtain breakfast although we came to no water. About noon we also
halted for half an hour at a muddy pool, which the
cattle drained to the dregs, whilst a sheep was being
slaughtered to satisfy the cravings of our guest's
stomach, to the empty state of which he had repeatedly drawn our attention, altogether forgetting that
he had secured the lion's share of a spring-buck
that I had shot the preceding morning.

During the early part of the day our road continued across a boundless ocean-like expanse, the
surface being broken only by ant-hills, or occasional
dwarf bushes, amongst which troops of ostriches
were grazing. Proceeding, we passed through
many extensive areas of waving grass, and the
country gradually became decorated with larger
shrubs, bearing a profusion of yellow flowers.
Occasionally, too, straggling clumps of mimosas,
from ten to fifteen feet in height, resting like islands
on the bosom of the sea of grass, afforded a pleasing
relief. The day was intolerably hot, dusty, and
disagreeable: we saw Motito indistinctly in the
distant glare some hours before we reached it. This
we did about sunset, having travelled altogether
twenty-two miles. We were immediately welcomed
by Mr. Lemue, the French Missionary, who, with
his agreeable wife, evinced, by great attention and
kindness to us, the gratification they experienced
from the arrival of two civilized strangers in the
desert, in which, from motives of the highest nature,

they have immured themselves. The elder of this
interesting young couple did not appear to be more
than twenty-two years of age.

I have not hitherto referred to the dress and
appearance of the Bechuana tribes, of which the
remnants have been collected by the Missionaries.
Of the habiliments of the men little need be said, as
they have generally adopted a rude imitation of the
European costume. The females, however, almost
invariably retain the garb of their ancestors. The
appearance of these ladies is masculine, and far
from attractive. Fat and grease of all kinds form
their delight: their bodies and skin cloaks being
also plentifully anointed with *sibilo*, a grey iron-ore
sparkling like mica, procured from mines in the
neighbourhood, which are visited from all parts of
the country. Their naturally woolly hair is twisted
in small cords, and matted with this substance into
apparently metallic pendules, which being of equal
length, assume the appearance of a skull-cap or
inverted bowl of steel. Tobacco having lately
undergone considerable depreciation by the introduction of the plant—beads are the medium through
which exchanges are usually effected amongst the
Bechuana. The more wealthy of their women are
adorned with a profusion of these, hung in cumbrous
coils round the waist and neck, along with ivory
tooth-picks and gourd snuff-boxes: but even the
indigent are not altogether without them. An apron
of leather, cut into thin strips, and clotted with an
accumulation of grease and filth, reaches to the ancles

—and with a rude skin cloak and mocassins, completes the costume.

We were subjected to continual interruptions from the visits and curiosity of crowds of these ladies, who appeared to have no domestic concerns to attend to : and, although the assertion may subject me to the accusation of want of gallantry, I am compelled to state that the effluvia arising from their persons, which are not always free from vermin, was far from agreeable. Their language, termed *Sichuana,* is exceedingly melodious. Few syllables end with a consonant, and the remarkable abundance of vowels and liquids give it a smoothness of sound to which both sexes do ample justice by the gentle tones of their voice.

Early the following day our waggons were surrounded by a tatterdemallion band of natives with skins and *carosses* * for sale. Foremost in the motley group was Mahura, the Batlapi chief—brother of Motibe, king of that tribe—a portly personage of exceedingly forbidding manners and unprepossessing exterior. He was habited in a thread-bare braided jacket and leathern trowsers, with a broad-brimmed white hat which obscured a large portion of his sinister physiognomy. His A. D. C.—another prominent figure—had inducted his shrivelled frame into a green surtout and military chaco, being withal the least martial character I ever beheld. We made them propitiatory offerings, and handed round the snuff-box: but far from

* *Vide* Note at Chapter V.

meeting our advances, they seemed disposed to quarrel, more especially when they discovered that we knew exactly how many yards of brass wire were esteemed an equivalent for a caross. At length, finding it impossible to come to terms, we closed our little shop, and were preparing to depart —when on a sign made by Mahura, a tall gaunt savage pounced upon a drinking cup, and declared his intention of retaining it in compensation for alleged injury to the fence of his field. Deaf to our remonstrances, he was moving off with his prize, when Richardson seized it from him, and threw it to the right owner. In the mean time another obtrusive savage deliberately seated himself on the pole of the waggon, from which he refused to move, although civilly requested to make way for the oxen. In this posture of affairs I found it necessary to resort to personal violence, which so exasperated him that he sprung at me, brandishing his weapons, and exclaiming that I had kicked him on his own premises. The clamour now became fast and furious, and the threatening attitudes of our assailants obliged us to protrude the muzzles of two or three fowling-pieces from the waggons, so as to bear upon their masses—when they instantly dispersed, leaving us to pursue our journey.

Mahura and Moselekatse are bitter foes. Shortly after Dr. Smith's expedition arrived at Kuruman, the former, who had carried off several head of cattle from the Matabili, expressed his determination of opposing the Doctor's advance—a threat

which he did not however carry into execution.
From that period, until within a few days of our
arrival at Motito, this boaster, dreading the vengeance of Moselekatse, had ignominiously concealed
himself—now, for the first time, venturing from his
hiding-place.   Before we had proceeded many miles
a savage, breathless with haste, met us as if by
accident, and implored the waggon-drivers to turn
back—representing Moselekatse as highly incensed
—and stating that that prince had attacked a party
of farmers with great slaughter, and that the same
fate awaited us if we advanced farther into his
territory.   He then decamped, leaving every face
blank with dismay.   We instantly suspected that
the whole was a plot of Mahura's, and it had the
effect he desired of creating such a panic among the
people, that they positively refused to advance
another step.   Andries was the first to declare this
determination, repeating the savage's story with
fifty exaggerations of his own, and confidently pre-
dicting an attack during the night.   The spirits of
the bolder were damped by the gloomy forebodings
of the more cowardly, nor would they have proceeded
if John April had not fortunately, though unwar-
rantably, presumed to broach the grog-cask during
the night: getting so drunk himself, that we were
obliged to leave him to come on behind, whilst the
rest became sufficiently courageous to resume the
journey in the dark—not, however, until they had
broken the pole of the waggon, which we soon
replaced.

As the morning's dawn slowly withdrew the
curtain from the landscape, we perceived the aspect
of the country completely changed.   Instead of the
dreary waste over which we had lately passed, we
might now imagine ourselves in an extensive park.
A lawn, level as a billiard-table, was everywhere
spread with a soft carpet of luxuriant green grass
spangled with flowers, and shaded by spreading
mokaalas—a large species of acacia* which forms
the favourite food of the giraffe.   The gaudy yellow
blossoms with which these remarkable trees were
covered, yielded an aromatic and overpowering per-
fume—while small troops of striped quaggas or
wild asses, and of brindled gnoos, which were for
the first time to be seen through the forest, enlivened
the scene.   After travelling four hours we reached
Little Chooi, an extensive salt-lake, surrounded by
troops of ostriches and spring-bucks, attracted thither
by the luxuriant, yet crisp and sour grass, which our
cattle refused to eat—and by a small pond of intolerably alkaline water, which we found it impossible to purify.

Several armed natives of the Barolong and Batlaroo
tribes, branches of the Bechuana, visited us for the
purpose of begging *muchuko* or tobacco, causing great
consternation by their approach.   Poor Richard in
particular, who till yesterday had considered himself a perfect Bayard " sans peur et sans reproche,"
had been rapidly sinking since the affair of the flying
savage, and now felt convinced that the threatened

*Acacia Giraffæ.

attack was at hand.   Enveloped in a great coat, with
a red worsted night-cap on his raven pate, and pouring out a flood of smoke from a broken clay pipe
which garnished one corner of his mouth, he sat on
the box of the baggage-waggon looking the very
picture of despair—and as he thought of his fat wife
and helpless family, with the improbability of his
never seeing them again, his feelings quite overpowered him and he wept aloud.   Never was the
heart of a hen partridge concealed beneath so bushy
and so black a beard.   We incontinently dubbed
him *Cœur de Lion*, and he bore the surname ever
afterwards.

CHAPTER VIII.

FROM LITTLE CHOOI, TO THE MERITSANE RIVER.

THE true zebra* is exclusively confined to mountainous regions, from which it rarely if ever descends: but the extensive plains of Southern Africa abound with two distinct species of the same genus, the quagga,† and the striped quagga or Burchell's zebra.‡ These differ little from each other in point of shape or size, both having the tail and ears of the horse, whilst the zebra has those of the ass. Of a pale red colour, the quagga is faintly striped only on the head and neck—but Burchell's zebra is adorned over every part of the body with broad black bands, which beautifully contrast with a pale yellow ground. The gnoo and the common quagga delighting in the same situations, not unfrequently herd together—but I have seldom seen Burchell's zebra unaccompanied by troops of the brindled gnoo,§—an animal differing materially from its brother of the same genus, from which, though scarcely less ungainly, it is readily distinguishable at a great distance by its black mane and tail, more elevated withers, and clumsier action.

* *Equus Zebra*
† *Equus Quagga*
‡ *Equus Burchellii*
§ *Catoblepas Gorgon*
} Delineated in the African Views.

D 5

We were preparing to leave Chooi, when a party
of Griquas arrived with three waggons.   They had
been hunting giraffes on the Molopo, and having
expended their ammunition, were returning to
Daniel's Kuil with the spoils.   Their horses and
oxen were perfect skeletons, and their waggons literally tumbling to pieces.   Tireless wheels were
lashed together with strips of raw hide, and festoons
of sun-dried meat, termed *Biltong*, occupied the
place of the awning; whilst a number of filthy
women and children were stowed away with an
odoriferous *melange* of garbage and fat.   These
people had approached to the western limit of
Moselekatse's territory without molestation—a circumstance which seemed to inspire our timid
followers with confidence.   Large parties are annu-
ally formed for the purpose of hunting the cameleopard and eland—the flesh of these animals being
held in great estimation, and the skins applied to
the manufacture of shoes and a variety of other
uses.   We would gladly have purchased some of
the miserable horses, but the owners declined receiving any thing in exchange but gunpowder,
which we could not have given without incurring
the risk of twelve months' imprisonment on our
return to the Colony, although a single pound would
have given us the choice of the stud.

After crossing the Saltpan, we passed a long line
of pit-falls used for entrapping game.   Upwards of
sixty of these were dug close together in a treble
line; a high thorn fence extending in the form of a

crescent a mile on either side, in such a manner that gnoos, quaggas, and other animals might easily be driven into them. They are carefully concealed with grass, and their circumscribed dimensions render escape almost impossible. Heaps of whitened bones bore ample testimony to the destruction they had occasioned.

We now entered upon the Chooi Desert, an extensive flat, denuded of trees—broken occasionally by low ridges, but still remarkable for its scorched and sterile uniformity. After travelling twenty miles across this " region of emptiness, howling and drear," we reached Loharon, at which there was a prospect of obtaining water, but unfortunately the only tank in the country was exhausted. The small supply that we had brought in the waggons was barely drinkable even in coffee; but *our* sufferings were nothing compared with those of the unhappy oxen, which, although tired to death with the sultry march, ran franticly in quest of some pool where they might slake their thirst—making the air resound with their mournful lowings. During the night the hyænas, attracted by the smell of our mutton, actually devoured a spring-buck within the limits of our camp.

As we advanced, the game became hourly more abundant, although still exceedingly wild. Groups of hartebeests,* quaggas, and brindled gnoos, were every where to be seen—the sleek variegated coats of the two former species sparkling in the rays of

* *Acronotus Caama,* Delineated in the African Views.

the sun; and the fierce little eyes of the latter glistening like fire beneath their shaggy forelocks. A short chase was sufficient to seal the fate of three quaggas—all males, averaging thirteen hands high. During the run I had not seen a human being, and fancied myself alone; but I had scarcely dismounted to secure my game, when a woolly head protruded itself from every bush, and in an instant I was surrounded by thirty Barolongs, who having by signs expressed their approbation of my performance, proceeded to devour the carcase with the greatest avidity—greedily drinking the blood, rubbing the fat upon their bodies, and not leaving so much even as the entrails for the birds of prey.

Our unfortunate cattle had now tasted no water for six-and-thirty hours, and we resolved to travel day and night in search of this necessary of life. The sun at length departed, darkness overtook us, and no moon succeeded to guide our course; when, by a singular instinct, the two horses that we had obtained from Captain Sutton, and which were consequently acquainted with the road—suddenly separated themselves from us, and galloped off. Following them up, the screaming of water-fowl sounded like music in our ears, and we had the gratification of perceiving a pond of mephitic water a little to the right of the road. Both man and beast appeared simultaneously apprized of the cheering discovery—water was the universal cry— the Hottentots rushed to the edge of the pond, and throwing themselves on their faces, swallowed large quantities—indifferent to the crowd of horses, oxen, and sheep, which followed close upon their heels. The oxen in the waggons were with difficulty restrained until the yokes had been removed, when, impatient of their burning thirst, they also rushed headlong into the now muddy pool.

An accident deprived us of the handsome dog that we had obtained from Brother Mark Graaff, the itinerant tutor : no bush presenting itself which could shelter him for a moment during the long march, from the scorching rays of a vertical sun, he had sought an asylum beneath the waggon, the wheel of which passed over his body. For many days past the feet of our canine companions had suffered greatly from their contact with the heated earth ; and, in some instances, had become perfectly raw. Ever and anon the unfortunate animals would voluntarily present a paw, and, with a supplicating whine, solicit another dressing of the tar and fat composition used for greasing the axletrees—from the application of which they experienced temporary relief.

In order to recruit the exhausted strength of the oxen, we halted a day at Great Chooi, another extensive salt-lake, which we reached early the following morning. No pen can describe the scene that here took place. The Hottentots, having first mutinied against Richardson, deputed Andries—who advanced to me with a step of defiance—to acquaint me with their determination not to obey his orders : the contracts at Graaff Reinet having, to save trouble, been made in my name only. The discussion having been suppressed by me, led to a disagreement among themselves; they fought with inconceivable fury for half an hour, and were with difficulty prevented from murdering each other. With blood streaming from many a ghastly wound, they at length retired to ablute themselves, and returned better friends than ever. The engagement had been witnessed by a party of savages, who carried umbrellas of ostrich feathers, twisted round a long stick so as to resemble the nodding plumes of a hearse. In honour of their own courageous bearing, the Hottentots purchased a number of these for a small piece of tobacco, and binding them round their hats, strutted forth knights of the sable plume.

And here, for the reader's especial information, I must be permitted to cast a little light upon the primitive mode in which transactions of a commercial nature are conducted by barter amongst these illiterate tribes, who, it may be supposed, are but imperfectly conversant with the rules of arithmetic. The savage, having spread on the ground his caross (which, be it known, is most commonly composed of the skins of the jackal, or wild cat, curiously sewn together with the animal's sinew), a piece of tobacco a span in length, a small string of beads, an ell of brass-wire, a button, or some other commodity equally valuable, is carefully placed upon the head of each skin composing the upper row. Having satisfied his suspicions as to the fairness of the proceeding by the most irksome scrutiny, the vendor suddenly makes up his mind, and closes the negociation by greedily scraping together the equivalent, with which he immediately makes off in triumph, leaving the happy purchaser in undisturbed possession of his bargain. By virtue of six yards of *pig-tail*, and a suitable stock of patience, it is practicable to become the proprietor of a caross, which, in an European market, would realize from fifty to a hundred rix-dollars. Traders, or *smouches*, as they are called by the colonists, constantly visit Latakoo and its neighbourhood, and often proceed to a considerable distance beyond it into the interior, for the purpose of thus collecting ivory and peltries for the Cape market; availing themselves of the opportunity of supplying the farmers and missionaries lying in their outward route, with the portable luxuries of life. We were constantly taxed with being itinerant pedlars, the profession of a gentleman being quite unknown in the colony. It must, however, be observed, that the field for traffic is extremely limited, and that fortunes are rarely made.

The scattered inhabitants of this part of the country are the remnants of various Bechuana tribes, which have been conquered by Moselekatze—and consist principally of the Barolong, Wangkets, Batlapi, and Baharootzi. These poor wretches live in small communities, and, being destitute of cattle, depend entirely for subsistence on locusts, or such game as chance may direct to their pitfalls. Crowds of them, attracted by prey, now hovered around me

in my hunting expeditions, which were here particularly successful ; and having obtained a supply of
meat, with the luxuries of snuff and tobacco, for which
they were constantly begging, under the denomi-
nations of *lishuena* and *muchuko*, they composed
themselves to sleep, appearing to be in the enjoyment of as much happiness as man in a state of
mere animal existence probably ever attains. Our
little band was also instinctively attended by a host
of hungry vultures, who, little disturbed by the presence of man, divided the office of carrion scavengers
with hyænas and jackals. Wheeling in circles
high above our heads, like small specks in the
firmament, these voracious birds were ever ready to
pounce upon game that might be shot, or upon the
carcases of oxen that perished on the road—devouring
the largest bodies with a promptitude truly surprising.

We had now crossed the unvaried level expanse
of the Chooi Desert, and were entering upon a
country, which, though equally remarkable for its
sameness of appearance, presented a different character. Immense sandy flats, with a substratum of
lime, were uniformly covered with mokaala trees,
low thorn bushes, and long grass, interspersed with
numerous dry tanks; but no hill or conspicuous
object that could direct the footsteps of a wanderer.
Before reaching the Siklagole River, twenty-two
miles, we passed many extensive villages totally
deserted; rude earthen vessels, fragments of ostrich
egg-shells, and portions of the skins of wild animals,
however, proving that they had been recently in-

habited.   During the whole of this and the following day we saw no human being, a circumstance which I note here, because it added in no small degree to the troubles I am about to detail.

On the morning of the 9th October, when the waggons had started on their way to the Meritsane River, our next stage, I turned off the road in pursuit of a troop of brindled gnoos, and presently came upon another, which was joined by a third still larger—then by a vast herd of zebras, and again by more gnoos, with sassaybys * and hartebeests, pouring down from every quarter, until the landscape literally presented the appearance of a moving mass of game.   Their incredible numbers so impeded their progress, that I had no difficulty in closing with them, dismounting as opportunity offered, firing both barrels of my rifle into the retreating phalanx, and leaving the ground strewed with the slain.   Still unsatisfied, I could not resist the temptation of mixing with the fugitives, loading and firing, until my jaded horse suddenly exhibited symptoms of distress, and shortly afterwards was unable to move.   At this moment I discovered that I had dropped my pocket compass, and being unwilling to lose so valuable an ally, I turned loose my steed to graze, and retraced my steps several miles without success; the prints of my horse's hoofs being at length lost in those of the countless herds which had crossed the plain.   Completely absorbed in the chase, I had retained but an imperfect

* *Acronotus Lunata.*   Delineated in the African Views.

idea of my locality; but returning to my horse, I led
him in what I believed to be a north-easterly direction, knowing, from a sketch of the country which
had been given me by our excellent friend Mr.
Moffat, and which, together with drawing materials,
I carried about me, that that course would eventually
bring me to the Meritsane. After dragging my
weary horse nearly the whole of the day under a
burning sun, my flagging spirits were at length
revived by the appearance of several villages. Under other circumstances, I should have avoided intercourse with their inhospitable inmates, but dying
with thirst, I eagerly entered each in succession,
and to my inexpressible disappointment, found them
deserted. The same evidence existing of their
having been recently inhabited, I shot a hartebeest,
in the hope that the smell of meat would as usual
attract some straggler to the spot. But no. The
keen-sighted vultures, that were my only attendants,
descended in multitudes, but no woolly-headed negro
appeared to dispute the prey. In many of the trees
I observed large thatched houses resembling hay-
stacks; and under the impression that these had
been erected in so singular a position by the natives
as a measure of security against the lions, whose
recent tracks I distinguished in every direction, I
ascended more than one in the hope of at least finding some vessel containing water. Alas! they proved to be the habitations of large communities of
social grosbeaks,* those winged republicans of

* *Loxia Socia.* Delineated in the African Views.

whose architecture and magnificent edifices, I had, till now, entertained a very inadequate conception. Faint and bewildered, my prospects began to brighten as the shadows of evening lengthened. Large troops of ostriches running in one direction, plainly indicated that I was approaching water; and immediately afterwards I struck into a path impressed with the foot-marks of women and children —soon arriving at a nearly dry river, which, running east and west, I at once concluded to be that of which I was in search.

Those only who have suffered as I did during this day from prolonged thirst, can form a competent idea of the delight, and I may add, energy, afforded me by the first draught of the putrid waters of the Meritsane. They equally invigorated my exhausted steed, whom I mounted immediately and cantered up the bank of the river, in order, if possible, to reach the waggons before dark. The banks are precipitous—the channel deep, broken, and rocky : clusters of reeds and long grass indicating those spots which retain the water during the hot months. It was with no small difficulty, after crossing the river, that I forced my way through the broad belt of tangled bushes which margined the edge. The moonless night was fast closing around, and my weary horse again began to droop. The lions, commencing their nightly prowl, were roaring in all directions, and no friendly fire or beacon presenting itself to my view, the only alternative was to bivouac where I was, and to renew

my search in the morning. Kindling a fire, I
formed a thick bush into a pretty secure hut, by
cutting away the middle, and closing the entrance
with thorns; and having knee-haltered* my horse
to prevent his straying, I proceeded to dine upon a
Guinea-fowl that I had killed, comforting myself
with another draught of *aqua pura*. The monarchs
of the forest roared incessantly, and so alarmed my
horse, that I was obliged repeatedly to fire my rifle
to give him confidence. It was piercingly cold, and
all my fuel being expended, I suffered as much from
chill as I had during the day from the scorching
heat. About 3 o'clock, completely overcome by
fatigue, I could keep my eyes open no longer, and
commending myself to the protecting care of Providence, fell into a profound sleep.

* Knee-haltering is the colonial method of securing a horse
when turned out to graze; a leathern thong attached to the neck,
is passed round the knee, and tied.

CHAPTER IX.

HUNTING AT MERITSANE.

On opening my eyes, my first thought was of my
horse. I started from my heathy bed in the hope
of finding him where I had last seen him, but his
place was empty. I roamed every where in search
of him, and ascended trees which offered a good
look-out, but he was no where to be seen. It was
more than probable he had been eaten by lions,
and I had almost given up the search in despair,
when I at length found his foot-mark, and traced
him to a deep hollow near the river, where he was
quietly grazing. The night's rest, if so it could be
called, had restored him to strength, and I pursued
my journey along the bank of the river, which I
now re-crossed opposite to the site of some former
scene of strife, marked by numerous human skeletons,
bleached by exposure. A little further on I disturbed a large lion, which walked slowly off,
occasionally stopping and looking over his shoulder,
as he deliberately ascended the opposite bank.
In the course of half an hour, I reached the end of
the dense jungle, and immediately discovered the
waggon road; but as I could detect no recent
traces upon it, I turned to the southward, and
after riding seven or eight miles in the direction of

Siklagole, had the unspeakable satisfaction of per–
ceiving the waggons drawn up under a large tree
in the middle of the plain.   The discharge of my
rifle at a little distance, had relieved the anxiety of
my companion and followers, who, during the night,
had entertained the most gloomy forebodings on
my account, being convinced that I had either been
torn piecemeal by lions, or speared by the assagais
of the cannibals!   A cup of coffee was immediately
offered me, which, as I had scarcely tasted nourishment for thirty hours, proved highly grateful; and
I learned that Richardson had been obliged to halt
in the plain the preceding night, in consequence of
the great length of the march, and the darkness
overtaking.him.   This accounted for my not meeting him on the river bank, which we again reached
in about two hours, encamping under a grove of
spreading mokaala trees.

Both the Siklagole and the Meritsane take their
source in the low range of hills called Kunuana,
considerably to the eastward of the point where
we crossed them ; and, joining about the same distance to the westward, empty themselves into the
Molopo.   Near their confluence the camp of Mr.
Bain, a trader to whose name I have already alluded,
was attacked in 1834 by Moselekatse.   A party of
marauding Griquas, whom he had imprudently
taken with him to assist in hunting, entered the
territories of that prince, and succeeded in capturing
several head of cattle, with which they had made
good their retreat.   A large party of warriors, how-

ever, overtook them when within sight of the camp;
nearly all the followers fled in disorder on the first
alarm, leaving their master to shift for himself, who,
finding the camp surrounded and resistance vain,
jumped on his horse, and, accompanied by four of
his people, narrowly escaped with life, by riding
through and killing some of the assailants. After
travelling several days, and suffering dreadfully
from want of food and water, the party reached
Motito nearer dead than alive.

The reports of four savages of the Batlapi tribe,
who joined us yesterday, determined us to halt a
day for the purpose of hunting. Richardson and
myself left the waggons at daybreak, attended by
these men, and crossing the river, took a north-westerly direction through a park of magnificent camel-
thorn· trees, many of which were groaning under
the huge nests of the social grosbeak; whilst others
were decorated with green clusters of misletoe, the
bright scarlet berries of which were highly orna-
mental. We soon perceived large herds of quaggas
and brindled gnoos, which continued to join each
other, until the whole plain seemed alive. The
clatter of their hoofs was perfectly astounding, and
I could compare it to nothing but to the din of a
tremendous charge of cavalry, or the rushing of a
mighty tempest. I could not estimate the accumu-
lated numbers at less than fifteen thousand; a
great extent of country being actually chequered
black and white with their congregated masses.
As the panic caused by the report of our rifles,

extended, clouds of dust hovered over them; and
the long necks of troops of ostriches were also to be
seen, towering above the heads of their less gigantic
neighbours, and sailing past with astonishing rapidity.   Groups of purple sassaybys, and brilliant
red and yellow hartebeests, likewise lent their aid
to complete the picture, which must have been
seen to be properly understood, and which beggars
all attempt at description.   The savages kept in
our wake, dexterously despatching the wounded
gnoos by a touch on the spine with the point of an
assagai, and instantly covering up the carcases
with bushes, to secure them from the voracity of
the vultures, which hung about us like specks in
the firmament, and descended with the velocity of
lightning, as each discharge of our artillery gave
token of prey.   As we proceeded, two strange figures
were perceived standing under the shade of a tree;
these we instantly knew to be elands,* the savages
at the same moment exclaiming with evident delight,
Impoofo, Impoofo, and pressing our horses to the
utmost speed, we found ourselves for the first time,
at the heels of the largest and most beautiful species
of the antelope tribe.   Notwithstanding the unweildy shape of these animals, they had at first
greatly exceeded the speed of our jaded horses, but
being pushed, they soon separated; their sleek
coats turned first blue and then white with froth;
the foam fell from their mouths and nostrils, and
the perspiration from their sides.   Their pace gra-

* *Boselaphus Oreas.*   Delineated in the African Views.

dually slackened, and with their full brilliant eyes
turned imploringly towards us, at the end of a mile,
each was laid low by a single ball. They were
young bulls, measuring upwards of seventeen hands
at the shoulder.

I was engaged in making a sketch of the one I
had shot, when the savages came up, and in spite
of all my remonstrances, proceeded with cold-blooded
ferocity to stab the unfortunate animal, stirring up
the blood and shouting with barbarous exultation,
as it issued from each newly inflicted wound, regardless of the eloquent and piteous appeal, expressed
in the beautiful clear black eye of the mild and in-
offensive eland.

In size and shape, the body of the male eland
resembles that of a well-conditioned Guzerat ox,
not unfrequently attaining the height of nineteen
hands, and weighing two thousand pounds. The
head is strictly that of the antelope, light, graceful,
and bony, with a pair of magnificent straight horns,
about two feet in length, spirally ringed, and pointed
backwards. A broad and deep dewlap, fringed
with brown hair, reaches to the knee. The colour
varies considerably with the age, being dun in some,
in others an ashy blue with a tinge of ochre; and
in many also, sandy grey approaching to white.
The flesh is esteemed by all classes in Africa, above
that of any other animal; in grain and colour it
resembles beef, but is better tasted, and more delicate, possessing a pure game flavour, and the
quantity of fat with which it is interlarded is sur-

E

prising, greatly exceeding that of any other game
quadruped with which I am acquainted.   The
female is smaller and of slighter form, with less
ponderous horns.   The stoutest of our savage attendants could with difficulty transport the head
of the eland to the waggons, where one of the
Hottentots had just arrived with the carcase of a
sassayby that he had dragged a considerable distance, assisted by upwards of twenty savages.   These
men were no sooner made acquainted with the
occurrences of the morning, than they set off at
speed upon the tracks of our horses, and were
presently out of sight.   About sunset the party
returned, gorged to the throats, and groaning under
an external load of flesh, which having been unable
to consume, they had hung round their necks.

About midnight an unusual commotion caused
us to start from our sleep.   The whole of the cattle
had burst through the thorn fence by which they
were surrounded, and, panic-stricken, were blindly
charging they knew not whither; oxen, horses,
and sheep, tumbling headlong over the waggon
poles, and over each other, in indescribable confusion.   The night was intensely dark, and all the
fires had gone out—Cœur de Lion had clambered
on to the top of the baggage-waggon, and was
screaming like a woman, whilst each Hottentot was
discharging his gun, loaded with ball, in any direction that the muzzle might happen to have
assumed.   The horses were the least alarmed, and
after floundering about in the dark for some time,

we succeeded in recovering all but one; but every
endeavour to reclaim the oxen and sheep proving
abortive, we retired again to rest, having first ascertained, by the light of a candle, that the consternation had been occasioned by three lions
that had entered the fold and slain two of the sheep.

At daybreak, both Hottentots and savages were
despatched on the tracks of the fugitives. Some
of the savages shortly returned with the sheep,
several more having, however, been devoured by
lions; but the former did not make their appearance until noon, when they informed us that the
oxen had divided into two parties, and, being dreadfully alarmed, would not stop in all probability until
they should reach the Kuruman; adding, that if
we wished to recover them, each Hottentot must
be provided with a horse and a supply of ammunition. Knowing from sad experience the fate that
awaited our steeds, upon whose well-being our sport
entirely depended, we resisted the application;
upon which all but Claas and Ethaldur begged to
throw up their commissions. No one had any
complaint to allege except April, who objected to
the fatness of the mutton, and Andries, who felt
aggrieved by a threat of retribution extended at
Chooi. The latter looked particularly black, and
it was not until after he had been despatched with
Cobus on horseback in quest of the oxen, that
we discovered him to have been the instigator of a
plot, which had been joined by all, to desert us in the
wilderness, and return to the Colony with the

horses and whatever else they could lay their hands upon.

Apprehensive of another attack from lions, we moved in the afternoon to the opposite side of the river, drawing up the waggons on the tops of a hillock, in such a manner as to flank the cattle enclosure—an arrangement which we ever afterwards observed. Our friends the Batlapi returned about sunset with the oxen, which they had found twelve miles off, a piece of service for which, according to agreement, they were rewarded with a yard of tobacco and a tinder-box. Cobus and Andries also came back during the night, having galled the backs of both the horses, without obtaining any tidings of the lost one. The whole of the following day was passed in fruitless endeavours to recover the truant, and it was not until six months afterwards, that we ascertained he had returned to the farm on which he had been bred in the New Hantam, a distance of five hundred miles.

CHAPTER X.

FROM MERITSANE TO MIMORI, AND HUNTING ON THE MOLOPO.

CONTINUING our journey on the 14th October, twenty-eight miles, through a beautiful country abounding with trees and grass, we reached the Lotlokane, the shallow channel of a periodical river, said in the rainy season to contribute its mite to the Molopo, which it joins at some distance to the westward.   At this season it was perfectly dry; but we had fortunately found a small pool of water on the road, at which we breakfasted, after killing several hartebeests and sassaybys.   The skins of both these animals, and especially of the latter, are in great demand amongst the savages, for *kobos,* or fur cloaks—both on account of their brilliant colour and their supple nature.   They are cured by means of continual rubbing, stretching, and scraping; and for this purpose are constantly carried about, and referred to as an amusement in moments of leisure. The operation is rendered less tedious by the constant addition of grease: and less irksome, by savage howlings and gruntings, intended to pass current for singing.

The sassayby, or crescent-horned antelope, and the caama, or hartebeest, are both members of the

Acronotine group, and are alike remarkable for their
elevated withers, drooping hind quarters, and triangular form.   The colour of the former is purple
violet, and of the latter bright orange; their legs
and faces being eccentrically marked, as if with the
brush of a sign painter; and their horns placed on
the very summit of the head, upon a prolongation
of the frontal bone, instead of above the eyes as in
most other antelopes.   Their brain, as well as that
of the gnoo, is filled with large white maggots—
a phenomenon, of which, until I had received ocular
evidence, I could not help being sceptical.

Rations of flour were here first served out to the
followers, in the measure of three-quarters of a
pound of meal to each man, and were continued
daily during the rest of the journey.   In the morning four savages volunteered to show us a rhinoceros.   We accompanied them amongst ruined stone
kraals of great extent, situated to the left of the
road, and so overgrown with thorn-bushes, that we
were not unfrequently obliged to exchange an erect
for a stooping posture, and at times even to travel
on our hands and knees.   We found nothing, however, but a pack of wild dogs* that had just hunted
down a hartebeest.   Like the wild dogs of India,
these animals take the field in organized packs, and
by their perseverance seldom fail to weary out the
swiftest antelope.   Of a slender form, the general
colour is ochreous yellow, blotched and brindled
with dingy black.   The ears are large and semi-

* *Hyæna venatica.*

circular: the muzzle and face black, and the tail bushy like that of a fox.

During the day we passed another extensive stone town, which once contained its "busy thousands," but now presents a heap of ruins. The walls extend more than a mile on each side of the road; and the plain on which it is constructed, is thickly covered with a species of wild basil, yielding an aromatic scent when crushed under the foot. We had scarcely passed this, when the lightning began to flash, and tremendous peals of thunder burst over our heads. A black cloud that had suddenly formed, then emptied its contents upon us; the rain pouring down like a sluice for five minutes, and obliging us to seek shelter in the waggons. Ceasing as abruptly as it commenced, we passed on at once to parched and dusty land, from a tract which had in an instant become covered with pools of water.

It was nearly dark when we reached the Molopo, a few miles below its source. This river, which forms the western boundary of Moselekatse's territory, exhibits a broad shallow bed, covered with turf, traversed by a deep stream about ten yards wide, completely overgrown with high reeds. The soil on both sides is black, spread with luxuriant grass, and detached clumps of acacia. We crossed, and encamped on the northern bank, under a solitary tree, around which was a ready-made fence for the cattle. During the night, the obtrusive visit of a hippopotamus—of which amphibious animals

there are abundance in the river—caused great consternation : Richard screaming, and the Hottentots
expending their ball-cartridge as usual.

The two following days were spent in hunting
the eland and gemsbok.* The latter, which is
doubtless the animal from which the delineations of
the fabulous unicorn have descended, is one of the
most magnificent antelopes in the universe. Although common in Namaqua-land, it is rare in this
part of the country, and we were fortunate in finding three, one of which I succeeded in riding down :
nearly, however, sacrificing my best horse in the
arduous achievement. The oryx is about the size
of an ass, and nearly of the same ground colour,
with a black list stripe down the back and on each
flank; white legs, variegated with black bands ;
and a white face, marked with the figure of a black
nose-band and head-stall. Its copious black tail
literally sweeps the ground : a mane reversed, and
a tuft of flowing black hair on the breast, with a
pair of straight slender horns (common to both
sexes), three feet in length, and ringed at the base,
completing the portrait. During the chase, I
passed under the noses of three rhinoceroses, which,
on my return, I was unable to find. Richardson
had fallen in with a troop of five lions, one of which
he wounded, but being deserted by the Hottentots,
was unable to follow among the brushwood ; and
my horse was so completely exhausted, that I was
obliged to drag him home, carrying the saddle myself.

* *Oryx Capensis.* Delineated in the African Views.

Prodigious swarms of locusts passed overhead to
the eastward during the greater part of the day, and
were followed by such dense flights of birds as almost
to darken the air. The *springhaan-vogel*,* as the
latter is called by the colonists, is about the size of
a swallow, with numerous speckles like the starling,
and is said to subsist almost exclusively upon the
destructive insects with which it literally vies in point
of numbers. The ravages committed by the locust,
whose desolating visits have been the theme of naturalists and historians in all ages, have too probably
been witnessed by the majority of my Indian readers;
but Africa, more especially the northern parts of it,
would appear to be a quarter of the globe even more
frequently and more severely subjected to the scourge
of their inroads than Asia. Often have the lands on
the frontier of the colony been totally laid waste by
their migratory swarms, which, as usual, have been
followed by all the horrors of famine ; whilst to the
wandering Bushman, who has neither flocks nor
herds to perish for lack of nourishment—no garden
nor corn-fields of which to lament the devastation,
the intrusion, so appalling to the grazier and agri-
culturist, proves a source of joy rather than of sorrow.
Following up their devouring hosts, he feeds upon
them as they advance, and preserving also a large
quantity for future emergencies, finds in the insect
army a ready and ample compensation for the wild
game which has been compelled to abandon the ra-
vaged pastures of the wilderness. Their hereditary
enemies are also numerous ; almost every animal,

* *Anglicè*, Locust-bird.   E 5*

domestic as well as wild, contributes to their destruction—fowls, horses, oxen, sheep, and antelopes,
alike swallowing them with the greatest avidity.

The night of the 17th was rainy and tempestuous;
and the lions, never failing to take advantage of such
an opportunity, prowled round the camp, roaring in
concert with the sighing of the reeds, which so alarmed the cattle that they thrice broke loose, and were
recovered with difficulty. There was nothing, however, to prevent our resuming our journey in the
morning, the thirsty earth having completely absorbed the deluge that had fallen. Our road lay
across a plain, with isolated groves of acacia, and we
frequently passed over a solid pavement of granite.
Visiting the scene of the occurrence detailed above,
and searching amongst a low belt of wooded hillocks,
which skirted a part of the road, I found a fine fat
eland, which I drove into the plain, and, assisted by
Richardson, brought up to the waggons, and then
despatched, the caravan being immediately halted.
We frequently afterwards adopted this plan, which
saved the trouble of carrying the meat from a distance; and the unfortunate animal once blown, was
much more manageable than a Smithfield ox.

Andries having donned his best apparel, here
proposed to proceed on horseback to Mosega, in
order to apprize the king of our approach—an
offer which we gladly accepted. From this point,
the summits of distant ranges of hills could be distinguished, across extensive plains covered with
grass waving to the breeze, which stretched away to
the northward and eastward, far as the eye could

reach. On the left, the low range of hillocks, already noticed, terminated at some distance in several detached hills—some conical, others table-topped—the white slabs on the sides of these strongly contrasting with the black charred bushes which grew amongst the crevices. A large portion of the country had been set on fire a few weeks before, in order to clear off the withered grass, and the bountiful thunder-clouds having caused the young green blades to make their appearance, large herds of game had been attracted to the spot. At the gorge of these hills was an extensive line of pit-falls, into one of which a hartebeest, whose leg I had broken, fell as I was riding him down—my horse being nearly ingulfed in a second, at the same moment. During the day I killed another impoofo, which actually measured nineteen hands two inches at the shoulder, and was even more remarkably un-wieldy than any we had hitherto seen.

Our road was now sometimes over a rocky pavement, at others over ground which threatened the destruction of the waggons. About 4 o'clock we halted at the Mimori River, only five miles from Mosega. A chain of lakes to the left of our camp contained a herd of wild buffaloes,* whose formidable heads, resembling masses of rock, were protruded from the water amid waving sedges, the whole of their bodies being immerged. I wounded one, which I attempted to ride down; but the sharp-pointed stones cutting the shoeless feet of my horse to pieces, I brought him back to the waggons dead lame.

* *Bubalus Caffer*. Delineated in the African Views.

CHAPTER XI.

ARRIVAL AT MOSEGA, THE CAPITAL OF THE CHIEF MOSELEKATSE.

LATE in the evening we were agreeably surprised by the auspicious arrival of four Matabili warriors from Mosega, bringing a civil message from the deputy-governor, who, in the absence of Moselekatse, and of his prime-minister Kalipi, had been apprized by Andries of our advent. Tall, straight, well-proportioned, and of regular features, these men, although of very dark complexion, were far superior in appearance to any tribe that we had hitherto seen. Their heads were shaven, and surmounted by an oval ring attached to the scalp; a large perforation in the lobe of one ear receiving a small gourd snuff-box. Their dress consisted of a leathern girdle, with a few strips of cat-skin attached to the front and rear; and each was armed with two short javelins, and a knobbed stick used for throwing. We made them heartily welcome to our fireside—filled their stomachs with beef, and their boxes with snuff, and left them making their nests among the sheltered bushes on the river bank. A strong disagreeable wind setting in, completely destroyed the fire; and after we had retired, it increased to such a perfect hurricane that sleep was out of the

question.   Our waggon was carefully closed and
drawn up under the shelter of a superb grove of
trees; yet the bitter blast that howled without, cut
so keenly through the blankets, that it penetrated
even to the marrow of our bones.   I wrapped my
sheep-skin coverlet closer about me, without any
sensible advantage; and my companion, after suc-
cessively inducting himself into every article of
wearing apparel upon which he could put his hand,
still declared himself as cold as ice.

At daybreak the mercury in Fahrenheit's thermometer stood at forty-four degrees, yet to the
bodily feelings, the air was still much colder than
we had felt it when down to eighteen degrees.   We
crossed the deep sedgy stream of the Mimori, and
ascending to a higher level, were presently met by
his Excellency the Deputy-Governor, a tall athletic
savage of commanding appearance, blind of the
left eye.   His attire was of the nature already described, and saving that he was unarmed, differed
in no respect from that of his attendants.   A
general greeting and hand-shaking ensued—the
snuff-box circulated briskly, and we all became
capital friends.

Smoking is not a fashionable vice amongst the
Matabili, but all classes are passionately addicted
to snuffing—indeed the sharing the contents of your
box with a stranger, is the greatest compliment
that can be paid to him.   The mode of taking it is
not unworthy of notice.   One-half of the powder
having been transferred to the palm of the hand,

by means of a small ivory spoon, which is usually hung round the neck, the recipient leisurely seats himself under a convenient bush—drawing every grain into his nostrils at once, with an eagerness which, although followed by a copious flood of tears, proves the extent of the enjoyment afforded. Worse than barbarian would that man be esteemed, who would wantonly interrupt a social party so employed.

After travelling about five miles, over undulating downs, covered with luxuriant grass, we descended into a lovely and fertile valley, in form resembling a basin, of ten or twelve miles in circumference, bounded on the north and north-east by the Kurri-chane range of mountains, and containing the sources of the Mariqua River. Prior to the occupancy of this valley by the Matabili, it formed the principal residence of the Baharootzi tribe. It is now extensively cultivated, and contains the military town of Mosega, and fifteen other of Moselekatse's principal kraals. On our way to the houses of the American Missionaries, we passed several of these, to the no small delight of their inhabitants, who, principally women and children, flocked round the waggons in great numbers, offering their greasy hands without compunction; at every step the crowd increased—both sexes were to be seen working in the fields, but they all quitted their occupation as they saw us, and adding themselves to the group, escorted us to the halting ground. We received a hearty welcome from Dr. Wilson, one of the American fraternity, from whom we learned, on delivering

a letter from Mr. Moffat, that he had had the misfortune to lose his wife a few days before; and
that the rest of the party were likewise dangerously
ill with fever, contracted from having slept in their
newly-built house before the floors were dry. This
gentleman likewise gave us accounts of the capture
of several waggons, the property of a farmer named
Erasmus, who was hunting on the Vaal River.
This was the event to which Captain Sutton had
referred, but Dr. Wilson further informed us, that
a very large Commando* under Kalipi, the minister
and governor of Mosega, had already been some
days gone to the river Vaal, to complete the destruction of the emigrant farmers—concluding by
strongly advising us not to visit the king at such a
conjuncture. Having come thus far, however, we
resolved to proceed, and with that view immediately
despatched messengers to his Majesty with a present of beads, and a request that we might be
suffered to pay our respects. These men received
a bunch of beads weighing one pound, and the promise of another if they returned on the third day—
Moselekatse was reported to be at a kraal fifty
miles to the northward, at which he had resided
ever since the establishment of the Missionaries at
Mosega, his head-quarters.

It rained during the whole of the night; and
during the whole of the following day we were
surrounded, without a moment's respite, by a crowd

* Commando is the colonial term for every expedition of a
military nature.

of people importuning for tobacco. They entered
the tent and clambered into the waggon without
ceremony, leaving a host of vermin behind them,
and becoming at length so troublesome, that we
were compelled, in self-defence, to drive them away
with the waggon-whips. A long line of women
and girls, however, still continued to stand at
a distance on tiptoe, attempting to gratify their
curiosity by peeping in at the back of the waggon;
whilst others sat and loitered about as if their time
were valueless. The governor invited himself to
dinner in the evening, and as it rained again, sat
so late, that we were at last obliged to send the
Parsee outside to start him, which he did by poking
a stick under his person from below the walls of
the tent, a hint which he good-naturedly took, and
departed.

We embraced an early opportunity of mentioning
to the Missionaries our intention of leaving the
country by the Vaal River; a scheme which they
discountenanced as fraught with peril. But whilst
they felt sure that Moselekatse would never listen
to such an arrangement, they obligingly consented
to allow one of their domestics, Baba, a converted
Bechuana who had accompanied Dr. Smith's expedition as interpreter, to attend us as far as the
king's residence, in the like capacity.

The next morning we rode through a pass in the
hills behind the mission-houses, towards the Mimori
Lakes, in order to obtain food for the people; it being
an object to husband our resources, as far as possible,

against our return.´ The plains here are broken by
low ranges of stony hills, with clumps of acacia. A
large herd of buffaloes on being pursued took to the
lakes, into which we followed them, the water reaching up to the horse's girths, and the reeds far above
our own heads.   We could hear the animals forcing
their way through immediately in front of us; but
after several hours' severe labour could only succeed
in driving out one, which breaking at the opposite
side of one lake had gained another before we could
overtake him. A general skirmish then commenced;
some of the followers wading up to their middles,
whilst others fired from the banks whenever a glimpse
of the buffaloes could be obtained. Several were
wounded; and Piet, in attempting to despatch one,
was charged and knocked over by another. Capless
and disarmed, we could see him through a telescope,
lying beneath a shady karree-tree, which reared its
venerable head in the middle of the lake, holding
his hands to his stomach as if mortally wounded;
his adversary drooping near him, the blood streaming from its nostrils, and the moment of dissolution
approaching. A broad deep stream, tangled over
with sedge, encircling this spot on three sides, defied
approach either on horseback or on foot, without
incurring the certainty of drowning, and compelled
us to ride three miles round before we could arrive
to the rescue. By that time the buffalo was dead,
and Piet appearing more frightened than hurt, we
removed his leathern doublet, which was much torn,
and ascertained that there were no holes in his skin.

A laborious search among the reeds brought his
cap and gun to light, and the wounded man being
borne out by the savages, was placed upon a horse
and conducted to Mosega, where he enjoyed the
advantage of Dr. Wilson's professional aid.

On our return, Mr. Lindley, one of the Missionaries, still very weak, though slowly recovering from
fever, came to apprize us of the return of the messengers from Kapain with a pressing invitation from
the king, who declared that we were " his own white
men," and must hasten our advance as much as possible, so as to arrive on the third day.   These men
had used extraordinary expedition, and allured by
the promise of beads had performed one hundred
miles in less than thirty-six hours.   Seeing us determined to continue our journey the next morning,
Mr. Lindley and the Doctor again endeavoured by
every argument in their power to dissuade us from
our intention of forcing our way out by the Vaal
River, which we were bent upon doing, whether
Moselekatse permitted it or not; but we at the same
time expressed our conviction that we had in the
waggons that which would bribe his majesty to accede to our wishes.   Without the least anticipating
the success of our project, Dr. Wilson then entrusted
us with a letter, announcing to his family the heavy
loss he had recently sustained.

The accounts given by these gentlemen were not
calculated to raise our spirits, or give us a favourable
impression of the treatment we should experience
from the despot, of whose inhuman executions and

horrible butcheries they could never speak with patience; representing him to be treacherous, oppressive, cruel, and capricious in an extraordinary degree, and to exact from his subjects an abject deference, little according with American notions of tolerance. Amongst his more recent enormities they adduced the murder of a trader, named Gibson, with the whole of his followers, and of two servants belonging to Captains Sutton and Moultry, the particulars of which shall hereafter be given. Although the tyrant had not opposed the establishment of the Mission, its presence was far from agreeable to him; and not only had he entirely withdrawn himself from Mosega, but he had also given great annoyance, by interdicting his people from entering the service of its members, alleging that they were capable of taking care of themselves. Under so despotic a government, it is not probable that the Matabili will ever derive much advantage from the exhortations of ministers of the gospel, were they even better disposed to receive them. In lieu of the reverence to which these worthy men were entitled, and which they would have received from other savage tribes, we not unfrequently observed groups of both sexes gazing in at the windows of the mission-houses as at wild beasts in a menagerie, with every demonstration of merriment at the expense of their inmates —behaviour, which the proceedings on the part of the king could not fail to induce on that of his subjects.

CHAPTER XII.

HISTORY OF CHAKA, SURNAMED "THE BLOODY."

But Moselekatse, with all his crimes, is no more than a humble follower in the sanguinary footsteps of Chaka, the liege lord from whom it has already been shown he revolted.   The reign of that inhuman despot, of whose singular career I purpose giving a brief outline,* was stained by a succession of enormities of so deep a dye that the blood curdles in the recital.   Even in the annals of savage nations his atrocities stand forth pre-eminent.   He was a fiend in human form, to whose vices and crimes history, neither ancient nor modern, can furnish the slightest parallel.

The family of this monster, whose name in the Sichuana language signifies " The battle-axe," was ever remarkable for its conquests, cruelty and ambition, and emerged from a tribe originally inhabiting a district about Delagoa Bay, of which tradition informs us the first king was named Zoola. Essenzinconyarna, the father of Chaka, made his way from the primitive location of his ancestors to the Umferoche Umstopic, or white river (a branch of the river St. Lucie), and colonizing within sixty miles of the coast kept the neighbouring tribes in

* Collected chiefly from Isaac's Travels in Eastern Africa.

terror and subjection.   In addition to thirty wives, he was possessed of concubines without number, and had many children, but from peculiar circumstances attending the birth of the infant Chaka, it was esteemed a miraculous event, and the child in consequence was held by the nation to be something superhuman.   Advancing towards manhood he did not disappoint the expectations formed of him.   His strength became Herculean, his disposition turbulent, his heart iron, his soul a warring element, and his ambition boundless.

The precocity, shrewdness, and cunning of Chaka speedily attracted the notice and jealousy of his father.   Knowing full well from the fate of his own progenitors that amongst the Zooloos, the son, whose ripening energies and developing physical powers, render him capable of setting an example for his subjects to imitate, experiences little difficulty in dethroning his aged and grey-headed sire, whose declining years render him no longer fit for feats of prowess, he resolved that the young prince should die, and began to plot his destruction.   Discovering this, Chaka fled with Umgartie, his younger and illegitimate brother, to a neighbouring tribe called the Umtatwas; by whose chief, Tingiswaa, being hospitably received, he soon distinguished himself, as well amongst the warriors by deeds of daring, as by his surpassing skill in punning and singing, both of which accomplishments are held in rare estimation—being, with the exception of dancing, almost the only amusements in which the Africans ever indulge.

On the sudden decease of Essenzinconyarna, one of his youngest sons assuming the crown of the Zooloos, Chaka at once resolved to dethrone him, and usurp his place at the head of the nation—with this view he formed a project which was speedily put in execution. Umgartie, his fraternal companion in exile, repaired to the residence of the young monarch with a story that Tingiswaa had slain Chaka, in consequence of which he had himself been obliged to fly for life and throw himself at his brother's feet for protection. This important and much wished for information being implicitly believed, Umgartie was presently installed in the office of chief domestic, and being thus constantly about the royal person, had every facility afforded him for the accomplishment of his bloody mission. Sending two of his confidential friends to secrete themselves in the long grass by the river side, while the king was taking his usual morning bath, the latter was speared to death on a preconcerted signal, and Chaka, at the head of the Umtatwas, took possession of the throne.

The putting to death all the principal persons of his brother's government, including every one that was suspected of being inimical to his own accession, was the first act that signalized his bloody reign. Tingiswaa dying shortly afterwards, the young king went to war with the Umtatwas—the nation that had so hospitably sheltered and protected him whilst in exile; and having destroyed the major part of the tribe, the remnant were fain to become his vassals. In a few years Chaka had depopulated the whole of the coast from the Amapoota River to the Ootagale—signal success also attending his incursions among the interior tribes, over which he exercised the most sanguinary persecution—pursuing them with a refinement in fiendish ferocity, too harrowing to be detailed.

Arriving at the zenith of his pride and ambition, and having, for a brief space, sated himself with the blood of his neighbours, the savage despot began to direct his thoughts towards the internal government of his realm—a measure which was rendered more than ever imperative from the circumstance of his extensive victories having placed him at the head of a gigantic and overgrowing nation. His first care was to discipline his rabble forces, which were already elated with achievements, originating chiefly from the dauntless and irresistible spirit of their leader. Ever in his own person did Chaka, surnamed " the bloody," set an example in the field well worthy the imitation of his followers; and whilst his ferocity kept his people in abject awe, dauntless intrepidity rendered him the terror of his opponents. Having once entered upon hostilities against a native power, his whole soul and energies were irrevocably bent on its extermination. Mercy was never for a moment an inmate of his bosom, and nothing short of rivers of blood, caused by the most lavish sacrifice of human life, was capable of gratifying his monstrous appetite. Partaking of this taste, his warriors were ever eager for battle,

and shouted for war from their love of plunder.
The magic of his name gained for them even more
renown than their actual prowess in arms, which
nevertheless was rendered desperately reckless by
the alternative he extended to them, of either returning victorious to participate in the spoils they
won, or being condemned to a cruel and immediate
death for alleged cowardice.

Chaka's army amounting altogether to near one
hundred thousand men, fifty thousand were mar-
shalled into regiments, and held in constant readiness for battle. These were formed into three
divisions, called *Umbalabale*, or the invincibles,
Umboolalio, or the slaughterers, and *Foogooso*, or
the hide-aways; a portion of each being incorporated with every force that took the field. Each
regiment was distinguished by shields of a different
colour, the great warriors having white ox-hides,
with one or two black spots ; the young soldiers,
black ; and those who possessed wives, were hence
denominated *Umfaundas*, or inferiors, red. Individuals distinguishing themselves in battle, were
honoured with a title, by which they were ever
afterwards accosted.

Having thus organized his army, the despot next
introduced a totally new system of discipline. The
slender javelins hitherto employed for throwing,
were abolished, and their use interdicted on pain of
death ; a single stabbing spear of stouter materials
being introduced in place of them. The superior
efficacy of this novel equipment, had previously been

established in a sham fight with reeds, which took place in presence of the assembled nation; and death by impalement was the penalty attached to the loss of the spear in battle. The warriors had now no alternative but to conquer or die; and as an additional spur to their valour, the commissariat of an invading army was never more than barely sufficient to subsist them to the scene of action. In order that the youths of the rising generation might imbibe a taste for military tactics, they were ordered to accompany the tried warriors in the capacity of esquires; and having attained an age which rendered them capable of wielding an assagai with effect, they were immediately supplied with arms, and duly incorporated.

With a view to render the troops as efficient as possible, the most unnatural abstinence was enforced, under the pretext that marriage deprives man of his relish for war, and causes his thoughts to be directed homewards, rather than towards his enemy. Commerce was likewise strictly forbidden, under the belief that it would enervate the people, and unfit them for their military duties. Every plan, in short, which ferocity and barbarity could devise, was resorted to by Chaka to inspire his men with a martial spirit; and under the excuse of perfecting the model of his army, the monster's unnatural propensities and insatiable thirst for blood, induced him, horrible to relate, to weed his warriors by singling out the maimed, the aged, and the infirm, to be put to the spear; observing, with savage

F

sagacity, that "such cripples were only in the way,
and without making him any return, did but consume his beef, which was required to make young
men stout and lusty!" Upon the occasion of this
foul slaughter of numerous brave veterans, to whose
valour and devotion Chaka owed a large portion of
his richest conquests, the wretch erected a kraal
upon which the name of *Gibbeklack*, signifying
" pick out the old ones," was humorously bestowed,
in commemoration of the base and barbarous deed!

Fully impressed with the conviction that his
warriors, thus organized and disciplined, would
prove themselves invincible, Chaka now indulged
in projecting movements upon a grander scale than
formerly; planning new predatory inroads upon
those independent tribes whose wealth in cattle
afforded the greatest inducements, and looking forward with a sort of prophetic spirit to a day not
far distant when all his ambitious schemes should
be achieved, when his expectations should be fully
realized, and he should find himself the sole and
undisputed " master of the world." A winter never
set in without its marauding expeditions; every
season also brought upon the weak and tributary
tribes, visits of violence, desolation, and plunder;
each in its turn sooner or later feeling the monster's
scourge for some alleged offence against majesty,
which alone had existence in his fertile invention.
The eve of going to war was with him always the
period of brutal and inhuman murders, in which he
seemed to indulge with the savage delight of the

tiger over its prey. A muster being taken prior to
his troops moving, those warriors who on any
previous occasion had not in his estimation properly
acquitted themselves of their duty, or (which was
held to be tantamount) were *suspected* of being
cowards, were singled out and publicly impaled.
Once determined on a sanguinary display of his
power, nothing could curb his ferocity. His
twinkling eye evinced the pleasure that worked
within. His iron heart exulted, and his whole
frame seemed as though knit with a joyous impulse,
at beholding the blood of the innocent flowing at
his feet! Grasping his Herculean limbs, his muscular hands exhibited by their motion a desire to
aid in the execution of the victims of his barbarity.
He seemed, in short, a being in human form endowed with more than the physical capabilities of
man; a giant without reason; a monster created
with more than ordinary power and disposition for
doing mischief, from whose withering glance man
recoiled as from the serpent's hiss or the lion's
growl.

Chaka constantly exercised a perfect system of
espionage which served to keep him minutely acquainted with the condition and strength of the
tribes, whether independent or tributary, by which
he was surrounded; his scouts being also enjoined
to make such observations regarding the country as
might enable them to lead his troops to the scene
of action with the least chance of discovery or surprise. Three months before he meditated an attack

F 2

he discoursed freely on war, and talked with confidence of routing his enemies—being withal exceedingly wary, and using every precaution to
conceal, even from his generals and chiefs, the real
power with which he designed to contend; precluding, by this crafty discretion, the possibility of
his enemies being in readiness for the march.
Should he not lead the army in person, his plans
were confided to a general-in-chief, who, however,
was never selected for command on a second occasion.
It was his invariable policy also to harangue his
warriors at their departure, in language calculated
to raise their expectations, and elate them in the
hour of battle; but in order to prevent any treacherous communication with the enemy, the true
object of the expedition was still studiously concealed, and the soldiers induced to believe that they
were about to attack any but the devoted tribe.
Achieving a signal triumph, the spoils were liberally
divided amongst them, as a stimulus to further
exertion; but defeat, under any circumstances, was
the watchword for a scene of woe and lamentation,
and for a massacre of no measured description—
numbers of brave men being hurried off, upon the
fiat of their ruthless and unappeasable master, to be
impaled as a warning beacon to future expeditions.

In all civilized countries cowardice in the army
is very properly punished with death, the testimony
of guilt having first been fully established; but
Chaka was neither remarkable for his nice discri-
mination, nor for his minute investigation of a

charge preferred. On one occasion, in particular, a whole regiment was indiscriminately butchered, together with the wives and families of the warriors that composed it—and who, although they had fought with signal bravery, had been overpowered by superior numbers, and thus compelled to retreat. The scene of this revolting tragedy was designated *Umboolalio*, or "the place of slaughter," in order to perpetuate its recollection in the minds of the people. But defeat was of rare occurrence. The predictions of the monarch were speedily verified by the success that attended his arms; and the fame of his troops spread rapidly over the whole country. Every tribe they encountered became an easy conquest; and no quarter being given, the inhabitants at once abandoned their villages and property to the mercy and rapacity of their insatiable invaders. Thus did Chaka spread devastation and terror throughout the whole country, from the Mapoota as low as the Umzimfoobo, or St. John's River. Tribe after tribe was invaded, routed, and mercilessly butchered: their huts were fired over their devoted heads, and the few that escaped of the ruined inmates, were driven to seek shelter in the depths of the forest—either to perish from hunger and want—to become a prey to wild beasts—or to be ultimately hunted down by the relentless and sanguinary Zooloo.

CHAPTER XIII.

HISTORY OF CHAKA, CONCLUDED.

DEATH ever reigned without a rival over the extensive dominions of Chaka, alike during the intervals of peace, as in time of war; the unexampled cruelties practised by the despot, and the plausible reasons assigned for their perpetration, being withal the surest means of governing his oppressed and wondering subjects. The nation were in the universal belief that their monarch dealt in necromancy, and held converse with the spirits of his forefathers; and so ably did he support this character, as to leave no doubt in their superstitious minds, that he possessed the power of reading their inmost thoughts, and of beholding their most secret actions; thus striking terror into them by his seeming unearthly power, and effectually checking any disposition to revolt against his inhuman decrees.

Having completed the re-organization of the army—elected rulers—abolished old laws—and enacted new ones—Chaka finally succeeded in establishing that which may with strict propriety be termed a *Zooloocratical* form of government. It is one that defies description or detail, and which neither can be comprehended nor digested; that affords protection to no living creature, and places

the trembling subject at the mercy of a despotic
monarch, whose nod may consign him, innocent or
guilty, to a lingering or instant death.   One that
may compel the agonizing father to butcher his unoffending child—brother to execute brother—the
husband to impale his wife—and the son to become
the inhuman mutilator of her that gave him birth!
The ties of consanguinity availed nothing with this
inhuman tyrant.   A sign given by the fatal pointing
of his blood-stained finger, or the terrible declination
of his head, must be promptly obeyed; and if, after
the perpetration of the revolting deed, the feelings
of violated nature should predominate, and manifest
themselves to this fiend in human form, the party
was ordered for instant dispatch, either by impalement, by having the neck twisted, or being stoned
or beaten to death with sticks.   The kith and kin of
the wretched victim likewise shared his fate; his
property being also seized and distributed amongst
the warriors.   Neither was any reason assigned for
the murderous decree, until it was too late to recal
the fiat of execution; the devoted subject frequently
thanking his savage monarch whilst he was undergoing the sentence that had been thus iniquitously
passed upon him.

To this enviable state of things, there succeeded
a dreadful lull, which may fitly be compared to that
which intervenes between the first and last shock of
an earthquake—when all are in consternation,
fearing that the next moment they may be swallowed
during the devastating convulsion.   This pause from

war and sanguinary executions, was devoted to the
superstitious ceremony of appeasing the manes of
the departed, and quieting the apprehensions of the
living, by great sacrifices of oxen, and by distributions
of the property of the murdered amongst the ex-
ecutioners.

Amongst barbarous tribes, it is a common custom
superstitiously to contend that their chiefs cannot
die naturally; that they are destined to live until
they fall in battle: and that death, proceeding
either from age or disease, is occasioned by the
"working of the wizard." This sanguinary superstition was carried to the fullest extent by Chaka,
who uniformly, on the death of a chief, endeavoured
to discover those who possessed the charm by the
test of their being unable to shed tears. On these
occasions numbers were put to death for not weeping—the forcing large quantities of snuff up the
nostrils in order to bring about a copious flood of
tears sometimes failing to have the desired effect.

As an example for his followers to imitate and
admire, Chaka married no queen, although at each
of his palaces he possessed from three to five
hundred girls, who were termed servants or sisters.
Becoming pregnant, a damsel was immediately put
to death upon some imaginary crime—the sturdy
executioner laying one hand upon the crown of the
head, placing the other under the chin, and dis-
locating the delicate neck by a sudden wrench.
The body was then dragged outside the kraal, and
left to be devoured by hyænas and carniverous

birds that were ever in attendance about the habitation of the destroyer, whose whole country had become a sepulchre white with the bones of his murdered subjects! Early one morning, Chaka took his seat as usual, and having with great earnestness enjoined his audience to secrecy, acquainted them that he had had a dream which greatly concerned him. The spirit of Umbeah, an old and favourite chief, had appeared, warning him of the designs of his people, and acquainting him that whilst he (Chaka) had been teaching songs to some of his warriors the preceding evening, others had been debauching his women, and polluting the imperial seraglio! This offence he declared himself determined to punish with rigour; and the courtiers applauding his resolution, he held a consultation with them as to the best mode of securing the whole of the people in the kraal. The place having been suddenly surrounded, the diabolical tyrant entered at the head of a party of warriors, and having first beaten his aged and infirm mother with inconceivable cruelty, "for not taking proper care of the girls," he caused one hundred and seventy persons, of both sexes, to be driven into the cattle enclosure; selecting several to be put to death with truly monstrous refinement by the hands of their own relatives, and leaving the remainder to be afterwards indiscriminately butchered. Upon the completion of this infernal work, his Majesty announced his intention of consulting Umbeah "in order that he might find out the rest of the delinquents;" adding,

that on the morrow he contemplated putting to
death all who had offended since the commencement of his reign, in order that nothing might be
wanting to complete his own happiness, and that of
his people.

Shortly after the perpetration of this satanic deed,
Umnante, the queen mother, died; and every
subject in the realm was expected to proceed, according to established custom, to the king's residence,
there to mourn for the illustrious deceased.   Umnante had been repudiated by Essenzinconyarna,
and had afterwards been guilty of signal infidelity
to the nation, by cohabiting with a commoner of her
father's tribe. Whether in consequence of this
lapse, or from some other circumstance, the usual
etiquette was somewhat laxly observed, and there
ensued an appalling tragedy, which had never been
exceeded either in brutality or foulness, by any of
the black and inhuman exploits detailed in the
long and bloody catalogue of Chaka's crimes! Upon
the grounds that "some of the subjects *must* have
been accessory by witchcraft to the death of the
queen mother, and did not therefore attend to mourn,"
several kraals and villages were fired; men, women,
and children, having first been cruelly tortured, were
roasted alive in the flames, by the ferocius agents of
a still more ferocius master; this act of unprecedented barbarity being followed up by a general
massacre throughout the realm—the tide of blood
flowing for a whole fortnight, and reeking of cruelties
too revolting to narrate!

But with this horrible and fiendish slaughter, terminated the unexampled reign of the bloody-minded Chaka. He had now subdued all the tribes, and laid waste the whole country, from the southern and western provinces lying about Delagoa Bay, as far as the nation of the Amaponda, two hundred miles south-west of Natal, and had begun to contemplate an attack on some of the frontier tribes. He, however, manifested the greatest apprehension of coming into collision with the white people, whose hostilities he was avowedly afraid to excite, and to whom, in his own country, he was hospitable from motives of prudence—and this consideration alone had restrained him from attacking those tribes that had thrown themselves under the protection of the Cape Government. Death arrested his merciless and ambitious career. He fell, as he deserved, by the hand of his own subjects, and by none was his fate mourned.

The assassination of Chaka had long been meditated by his brother Dingaan, and the diabolical massacre just detailed hastened the execution of his design. The tyrant was sitting one evening after sunset, with one or two of his principal chiefs, admiring the vast droves of sleek cattle returning to the kraal from pasture, and probably contemplating the murder of innocent beings, when he was startled by the audacity and unwonted demeanour of Boper, his principal attendant, who approached him with a spear used for slaughtering oxen, and in an authoritative tone demanded of the old chieftains,

who were humiliating themselves in the royal presence, " what they meant by pestering the king
with falsehoods and accusations?" An effort was
immediately made on the part of the exasperated
warriors to secure the traitor; and at that moment
Umslungani and Dingaan, the two elder brothers
of the despot, stealing unperceived behind him,
buried their assagais in his back. Chaka was enveloped in a blanket, which he instantly cast off,
making an ineffectual attempt to escape that death
to which his odious decrees had consigned so many
of his unoffending and loyal subjects. Being overtaken in his flight by his pursuers, the domestic
Boper transfixed him with his weapon. Falling at
their feet, the wretch besought his assassins in the
most abject terms to let him live, that he might be
their slave. To this dastardly appeal, however, no
heed was given; he was presently speared to death,
and the assassins then left him in order to execute
a similar deed upon the chiefs who were with him,
and who had also attempted to escape, but were
arrested in their flight, and shared the fate of their
ferocious master. One of these was an old grey-
headed warrior, who had. only a short time before
put to death his seven concubines, together with
their children, for having neglected to mourn for
the death of Umnante. Returning to the prostrate
body of their oppressor, the regicides then danced
and howled around it, as round the carcase of a
vanquished panther, an animal they greatly dread.
The inhabitants of the kraal fled in consternation,

and during the confusion that ensued, Dingaan ascended the throne.

So fell Chaka.   The Zooloo nation had too long
groaned under the weight of his tyranny, and had
superstitiously bowed to the yoke of his oppression,
until they could no longer bear up under his
insatiable and wanton cruelties.   His fall was
followed by a general rejoicing throughout the
country.   It afforded to the nation an interval of
repose from the horrors of war, and from the terror
which his savage decrees had constantly excited.
During his life there had been no security either for
person or property; no escape from his barbarous
innovations and inhuman butcheries.   His subjects
each had lived from day to day in increasing dread
lest the reeking finger of the tyrant should next
point at him as a signal for death and devastation.

To his savage propensities, Chaka added the
most extraordinary caprices and singular whims;
he lay on his belly to eat his meals, and compelled
his chiefs to do the same in token of their dignity,
and it was his custom to bathe every morning in
public at the head of his kraal, first anointing his
body with bruised beef, and then with an unguent
of sheep's-tail fat, or native butter.   Though not a
cannibal, he was a savage in the truest sense of the
word, and inherited no redeeming quality.   In war
an insatiable and exterminating fiend, in peace an
unrelenting and sanguinary despot; he kept his
people in awe by his monstrous executions, and was
unrestrained in his vicious career because they were

ignorant of their power.   Ever thirsting for the
blood of his subjects, the base dissembler could
stand unmoved, and blandly smile, while he feasted
on the execution of his atrocious decrees ; or he
could assume an expression of deep sorrow at the
necessity which had called him to issue them.   The
world has been scourged by monsters.   Rome had
her Nero, the Huns their Atila, and Syracuse her
Dionysius, the East has likewise produced her
tyrants ; but Chaka immeasurably eclipsed them
all.   In sanguinary executions, and in refined cruelties, he outstripped all who have gone before him
in any country.   He was a monster—a compound
of vice and ferocity—without one virtue to redeem
his name from the infamy to which history has consigned it.

CHAPTER XIV.

FROM MOSEGA TO THE KURRICANE MOUNTAINS.

LEAVING the Mission-house on the 22nd October, and repassing the town of Mosega, within the fence of which we saw Erasmus's captured waggons, our road wound for some distance, in a north-westerly direction, amongst numerous Matabili villages, having all the same form and appearance, though varying considerably in size and extent. A circular thorn fence, six or eight feet in height, with only one entrance, encloses a sloping area; around the circumference of which the dwellings or huts are constructed. The cattle are kept during the night in the space so surrounded. The domiciles are paltry low wigwams, of a circular form, having one small doorway directed towards the centre; it is of very narrow dimensions, barely affording space for a man to crawl through upon his hands and knees. Crowds of women and children poured down from each kraal as we passed, holding out their hands and then placing their noses in the hollow of the palm, snuffing and sneezing violently, as a hint that they required *Qui*, or snuff, for which, to them the greatest of all luxuries, they became as usual extremely clamorous. We saw comparatively few men, the larger proportion of the able-bodied being absent with Kalipi on the commando against the emigrant farmers.   The Missionaries estimated this force to consist of near five thousand warriors.

On the north and north-east, the Kurricane range of mountains rose in majestic grandeur, a great treat to us after the extensive unvaried flat over which we had travelled since leaving Kuruman, and indeed almost ever since passing the Sneuwbergen. The cultivated land in all parts of the basin was extensive ; and countless herds of sleek oxen were grazing on the slopes.   Our one-eyed friend, the deputy-governor, who was exceedingly reluctant to leave such amiable society, had taken his seat on the fore-chest of the leading waggon, having first paid Cœur de Lion the compliment of removing his camlet cloak, and enveloping his own greasy person therein as a protection against the cold, which was far from moderate.   The old man's elliptically crowned bald pate protruded above the high collar, contrasted with the grotesque solemnity of his deportment, had a sufficiently ludicrous appearance. Baba, the interpreter, had brought two horses, one of which he rode.   Piet, who fancied himself at the point of death, had composed himself upon my cot, of which he held the monopoly for several days ; and the two savages who had announced our advent to the king, accompanied us as guides, or more correctly speaking, as spies.   These fellows rendered themselves particularly obnoxious during the whole journey, by their peremptory interference in our affairs, as well as by their offensive familiarity

They often clambered into our beds without ceremony, and obtruded themselves stark naked when
least required.

We unyoked for breakfast on the bank of one of
the numerous streams that here form the source of
the Mariqua, a river of which I shall have occasion
frequently to speak. A spacious and level valley,
hemmed in on three sides by the skirting hills of the
Kurricane range, was intersected by three or four
of these rivulets, whose serpentine course could be
traced by the sedges that rose high above their banks.
As soon as the governor had completed his breakfast, and the waggons were ready to proceed, the
extension of his excellency's greasy hand announced
his intention of leaving us and returning to Mosega.
A severe *pump-handling*, and the presentation of
two bunches of beads to himself, and a brass-wire
collar to his little son, whilst it firmly cemented our
friendship, terminated our acquaintance for ever,
under a parting assurance, that he had made a favourable report of us to his royal master, who was,
he said, " *Monanti, Monanti, Monanti,*" or in plain
English, the most gracious of sovereigns.

As the waggons proceeded, we turned off the road
in search of a rhinoceros, and speedily became so
entangled in a labyrinth of thorn fences, newly constructed to entrap game, that we had great difficulty in extricating ourselves. Stiff thorn branches,
too high to be surmounted, were firmly fixed in the
ground, and so entwined amidst a dense grove of
mimosas, that after fruitless endeavours to force a

passage in various places, we found that we had ridden completely round the enclosure, to the point at which we had first entered.

In the course of two hours the waggons had reached the termination of the plain, and were beginning to ascend the ridge which bounds the valley of Mosega.   We shortly afterwards entered a pass, or gap, which conducted us between two ranges of the Kurricane hills; the slopes on either side were covered with stately trees, from which depended clusters of moss and festoons of various parasitic plants.   The ground was broken and stony, and in parts abounded with deep holes.   In the act of killing a sassayby, my horse put his feet into one of these, and came down with frightful violence, cutting my knees and elbows to the bone, breaking his own nose, and, what was a far greater misfortune, and one that I had long anticipated, fracturing the stock of my only and especially favourite rifle.   I could have wept, if the doing so would have availed any thing.   A strip of the sassayby's hide rectified the damage, for the present at least; and having packed the flesh in the waggon, we continued winding among the hills, constantly assured by the guides that the kraal at which they had resolved we should pass the night, was close at hand, but still not reaching it until we had travelled full thirty miles from Mosega, by which time it was fairly dark.   At last we perceived fires in the valley beneath us, and soon drew up under the fence of a little village, constructed as usual on a slope.

Scarcely were the oxen unyoked, when the clouds, which had been collecting for some hours, burst at once upon our devoted heads. Deafening claps of thunder peeled above us, preceded by forked and vivid lightning, which cast upon the surrounding landscape a lurid and almost incessant glare. The windows of heaven were literally opened, and a pelting pitiless deluge descended, which in an instant extinguished the fire, and put an end to all culinary operations. We, however, succeeded in obtaining a little milk from the village, and in a few minutes Morpheus strewing his poppies over us, we ceased to trouble our heads about the state of the weather, or our soaking supperless condition.

A tranquil morning succeeded the most tempestuous of nights. The inhabitants of the kraal were anxious that we should shoot a rhinoceros, which they pretended to have seen at no great distance; but although we sacrificed one-half of our raiment in the attempt to oblige them, the animal was no where to be found. The road still wound among the mountains; three hours travelling brought us to a kraal at no great distance from the ancient town of Kurricane, in which Mr. Campbell found the Baharootzis about ten years ago. This once populous city was destroyed by Moselekatse, and the inhabitants scattered in various directions. Here the guides declared it was the king's command that we should tarry until the following day, when he expected to see us. But as the royal lodge was still far distant, we obstinately

insisted upon continuing our journey after breakfast,-
so as to get clear of the hills in the course of the
day; and were accordingly preparing to start when
a herald, called, in the Matabili language, *Imbongo,*
a proclaimer of the king's titles, suddenly made
his appearance outside the kraal, to give us a little
insight into his Majesty's biography. Advancing
slowly towards the waggons, he opened the exhibition by roaring and charging, in frantic imitation
of the king of beasts—then placing his arm before
his mouth, and swinging it rapidly in pantomimic
representation of the elephant, he threw his trunk
above his head and shrilly trumpeted. He next
ran on tiptoe, imitating the ostrich; and lastly,
humbling himself in the dust, wept like an infant.
At each interval of the scene, he recounted the
matchless prowess and mighty conquests of his
illustrious monarch, and made the hills re-echo
with his praise. He was a brawny athletic savage,
upwards of six feet in height, naked as he was
born. Frenzied by his energetic gesticulations, the
perspiration trickled from his greasy brow, and
white foam descended in flakes from his distorted
mouth, whilst his eye glared with excitement.

The road now became almost impassable—
large trees overhung the way, and threatened the
destruction of the waggon tents; we proceeded very
slowly, and narrowly escaped being upset, the
jungle becoming more and more intricate as we advanced. Game-traps and pit-falls were to be seen
through every avenue, many of the thorn fences

extending across the path, and impeding the waggons until cut away with the hatchet. A party of
six natives had followed our tracks and volunteered
to show a giraffe.*   I emerged under their guidance from the forest we were threading, into a wide
plain, on which I saw, for the first time, the footsteps of four of these gigantic quadrupeds, but no
living objects, save a few sassaybys, one of which I
foolishly shot, when four of my savages immediately
slunk behind to eat him.   I was much struck with
the *spoor* or track of the cameleopard—it was different from every thing I had seen or imagined it
would resemble. The largest impression was eleven
inches in length, of parallelogramatic form, tapered
at the toe, and rounded at the heel. I felt singular
satisfaction in finding myself at length treading on
ground imprinted with the recent footsteps of that
extraordinary animal.

I had by this time ridden far in advance of the
waggons, and as night was fast closing around, I
began to be apprehensive that I should have to
bivouac in the bush. The savages appeared to
contemplate the same contingency, and evinced a
vast longing to join their companions, who had
wisely remained with the flesh-pots. I gave them
by signs to understand that I disapproved of such a
measure, and we all pushed on as briskly as possible. A contumacious rhinoceros † was standing
directly in our path, and, although hailed repeat-

* *Cameleopardalis Giraffa.* }Delineated in the African Views.
† *Rhinoceros Africanus.*   }

edly, refused to make way. There was just light sufficient to admit of my discharging both barrels of my rifle into his unwieldy sides. Sneezing violently, and wheezing, he ran off in the direction we were taking, and presently subsided in the path. We approached him with caution, but he was dead. At the same moment a discharge of musketry, and a bright beacon fire bursting forth, directed our benighted steps to the encampment. It was at the termination of the forest, and not more than two hours' journey from the residence of the king.

CHAPTER XV.

ARRIVAL AT KAPAIN, AND VISIT FROM THE CHIEF MOSELEKATSE.

THE absence of water, added to our anxiety to kiss the hand of his Majesty, induced us to yoke the oxen much earlier than usual on the 24th. The Hottentots were all in high spirits, their timidity having actually left them for a season. It seemed as if some new and exciting emotion were felt at our near approach to the king, which they considered as a crisis in their fate. Even Cœur de Lion was resigned to his doom—he had dried his eyes, and went like a lamb to the slaughter. It was a soft golden morning, and five miles travelling over a fertile plain, broken occasionally by isolated hills of inconsiderable altitude — and covered with large herds of oxen, brought us within a short distance of three conical mountains, disposed in a triangular form, within the area enclosed by which we were told that the royal kraal would be found. As our approach was discovered, the tops of the hills became lined with natives, some of whom ran down at intervals to report our progress, but it was not until we had actually entered the gorge, that a miserable hamlet was perceived, which Baba immediately pointed out as the imperial residence.

Piet and the Parsee now guided the waggons: Cœur de Lion, not wishing to find himself in the front of the battle, volunteered to drive the cattle in the rear, and the other six Hottentots proceeded in advance with solemn step, saluting the king with repeated discharges of musketry, as a complimentary mode of announcing our arrival. Several of the subordinate chieftains, who were standing near the gateway of the kraal, then advanced, and as the waggons ascended the acclivity, took the hand of each of our party in succession, repeating the word *Fellow! fellow! fellow!* several times. The principal of these men was Um'Nombate, a peer of the realm. He was an elderly man of slight figure, benevolent aspect, and mild but dignified demeanour. He wore the usual tails, consisting of a few strips of wild cat and monkey skin dangling in front, and some larger and more widely apart behind. The elliptical ring, or *issigoko*, was surmounted by the inflated gall-bladder of a sheep. Andries, Piet, and April, were old acquaintances, and he appeared glad to see them. In reply to our inquiries respecting the health of the king, and whether it was the royal pleasure that we should visit him, he observed that his Majesty was very glad we had arrived, and would come to the waggons anon, at the same time directing them to be drawn up outside the gate. The next in rank was a chief of mean and contemptible exterior, whose repulsive manners were but too exactly indicated by his scowling profile. He was deeply scarred with

small-pox; and excepting a necklace of lions'
claws, three inflated gall-bladders on his pate, and
a goodly coat of grease upon his hide, was perfectly
naked. I saw nothing remarkable about any of the
others. They all carried snuff-boxes stuck in their
ears; a collection of skin streamers, like the tails of
a lady's boa, attached to a thin waist-cord, being
the nearest approach to an habiliment amongst
them. All their heads were shaven, sufficient hair
only being left to attach the *issigoko*, which is composed of sinews sewn to the hair, and blackened with
grease.

Shortly after the oxen were unyoked, and the
tent erected, Mohanycom, the king's page, came
forth from the kraal bearing the congratulations of
his Majesty. He, too, was unincumbered with
raiment of any sort; but wore a red feather from
the long-tailed finch in his hair, which, unlike that
of the rest, was unshorn, and destitute of the *issigoko*.
The dimensions of his mouth were calculated to
excite the astonishment of every beholder, that
feature literally extending from ear to ear. An
inspection of our property then took place. Not a
word was spoken; neither did any of the party
betray the smallest symptom either of surprise or
even of gratification. An imperturbable gravity
pervaded the countenance of every one, and as soon
as they had sufficiently scrutinized, they retired to
report to the chieftain the result of their observations.

It was some hours before we could obtain any
breakfast, the nearest water being three miles from

G

the kraal. We felt quite certain that the king must
be dying with impatience to obtain possession of
the various presents we had brought for him, but
he thought it dignified to affect indifference, and
prosecuted his ideas of propriety so rigorously, that
his non-appearance became at length alarming.
We therefore dispatched Baba to say that everything was prepared for his reception, and that we
were extremely anxious to pay our respects.   In
the course of a few minutes, loud shouting and yelling announced his approach.   He was attended by
the spies that had accompanied us from Mosega,
several of his chiefs, and most of the warriors who
were not absent on the expedition I have alluded to,
armed with shields and assagais.   As he advanced
others rushed up with a shout, brandishing their
sticks.   A number of women followed with calabashes of beer on their heads; and two pursuivants
cleared the way, by roaring, charging, prancing,
and caricoling as already described, flourishing
their short sticks in a most furious manner, and
proclaiming the royal titles in a string of unbroken
sentences.   As we advanced to meet him, several
of the crowd exclaimed " *Haiyah! Haiyah!*" a
shout of congratulation and triumph.   Having
shaken hands, we led him into the tent, and seated
him on a chair; the courtiers and great men squatting themselves on their hams on the ground in
semicircular order on either side.   He was particularly glad to see Andries, and shook him by
the hand several times.

MOSELEKATSE, KING OF THE AMAZOOLOO.

The expression of the despot's features, though singularly cunning, wily, and suspicious, is not altogether disagreeable. His figure is rather tall, well turned, and active, but through neglect of exercise, leaning to corpulency. Of dignified and reserved manners, the searching quickness of his eye, the point of his questions, and the extreme caution of his replies, stamp him at once as a man capable of ruling the wild and sanguinary spirits by which he is surrounded. He appeared about forty years of age, but being totally beardless, it was difficult to form a correct estimate of the years he had numbered. The elliptical ring on his closely shorn scalp was decorated with three green feathers from the tail of the paroquet, placed horizontally, two behind and one in front. A single string of small blue beads encircled his neck; a bunch of twisted sinews encompassed his left ankle, and the usual girdle dangling before and behind with leopards' tails completed his costume.

The interpreters, three in number, were ranged in front. After a long interval of silence, during which the chieftain's eyes were far from inactive, he opened the conversation by saying he rejoiced we had come to bring him news from his friends the white people. Mohanycom put this speech into Sichuana, Baba translated it into Dutch, and Andries endeavoured to render the meaning intelligible in English. To this we replied, that having heard of the king's fame in a distant land, we had come three moons across the great water to see

G 2

him, and had brought for his acceptance a few
trifles from our country, which we thought would
prove agreeable.   He smiled condescendingly, and
the Parsee immediately placed at his august feet
the *duffel* great coat which I have already described, as being lined and trimmed with scarlet
shalloon; a coil of brass wire weighing fifty pounds;
a mirror two feet square; two pounds of Irish
blackguard snuff, and fifty pounds weight of blood-
red beads.   Hitherto the king had considered it
beneath his dignity to evince the slightest symptom
of astonishment—his manner had been particularly
guarded and sedate, nor had it been possible to
read in his countenance aught that was passing in
his bosom—but the sight of so many fine things at
once threw his decorum off the balance, and caused
him for the moment to forget what he owed to
himself in the presence of so large an assembly.
Putting his thumb between his teeth, and opening
his eyes to their utmost limits, he grinned like a
school-boy at the sight of gingerbread, patting his
breast, and exclaiming repeatedly, " *Monanti, mo-*
nanti, monanti; tanta, tanta, tanta! "* Having
particularly brought to his notice that the device of
an uplifted arm grasping a javelin, on the clasp of
the great coat, referred to his extensive conquests,
of which all the world had heard, we placed before
him a suit of tartan sent by Mrs. Moffat, with a
note which he requested me to read; and hearing
his own name, coupled with that of Ma Mary, as

* Good, good, good; bravo, bravo, bravo!

he termed that lady, and the word *tumerisho*
(compliments) he grinned again, and clapped me
familiarly on the back, exclaiming as before " *Tanta,
tanta, tanta !*"   He now rose abruptly, big with
some great conception, and made signs to the
Parsee to approach and assist him on with the coat;
habited in which he strutted several times up and
down, viewing his grotesque figure in the glass
with evident self-applause.   He then desired Mohanycom to put it on and turn about, that he might
see if it fitted behind ; and this knotty point settled
to his unqualified satisfaction, he suddenly cast off
his tails, and appearing *in puris naturalibus,* commanded all hands to assist in the difficult undertaking of shaking him into the tartan trowsers.   It
was indeed no easy work to perform—but once
accomplished, his Majesty cut a noble figure.   The
Parsee wore a pair of red silk braces, which he
presently demanded, observing that they would
supply the place of those that Mrs. Moffat *had forgotten* to send.   Shortly after this, he directed an
attendant, who was crouching at his feet, to take
every thing to his kraal; and resuming his solemnity and his seat, tea was brought in.   A number of gourds filled with *outchualla,* or beer, were
placed by the king's orders before the assembly,
who, passing them from one to the other, emptied
them on the spot.   Richardson and myself drank
tea out of two battered plated goblets, whilst the
king's mess was served in a flowered china bowl,
as being a more attractive vessel, and less likely to

retain the heat; but having eyed the different
drinking-cups for some time suspiciously, he handed
his own to his attendants, and then extending his
arm abruptly seized upon my goblet, and greedily
drained the contents. It is well known that savages,
however debased they may be in the scale of
humanity, are keenly susceptible of indignity; and
he either considered himself slighted, or had prudently determined, until we should become better
acquainted, to taste nothing of which we had not in
the first instance partaken ourselves.

It was now time to allude to our affairs, and
having repeated that our principal object in coming
into his country, was to make his acquaintance, we
proceeded to ask permission to hunt elephants.
This request was readily granted: but on stating
that we had little time, and should wish to return
to the colony by a nearer route than the one we
had come, he shook his head and gravely remarked
that there was no other road. As this reply passed
through Andries, he became dreadfully agitated,
and opening both eyes, he stuttered forth, with a
vehemence of manner which drew upon him the
attention of the whole assembly, that the king never
would consent to let any person depart by the Vaal
River, and that we should all have our throats cut if
we hinted further at such an arrangement! At
this moment, however, the opportune return of a
messenger, gave a fortunate turn to the conversation
The king had sent for his dress of state, that we
might have an opportunity of admiring the match-

less taste with which he had arranged some materials that had been presented to him by Sir Benjamin D'Urban. It was an apron composed of black goat-skin streamers, loaded with beads of every size and colour, and with a profusion of brass chains and ornaments disposed in an endless variety of patterns that did ample honour to his inventive genius.

The production of this article led the king to inquire after the health of our most gracious Sovereign, of whom he said he had heard, and whom he declared to be, next to himself, the greatest monarch of the universe, adding, that the white king's nation was undoubtedly second to his own in power. The dialogue proceeded very slowly, in consequence of the necessity of its being conducted through the tiresome medium of four different languages. Andries did not perform *his* duties with much regularity, and seemed to consider that the colloquy was intended for his own instead of for our edification. Under this delusion, he fancied that he had acquitted himself of the obligation we had imposed, if he favoured us with an occasional scrap. The king sometimes understood what Baba said in Sichuana to Mohanycom, nodding his head graciously, smiling, and repeating "*Tanta, tanta, tanta.*" At length the conversation flagged. Directing a sheep and sundry calabashes of beer to be placed before us, the despot arose, and abruptly, without the slightest compliment, made his exist amid the congratulations of his loyal subjects. The heralds

preceding him as before, rent the air with shouts
and acclamations, until " the great black one" had
re-entered his kraal.

During this serious yet laughable interview, we
were not a little surprised to observe that the guides,
who had by their freedom rendered themselves so
highly offensive to us, continued bruising and snuffing tobacco, without appearing the least abashed
in the royal presence. Whilst every one else cringed
beneath the tyrant's glance with obsequious humility,
they alone appeared at ease, nor were we able to
account for this behaviour, otherwise than by conjecturing that their too palpable office of spies upon
our actions admitted them to these liberties. They
had never quitted the waggons for a single instant
since we left Mosega, had watched all our actions
with the most provoking attention, and on our
arrival at Kapain, had doubtless reported to the
king every, the most minute, circumstance that had
transpired.

CHAPTER XVI.

RESIDENCE AT KAPAIN.

We were shortly afterwards visited by the king without either pageant or ceremony. This he considered a confidential interview, and said he had come " to see what we had got for him." The weather being cold, he was attired in a handsome black leathern mantle ; its ample folds, reaching to his heels, well became his tall and manly person ; and he looked the very *beau ideal* of an African Chief. He had completely thrown aside that reserve and gravity which in a public assembly he had conceived most becoming, and now appeared in high good humour, joking, laughing, and familiarly pulling our beards, of which the luxuriant growth elicited his admiration and surprise. He frequently asked us how many wives we had, and whether they also had beards. We thought this an auspicious moment in which to revert to the subject of our desired exit by the Vaal River, but took especial care to exclude Andries from the conference. Besides being a bad interpreter, we had seen that he was personally opposed to the measure, and we consequently preferred Richard, who had now recovered his self-possession, and was a much more impartial dragoman.

G 5

Arrowsmith's map of Africa having been produced, we placed a finger upon Graaff Reinet,
Kuruman, and Mosega, explaining to the king how
many days journey would be saved, if we were to
return to the Colony by the Vaal River.   He shook
his head as before, and petulantly observed, that
he had already said there was no road through that
country.   We laughed, and expressed a wish to
look for one ; but he rejoined, that his anxiety for
our safety would not allow him to hear of our travelling in that direction,—that should any accident
befal us, the white king would undoubtedly attribute
blame to him, and he therefore must insist upon
our giving up the intention.   Through this flimsy
veil, however, we could distinguish motives that
were in no way connected with our safety.   The
chieftain was naturally desirous of concealing, as
far as possible, the havoc that his people had made
amongst the emigrant farmers; and he was above
all things anxious to obtain further presents on our
return from the interior.   We saw the necessity of
waiving the subject for the present, but secretly
determined to attack him anon with his own weapons.

He soon became extremely eager to have a sight
of our various wares, but we steadily resisted his
teasing importunities to examine the contents of the
boxes.   Knowing that all savages possess the sor-
did passion of avarice in an extraordinary degree,
and have the insatiate desire of accumulating property for the mere pleasure of possessing it, we had
omitted no precaution to keep his Majesty in pro-

found ignorance of the nature and extent of our supplies. To have permitted him to see the contents of the waggons, would most assuredly have tempted him to practise every unfair and extortionate stratagem to obtain possession of them. We only therefore placed in his way, as baits, those trinkets that we designed he should take, and these, as well as everything else that met his eye, he never failed to appropriate. A pair of my shoes having been casually exposed, though much too small, were instantly seized and donned, and the operation of trying them on was highly diverting. A silken waist-cord was quickly transferred from my Indian sleeping drawers to his own neck, the tassels dangling in front; a red woollen night-cap was drawn over his bald pate, and a comforter over his shoulders, and he repeatedly desired the interpreters to explain that "he liked all and everything!" He crawled through the waggons, and diligently rummaged in every corner for beads, of which he frequently spoke. On this most important topic with all savages, he was particularly urgent; he said he liked every colour and size, sending at the same time to his seraglio for a vast variety, that we might distinctly comprehend his wishes on the subject. With the greatest reluctance, he at last prevailed upon himself to part with a single grain of each colour, as a sample to guide our selection when we should next visit him, and having gained this victory over his niggard nature, he repeated several times significantly, that we "now knew exactly what he wanted." The visit was a very long one : the king begged that we would publish to the white traders in the colony, his anxiety to obtain muskets and ammunition in barter for elephants' teeth. He spoke also on various subjects that interested him, particularly respecting the productions of the white men's country. His eyes had repeatedly wandered towards, and latterly been riveted upon a coil of brass wire, a portion of which protruded from the waggon, and before quitting us, he darted suddenly upon it, grinning with triumph, and bearing it along with him with the greatest exultation.

In the evening, as his numerous herds of cattle were returning from pasture, the king gave us a proof of the munificence of his nature, by selecting two of the worst oxen and a toothless cow, of which he begged our acceptance. We had repeatedly introduced the subject of cattle, bringing to his notice the miserable condition of our own teams, and hinting an expectation that he would recruit them. He had always replied with great readiness that they would soon get fat, as there was abundance of grass and water in the country to which we were journeying ; but we were certainly not prepared for so unequivocal a specimen of the royal bounty. About dark he sent to *borrow* some wax candles, at the same time sending by Um'Nombate the stewed breast of an ox, and a supply of beer. We requested the old man to honour us with his company, which he readily did, emptying his plate faster than we could fill it, and swallowing at a draught the

contents of a whole calabash of the native malt
liquor.   This detestable beverage, which is denominated *outchualla,* is of a whitish colour, frothy, and
produced from fermented Kafir corn.   Moselekatse
avowed himself an ardent admirer of it, and we
understood frequently drank it to intoxication. Out
of compliment to him I partook of it, but found it
very unpalatable.   The Hottentots averred that it
was not stronger than water, but they invariably
talked more at length and louder after drinking it,
and Claas was lying the whole day under a bush,
sealed in a torpor induced by the potations of it he
had swallowed.   Long files of women, singing as
they walked, were constantly to be seen arriving
from the adjacent kraals with bowls of this nectar
upon their heads ; and our guides were ready re-
cipients for any quantity that might be sent for our
consumption, loudly in their cups shouting the
praises of the king,

The full moon rose in cloudless beauty, rendering
the night nearly as light as day. We had been a
short time in bed when Um'Nombate aroused me
stealthily, offering me an elephant's tooth in exchange for beads, and assuring me that the king
should never know of the transaction. We were
too well acquainted with Moselekatse's character
to be lured by Um'Nombate's proposal, and never
doubting that he was a mere tool in the hands of
the king, dismissed him without ceremony, appriz-
ing him that we could make no exchange, except by
his Majesty's order.   The courtier retired discom-

fited, and the result proved that we were not wrong in our conjecture.

Shortly after daybreak, and almost before we had dressed, the despot himself was seen approaching with solemn step, accompanied by Um'Nombate, and a man bearing the identical elephant's tusk on his shoulder. He was instantly surrounded by ten or twelve persons, who ran from a distance and crouched before him. All this looked exceedingly ominous. We had heard of the execution of two culprits some time before, in presence of a trader, and were half afraid that the old man, having been detected in his delinquency by some of the spies about the waggons, was about to suffer condign punishment. The king seated himself upon a chair and looked mysterious; Um'Nombate squatted himself upon the ground with the dejected air of a criminal, and the rascally tooth was placed before them. We felt very uneasy, but pretended not to notice it, until his Majesty himself drew our attention to it by kicking it with his foot, and observing that Um'Nombate wished to receive some beads in exchange for it. This speech, although bearing more the character of a demand than a request, relieved our anxiety, but we replied that ivory was of no use to us, our oxen being quite unable to transport so heavy a commodity,—that we were ready to barter beads, or indeed anything we possessed, for fat oxen, adding, that if the king wished, we would gladly present a few beads to our friend Um'Nombate, but begged to decline accepting the ivory. The king did wish this very particularly, and the beads were accordingly given, the tusk being, however, left on the ground, to give to the transaction the colour of an equitable exchange.

We very justly took credit to ourselves for the way in which we had brought this affair to so amicable a conclusion. It was now evident that Moselekatse, as we suspected, had been privy to the whole transaction, and had availed himself of this pitiful stratagem to gratify his insatiate appetite for beads, and, if possible, to ascertain the extent of our resources. The villain Andries was clearly in the king's confidence, and had doubtless given him all the information in his power; and it is more than probable that the realization of half a dozen bunches of beads, by this paltry contemptible scheme, had afforded his Majesty infinitely greater gratification than he had been capable of deriving from the receipt of our liberal, and in his judgment, no doubt, princely presents.

But we had soon an opportunity of turning this greediness to account, and dealing with the king in his own fashion. In order to avoid creating suspicion as to the object of our desired return by the Vaal River, we lost no opportunity of impressing upon him that our leave was limited, that we were not colonial subjects, but that we had come in a ship from a far country of which the Parsee was a native. His Majesty frequently expressed amusement at his dress, remarking that he was a fine fellow to come so great a distance, and must not forget to make his *tumerisho* to the Parsee king, inquiring if that potentate too had a black beard, and wore a high turban—how many wives he had, &c. He even paid Nesserwanjee the compliment of desiring to inspect his pocket-knife, with six blades, nippers, picker, and corkscrew, complete, which, however, he forgot to return. We ever carefully abstained from making any allusion to the capture of Erasmus's waggons, or to the military proceedings against the emigrant farmers.

This morning messengers were seen running breathless with haste to acquaint the king with the success of Kalipi's attack. There was an unusual stir in consequence, and warriors were continually coming and going during the greater part of the day. The king appeared in high glee, but we carefully affected ignorance of all that was passing, and were thus gradually securing his confidence in the honourable nature of our intentions, regarding which he had evidently been distrustful. In spite, however, of all we could do, our Hottentots were perpetually prying round the imperial kraal, and putting impertinent questions to persons about the waggons; all which being scrupulously reported, had an exceedingly mischievous tendency, and caused us constant annoyance and anxiety.

CHAPTER XVII.

RESIDENCE AT KAPAIN, CONTINUED.

A DESIRE to see something of the king's domestic economy induced us repeatedly to ask permission to visit him, but he invariably replied that he had no place in which to receive us, and indeed he passed the greater part of his time in lounging on our beds or in the tent. To-day, 25th October, he was in unusual spirits, in consequence of the success of his arms against the emigrants. We affected to be alarmed at the possibility of an attack from Dingaan whilst hunting elephants to the eastward, but he ridiculed the idea, adding bitterly, that Dingaan was a cowardly rascal and not fit to live. We had observed him for some minutes plucking blades of grass from below his chair, apparently lost in thought, and at times scanning our countenances with great intenseness, when all of a sudden he exclaimed that he wanted our tent. This was the very opportunity we had been looking for; we had foreseen that he would become enamoured of it, and had determined to make it the stepping-stone to the attainment of our wishes. With affected indifference we accordingly replied, that if he had determined that we should return by the circuitous route of Kuruman, we could not dispense with the accommodation the tent afforded; but that if we could proceed by the Vaal River, it should be sent to him as soon as the hunting was over.   The high road to his heart was gained; his eyes twinkled, and after a moment's hesitation he said that he had been thinking the matter over, and that we were at liberty to go wherever we pleased!   Having made this gratifying announcement the king withdrew.

Our object was now accomplished, but the miscreant Andries no sooner heard that his predictions had been falsified, than he industriously circulated a report that the bushmen across the Vaal were so cruel and vindictive that there was not the most remote probability of our regaining the colony by that route; and from that moment the fear of death by poisoned arrows took the place of the dastardly dread of the "great black one," whom our followers now pronounced to be a "very fine gentleman."   I need scarcely add, that the despot's beer had no small effect in producing this revolution of sentiment.   In about half an hour the king sent for the tent.   This we had anticipated in the natural train of events; but in order to enhance the value of the bribe, we took the liberty of reminding him of the terms of the agreement, and declined to part with it until the hunting should be over, inwardly hoping that this *ruse* would hasten our dismissal, for which we were hourly becoming more anxious.

The wealth of this barbarous sovereign may be said almost to consist in his innumerable droves of horned cattle. These are herded in various parts of the country, and furnish employment to a considerable portion of his lieges, who are precariously maintained by his bounty, but depend chiefly for support upon their success in hunting. The deaths and casualties which occur amongst the oxen at different out-stations are regularly reported, and we had an opportunity of seeing this frequently done during our visit. Running with all speed to within about fifty yards of the king, a warrior places his arms upon the ground, and assuming a subdued posture, with his head bowed to the dust, crawls within ear-shot, when all those about the royal person exclaim " *Haiyah! Haiyah!*" and the report is made in a raised tone. This done, the soldier remains crouched a few seconds, his eyes bent on the ground, and if the king has no questions to ask, suddenly springs on his feet, exclaiming " *Haiyah!*" and runs back to his arms.

Moselekatse frequently inquired about King William's flocks and herds, asking if they were very extensive, a subject on which we could not enlighten him. He also spoke of our Sovereign's armies. The king's own warriors, who were present, we could not but admire, although the despot described them as young unfleshed soldiers, who had not yet gained a name in arms. They were, generally speaking, tall and handsome; clad with the usual tails, and the addition of two long red feathers in the hair when it was unshorn, or a cluster of variegated white and black feathers from the kingfisher or jay, falling gracefully so as to obscure one eye. They carried a short thrusting-spear—a club of rhinoceros horn, which is thrown with unerring precision—and an elongated elliptical shield of ox-hide, with the hair displayed. The size of this buckler is regulated by the stature of the warrior, reaching in all cases from the ground to his chin. A stick variously decorated at the ends is secured on the inner side, and two parallel strips of hide, differing in colour from the shield, are so interlaced as to traverse its whole length, imparting a striking effect to the accoutred warrior.

Excepting those individuals of distinction by whom he was generally attended, no subjects, or "dogs," as he termed them, ever passed the royal person without bending their bodies almost double, preserving that obsequious posture several paces before and after passing. The king seldom moved without half a dozen magnates in his train, the heralds howling at intervals, leaping about in imitation of some wild beast, and loudly praising "the noble elephant." The usual answer to an order was "*Ya, bo ba*,"—"yes, my father;" and no one quitting or approaching the presence omitted to exclaim "*Hai-yah!*" Any attempt to have taken the king's portrait openly would probably have been attended with disastrous consequences, drawing being supposed to be connected with witchcraft, but I seized the first opportunity of giving his Majesty a sitting unobserved. I exhibited several drawings of animals, and was surprised to find him so quick of apprehension. He instantly recognized them all, repeating the Matabili name. He inquired if we did not wish to visit the Great Lake in the interior, which he said we might easily do, as there had been plenty of rain, and he would send a commando to take care of us. This was a very tempting offer, but we replied we were sadly pushed for time, and were afraid of displeasing the white king by overstaying our leave. He rejoined that he would take care and prevent any unpleasant consequences by sending the white king a message about us.

This afternoon he was reclining on Richardson's bed, his little dark eyes moving with restless activity in every direction, when the well-known sound of a box, which had been imprudently opened by the Parsee, drew his attention to the baggage-waggon. He pricked his ears, hastily sprung from the bed, and, before the alarm could be given, had plunged both arms into the bead chest. Never shall I forget the triumphant expression of his face at that moment. The lid having been closed upon his arms, his idols were hidden from his sight, but he consoled himself by feeling them, and conjecturing their colour, grinning the while with extacy, and, if so mild a term can express his manner of asking, *requesting* to have them all. We said that they were all we had left, and that they were brought expressly for him ; but that we must be allowed to keep them until he granted us permission to depart, it being in our country the custom to make a present on taking leave of a great man. Looking eagerly at the beads, he exclaimed " *Mooe, mooe ! monanti,*

monanti! tanta, tanta, tanta!" and added, that although he deplored our departure, yet trustworthy
guides should be provided to conduct us on our
journey early the following morning, pointing at the
same time to the eastern horizon.   This bargain being
fully settled, his Majesty marched off iu triumph, a
man before him carrying the box, containing thirty
pounds of blue and white beads.

We were a little surprised at his having so readily
consented to part with us, and were half afraid he
might alter his mind before the morning.   The desire of obtaining immediate possession of the beads
without infringing appearances, had of course due
weight with him; and there can be no doubt that
he felt considerable uneasiness at our presence, now
that the return of Kalipi's commando from the Vaal
River drew so near.   His anxiety to get rid of ourselves, therefore, overcame the reluctance he felt at
parting with the small remnant of our property
which had escaped his two successful forays.   It
was the expected return of the commando, too, that
rendered him so anxious to send us to the Great
Lake, or indeed in any direction but that in which
we were bent on proceeding.   We had every inclination to avail ourselves of this most tempting offer,
but our leave from India being limited, it would have
been imprudent to have undertaken this journey,
which might have detained us beyond the Desert
until the next rainy season.   And although every
other circumstance subsequently conspired to favour
the project, and, by smoothing the path, to render it

probable that two "poor Indian gentlemen" could
have achieved so desirable and arduous an undertaking, we were yet compelled to sacrifice to circumstances our thirst for geographical discovery beyond
the tropic of Capricorn.

In order that there might be no excuse for delay-
ing our departure, we sent Baba in the afternoon to
ask the king's permission to pitch the "house" in
his kraal. He was taking a siesta in Mr. Bain's
waggon, but came out immediately in high spirits,
and pointed out the spot upon which he had determined that it should be erected. Whilst this was
being done, I had an opportunity of leisurely ex-
amining the imperial kraal. The plan of the enclosure was circular, a thick and high thorn fence
surrounding an area which was strewed with the
skulls, paws, and tails of lions, some of them quite
fresh, others bleached by long exposure to the sun.
Below the waggon I observed a pile of old muskets,
probably some that had been taken on the defeat of
Barend's Griquas in 1831. The royal lodge, and the
apartments of the ladies, were shut off by a rough
irregular palisade ; and a portion of this enclosure
was surrounded by a very closely woven wattle fence,
having only one aperture of barely sufficient dimensions to admit the king's portly person upon all
fours. The space was smeared with a mixture of
mud and cow-dung, resembling that used in all parts
of India for similar purposes. In the centre stood
a circular, plumpudding-shaped hut, about twelve
feet in diameter, and perhaps four in height, sub-

stantially thatched with rush matting, and exhibiting in its economy the most philosophic indifference to cleanliness and comfort. A low step led up to the entrance, which was very confined, and provided with a sliding wicket. The floor was sunk to the depth of three feet below the surface of the ground, and two more steps led down to it. The furniture consisted exclusively of calabashes of beer ranged round the wall.

Thirty ladies only of the imperial seraglio were present on this eventful occasion, and they remained standing round the king, who was seated in the open air. They were generally swarthy and somewhat *en-bon-point*. Many were even obese, with enormous pendant bosoms, and their heads were shaved, a small tuft of hair only being left on the crown, which was decorated with feathers. Their dresses consisted of short black kilts of leather, the fur worn inside, and the outside rubbed with some hard substance and charcoal until it had acquired the appearance of black clotted wool. These were studded with brass ornaments and a profusion of beads of divers colours ; they had besides a vast accumulation of these ornaments upon their bodies. Some wore blue from top to toe, others were enveloped in one mass of red, the endless variety of patterns in which they were disposed having doubtless emanated from the inventive brain and prolific fancy of his Majesty, a large portion of whose valuable time is passed in devising and superintending the construction of ornaments for the *Harem*.

Amongst the ladies, I observed a captive Griqua, called Truëy. This is the familiar name for Gertrude. She is the unfortunate daughter of Peter Davids, chief of the Lishuani Bastards, and successor to Barend Barends. This chief had, about three years before, undertaken a hunting expedition to the Vaal River, and in the natural course of events was attacked by a party of Moselekatse's warriors who were scouring the country in that direction; he narrowly escaped with his life, but the whole of his property was carried off, and his nephew and daughter were taken prisoners.

When the tent was nearly pitched, the king suddenly changed his mind, and resolved to have it immediately in front of the palace door. In order to accomplish this, it became necessary to remove a portion of the wattle fence—a work of considerable labour, in the progress of which *outchualla* was liberally circulated to the perspiring Hottentots. It was about three o'clock, and the pavilion had reared its head a second time. A bright thought then suddenly crossed the royal mind. Investing himself with the *duffel* great coat, placing a red night cap on his head, and commanding two wax candles to be lighted and placed before him, he seated himself with a dignified deportment upon an inverted calabash, the contents of which he had previously swallowed, and became totally absorbed in the contemplation of his surpassing importance. It was with difficulty that I preserved my gravity, and having hastily complimented the king on his accession

H

of property, and reminded him of our wish to leave the following day, I left him to his domestic enjoyments.

In the evening Truëy brought to the waggons a dish of stewed beef from the king.   Despite of our assertions to the contrary, he could not help suspecting that we still had beads in our possession, and thought that the attractive Griqua maid might find means of inducing us to part with some more before we departed.   The poor girl shed tears when she heard spoken the language of her tribe, and begged us to convey to her father, should we see him, the intelligence of her safety and that of her cousin Wilhelm, who had been sent to a distant kraal, the day before our arrival, in charge of a waggon containing two Dutch girls, prisoners of war, of whose presence the king was anxious that we should, if possible, be kept in ignorance.   She had herself resided for some time at the kraal in question with the king, who is in the habit of passing several months of the year there with one hundred of his wives, all of whom are decorated with bead dresses of the nature I have described.   Every female, married or single, is at his command; his subjects not having it in their power to call even their wives their own. The king alone is rich—his subjects are all equally poor, and can be said to possess nothing in the shape of property beyond the skins with which nature has clothed them,—

> " And that small model of the barren earth
> Which serves as paste and cover to their bones."

CHAPTER XVIII.

DEPARTURE FROM KAPAIN, AND ARRIVAL AT THE MARIQUA RIVER.

WE had been some time ready to depart on the morning of the 26th October, ere the king made his appearance. This he at length did, limping, and attended by the whole of his court. Andries, ever ready to create mischief, lost no time in spreading a report that he had overheard the discussions at a council held the preceding evening, when it had been determined to revoke the permission granted us to depart by the Vaal River—a measure to which ministers were very averse. The chairs having been put away in the waggons, we conducted the king to his old seat on Richardson's bed. In the act of ascending to this post of honour, having to climb over the chest which contained my wardrobe, he opened it eagerly, and darting his hand into the medley, triumphantly clawed up a pair of thick shooting shoes, which, unfortunately fitting him exactly, I was compelled to make a sacrifice of, at the risk of returning bare-footed to the colony. He now stated for our information, that his lameness had been occasioned by the tightness of the shoes he had taken the preceding day, and obstinately worn until they had raised large blisters on the royal heels. Having desired an attendant to advance with a very handsome weasel-skin cloak, which I had seen him wearing the day before in the kraal, he invested me with the greasy robe, saying that I looked very cold, and must keep it as a token of his friendship. A similar speech to Richardson was accompanied with a leopard-skin girdle. Determined not to be out-done in generosity, we presented him in return with a rich Persian carpet, which had formed the basis of my bedding. This being spread on the ground, had the desired effect of enticing him down from his seat, with the design of inspecting it narrowly, and we instantly gave orders to yoke the oxen, which had purposely been kept close to the waggons.

Having informed his Majesty that we were ready to start, and the whips being cracked, he accompanied us a considerable distance—at last stopping, and extending his hand, when a general leave-taking took place, the word *"Fellow! fellow! fellow!"* being repeated as before by each great man, the bystanders shouting *"Haiyah!"* He desired us to convey his *tumerisho* to the white king—to Sir Benjamin D'Urban, to whom he sent a special message—and to Dr. Smith, adding that Mohanycom would accompany us to the Vaal River—but that we must make haste back to the colony, lest the governor should think that he had slain us. Upon my repeating that I should shortly come again, bringing for him a double-poled tent, he replied that that was *mooe, mooe, mooe! monanti, monanti, monanti!*

tanta, tanta, tanta! that we must bring him
" every thing," and take care to visit him viâ Mr.
Moffat's station, and not by the Vaal River, lest
mischief should befal us by the way.

We now paid and dismissed the interpreter, with
a supply of provision for the road, and a note to Dr.
Wilson, thanking him for Baba's services, and informing him of the complete success of our nego-
ciations with the king.   Upon this point we had
certainly good reason to congratulate ourselves.
Visiting this capricious savage as we had done, at
an inauspicious juncture, when he was embroiled
with white men, and might not unreasonably have
regarded us in the light of spies upon his land—a
suspicion which the pusillanimous conduct of our
Hottentots, and of Andries in particular, was calculated to inspire and confirm—we had had throughout a difficult and somewhat hazardous part to
perform.   The probabilities were in favour of our
being detained, and were certainly greatly against
our obtaining permission to make our exit by the
hitherto proscribed route of the Vaal River, con-
ducting, as it would, directly through the scene of
his operations against the migratory farmers; but
by closing our eyes upon passing events, and preserving throughout our intercourse with the despot
a firm, conciliatory, and confiding demeanour—
not only had we succeeded in convincing him of
the honesty of our intentions—but now pursued our
journey with every reason to believe in the good
faith of his professions towards ourselves.

As we were now considered to be on terms of close intimacy with his Majesty, we had no danger whatever to apprehend from any of the native tribes, through whose territories we might have occasion to pass. All those that inhabit the country between the Vaal River and the tropic of Capricorn, were his tributaries, and the terror of his name filled the surrounding nations. None of his own subjects indeed would dare to refuse us assistance, without incurring the certainty of his summary vengeance.

Our course, in order to reach the Cashan range of mountains, where it had been resolved that our operations against the elephants should commence, was for the first three days a little to the southward of east. Mohanycom, now armed to the teeth, had relinquished his appointment in the imperial household for that of guide. He had received in our presence, more than once, the most positive injunctions to accompany us wherever we pleased to go within the king's dominions, and not to return until he had safely conducted us to the Vaal River, and he had been further directed to obtain from one of the kraals on our route a subordinate captain named Lingap, to assist in protecting us. Mohanycom having accompanied Um'Nombate, when that minister visited the colony under Dr. Smith's escort (for the purpose of forming an alliance on the part of his Majesty with the Cape Government), could understand the general tenor of conversation held in Dutch, and could even express himself intelligibly. Andries could stutter tolerably in

Sichuana, and possessed a smattering of Zooloo, and we thus hoped to be able to proceed without the aid of a sworn interpreter.

Owing to our unlooked for detention in the morning, we were glad to halt for breakfast after an hour's travel. Our long and wearisome marches through a parched and sterile country, in the course of which, as will have been remarked, our cattle were frequently deprived of all sustenance for many hours, had so reduced them in condition, that they could hardly support the weight of their own emaciated bodies. The last feed of corn was here divided amongst three of the horses that appeared most in need of it, the other half-starved wretches thrusting in their noses for a share, at a loss to understand why they should be excluded from so rare a feast.

Shortly after leaving Kapain, we observed a dog, with neatly trimmed ears and tail, following Mohanycom, who repeatedly endeavoured to drive him away, saying that he was the king's dog, and had been captured with Mr. Bain's waggons. Two messengers were speedily sent to bring back this pet, and his Majesty, unwilling to let slip so good an opportunity of asking for something, had desired them on no account to return without a fresh supply of wax candles. Conceiving, however, that our compliance with this unreasonable request would but lead to further exactions, we excused ourselves, sending in lieu a tin mould and a bundle of cotton wicks, with abundant compliments, and brief instruc-

tions in the art of manufacturing " tallows" from
the fat of the eland.

Having thus freed ourselves from the duns, it was
discovered that the oxen had gone off in search of
water—not one of the Hottentots having thought
proper to remain with them, although positively enjoined to do so. Three hours elapsed ere they were
recovered, and before we had proceeded many miles,
the sheep were missed. Andries being immediately
sent back upon horseback, found Frederick lying
under a bush in a state of stupefaction, the consequence of his frequent libations to the jolly god.
The sheep, as might have been expected, had availed
themselves of his drowsiness to *levant,* but were
traced up and recovered.

In spite of all these provoking delays, we contrived early in the afternoon to reach the Mariqua,
about thirty miles below the point whence it issues
from the mountain chain. The approach to this
small, but beautiful river, is picturesque in the
highest degree. Emerging suddenly from an extensive wood of magnificent thorn-trees, we passed
a village surrounded by green corn-fields, and then
descended by a winding path into a lawn covered
with a thick and verdant carpet of the richest grass,
bounded by a deep and shady belt of the many
stemmed acacia. These beautiful trees margined
the river on either hand far as the view extended—
and clothed with a vest of golden blossoms, diffused
a delicious and grateful odour around. Single
mokaalas, and detached clumps of slender mimosas,

hung with festoons of flowering creepers, heightened
the effect, screening with their soft and feathery
foliage considerable portions of the refreshing
sward, across which troops of querulous pintadoes
and herds of graceful pallahs* were to be seen
hurrying from our approach.

As we threaded the mazes of the parasol-topped
acacias, which completely excluded the sun's rays,
a peep of the river itself was unexpectedly obtained.
A deep and shaded channel, about twenty yards in
breadth, with precipitous banks overgrown with
reeds, was lined with an unbroken tier of willows.
These extended their drooping branches so as
nearly to entwine, had they not been forbidden by
the force of the crystal current, which swayed them
with it as it foamed and bubbled over the pebbly
bottom.   A plain on the opposite side, bounded by
a low range of blue hills, was dotted over with
mokaala trees, beneath which troops of gnoos,
sassaybys, and hartebeests, were reposing.

We drew up the waggons on a verdant spot on
the river bank, at a convenient distance from an extensive kraal constructed on the slope.   Although
the sun shone, the cold occasioned by a dry cutting
wind was scarcely to be endured, even with the assistance of a great coat ; and the inhabitants being
clamorous for food, I readily placed myself under
the guidance of their chief with ten of his men, and
diving into the heart of the extensive groves, soon
furnished them with the carcass of a black rhinoceros

* *Antilope Melampus.*   Delineated in the African Views.

upon which to whet their appetites. This huge
beast crossed the river twice after being mortally
wounded at duelling distance ; and I was compelled,
cold as it was, to wade after him through water
reaching to my middle—following his trail by the
blood, until from single drops, the traces became
splashes of frothy crimson. Struggling to force his
tottering frame through the tangled cover, the
wounded monster at length sank upon his knees,
another bullet from the grooved bore ending his
giant struggles, while he was yet tearing up the
ground with his ponderous horn.

CHAPTER XIX.

FROM THE MARIQUA RIVER TO TOLAAN, THE RESIDENCE OF MOSELEKATSE'S SON.

AT daybreak the following morning, a large party of hungry savages, with four of the Hottentots on horseback, accompanied us across the river in search of elands, which were reported to be numerous in the neighbourhood. We formed a long line, and having passed over a great extent of country, divided into two parties; Richardson keeping to the right, and myself to the left. Beginning to despair of success, I had shot a hartebeest for the savages, when an object which had repeatedly attracted my eye, but which I had as often persuaded myself was nothing more than the branchless stump of some withered tree, suddenly shifted its position, and the next moment I distinctly perceived that singular form, of which the apparition had ofttimes visited my slumbers—but upon whose reality I now gazed for the first time. It passed rapidly among the trees, above the topmost branches of many of which its graceful head nodded like some lofty pine—it was the stately, the long sought giraffe. Putting spurs to my horse, and directing the Hottentots to follow, I presently found myself half choked with excitement, rattling at the heels of the tallest of all

the Mammiferes, whom thus to meet, free on his
native plains, has fallen to the lot of few of the
votaries of the chase.   Sailing before me with incredible velocity, his long swan-like neck keeping
time to the eccentric motion of his stilt-like legs—
his ample black tail curled above his back, and
whisking in ludicrous concert with the rocking of
his disproportioned frame, he glided gallantly along
" like some tall ship upon the ocean's bosom," and
seemed to leave whole leagues behind him at each
stride.   The ground was of the most treacherous
description ; a rotten black soil overgrown with
long coarse grass, which concealed from view innumerable cracks and fissures that momentarily
threatened to throw down my horse.   For the first
five minutes I rather lost than gained ground, and
despairing, over such a country, of ever diminishing
the distance, or improving my acquaintance with
this ogre in seven-league boots, I dismounted, and
had the satisfaction of hearing two balls tell roundly
upon his plank-like stern.   But I might as well
have fired at a wall : he neither swerved from his
course, nor slackened his pace, and had pushed on
so far ahead during the time I was reloading, that
after remounting, I had some difficulty in even
keeping sight of him amongst the trees.   Closing
again, however, I repeated the dose on the other
quarter, and spurred along my horse, ever and anon
sinking to his fetlock ; the giraffe now flagging at
each stride, until, as I was coming up hand over
hand, and success seemed certain, down I came

headlong—my horse having fallen into a pit, and lodged me close to an ostrich's nest, in which the old birds were sitting.

There were no bones broken, but the violence of the shock had caused the lashings of my rifle to give way, and had doubled it in half—the barrels only now hanging to the stock by the trigger guard. Nothing dismayed by this heavy calamity, I re-mounted my jaded beast, and one more effort brought me ahead of my wearied victim, which stood still and allowed me to approach.   In vain I attempted to bind my fractured rifle with a pocket handker-chief, in order to admit of my administering the *coup de grace*—it was so bent that the hammer could not by any means be brought down upon the nipple.   In vain I looked around for a stone, and sought in every pocket for my knife, with which to strike the copper cap, and bring about ignition, or hamstring the colossal but harmless animal, by whose side I appeared the veriest pigmy in the creation—alas! I had lent it to the Hottentots to cut off the head of the hartebeest.   Vainly did I wait for the tardy and rebellious villains to come to my assistance, making the welkin ring, and my throat tingle, with reiterated shouts—not a soul appeared —and, in a few minutes the giraffe having recovered his wind, and being only slightly wounded in the hind quarters, shuffled his long legs—twisted his tail over his back—walked a few steps—then broke into a gallop, and diving into the mazes of the forest, disappeared from my sight.   Disappointed

and annoyed, I returned towards the waggons, now
eight miles distant, and on my way overtook the
Hottentots, who, smoking their pipes with an air of
gentlemanly laziness, were leisurely returning,
having come to the conclusion that "Sir could not
catch the kameel," for which reason they did not
think it worth while to follow as I had directed.

My defeat did not cause me to lose sight of the
flesh-pots. Any change from the monotony of an
unvaried bread and meat diet being highly agreeable, I went back to the nest of the ostrich with a
view of obtaining the eggs. So alarmed were the
old birds by my unceremonious intrusion in the morning, that they had not returned. Twenty-three
gigantic eggs were laid on the bare ground without
either bush or grass to conceal them, or any attempt
at a nest beyond a shallow concavity which had
been scraped out with the feet. Having broken one,
to ascertain if they were worth carrying home, a
Hottentot took off his trowsers, in which (the legs
being first tied at the lower end,) the eggs were securely packed, and placed on the saddle. Although
each of these enormous eggs weighs about three
pounds, and is equivalent to twenty-four of the
domestic fowls', many of our followers could devour
two at a single meal, first mixing the contents, and
then broiling them in the shell. When dressed in
more orthodox manner, we found them a highly
palatable omelette.

Richardson shortly returned, having been engaged in deadly conflict with a rhinoceros. Aroused

from a siesta by the smarting of a gun-shot wound, the infuriated animal had pursued his assailant so closely that it became necessary to discharge the second barrel into his mouth, an operation in the performing which the stock was much disfigured by the animal's horn.	I employed the rest of the day in repairing my own weapon with the iron clamp of a box, binding it with a strip of green hide from the carcase of an eland.

There being no practicable road across the Mariqua within several miles of our position, we were compelled, on the 28th, to make one by paring down the steep banks : and even then, experienced great difficulty in towing our heavy vans to the opposite side by the united strength of the teams.	The descent was almost perpendicular, requiring both wheels to be locked : the bed of the river, covered with loose stones, was too confined to admit of the oxen acting in concert :—and the current, straightened by the narrowness of the channel, was rapid, and rose to the floors of the waggons.

Shortly after we had crossed, a large mixed herd of sassaybys and quaggas, alarmed by the sudden appearance of our cavalcade, charged past me so close, that one of the latter fell at my feet at each discharge of the rifle.	Several savages had followed us to obtain a supply of dried meat and assist in hunting ; but although they were greatly delighted at this performance, it was not until an unwieldy white rhinoceros * had bit the dust, that they were

* *Rhinoceros Sinusus.* Delineated in the African Views.

perfectly satisfied.　Smacking their thick lips, patting their stomachs, and repeatedly exclaiming
"*Chikore, Chikore,*" they pointed out this huge beast
standing stupidly under the shade of a spreading
acacia.　I crept within thirty yards before firing,
but it was not until he had received six two-ounce
bullets behind the shoulder that he yielded up the
ghost—charging repeatedly, with his snout almost
touching the ground, in so clumsy a manner, that
it was only necessary to step on one side to be perfectly safe.

This grotesque-looking animal, which in many
points bears a ridiculous resemblance to, or rather
is a gross caricature upon, the "half reasoning
elephant," is upwards of six feet high at the
shoulder, its shapeless head exceeding four feet in
length.　It is the larger, but less ferocious, of the
two species of African rhinoceros, neither of which
is clad in shell armour like their Asiatic brethren;
they have in lieu, tough hides an inch and a half in
thickness, of which the whips known at the Cape,
under the denomination of *Sjamboks,* are usually
manufactured.　Both have double horns: those of
the black species are short, and sometimes nearly
of equal length—whilst the anterior horn of the
white rhinoceros is upwards of three feet in length,
the second being a mere excrescence.　These animals
may be readily approached within a few yards,
against the wind, and being heavy and inert, their
attacks are easily avoided.

Rejoining the waggons to breakfast, we found

many savages assembled from neighbouring kraals, clamorous for snuff. One old lady inhaled it in large quantities, and without wasting a single grain, by means of a long tube of wood, the ends of which were respectively applied to her nose and to the back of her hand on which the powder was placed.

The country through which we passed this day was more thickly wooded than any we had seen since leaving Kurrichane: and I for the first time observed several pit-falls constructed for the purpose of taking the rhinoceros. They differed from others in being dug singly instead of in groups—very deep and large—at the extremity of a narrow path cut through the bushes, and fenced outside with thorns —a sharp turn leading directly upon the trap, so that an unwieldy animal, being driven furiously down the avenue, could have no chance of avoiding the snare. Many skulls and bones of these huge beasts were lying at the bottom of the sepulchres that had swallowed them up alive.

After travelling upwards of fifteen miles, and passing three or four very large kraals, we arrived at the Tolaan River, a deep, narrow, and rocky channel, containing several extensive pools—the hollowed banks bearing testimony to the depth and rapidity of the current at certain seasons. The bed was perfectly dry where we crossed, but covered with huge fragments of granite, which threw the waggons from side to side with frightful violence—and, added to the almost perpendicular character of the banks, rendered the passage extremely perilous. We

halted on an isthmus, formed by a double bend
of the river; a grove of large acacia trees proving
an agreeable shelter, and rendering the spot delightful.   Here we were visited by Moselekatse's
son, an aristocratic and intelligent lad, fourteen or
fifteen years of age.   His dress consisted of the
usual girdle with long fur streamers, and a chaplet
of white beads bound about his forehead, to which
were attached three tufts of clipped quills, resembling
in size and shape the flower of the African marigold.
A lad of his own age attended him.   The blood of
the despotic sire flowing in the veins of the heir apparent to the throne of the Matabili, his first step
was to deprive Mohanycom of a clasp-knife that we
had given him, which he immediately hung about
his own neck, with a look of absolute superiority
hardly to be expected from such a youth.

CHAPTER XX.

THE MATABILI DESCRIBED—ARRIVAL AT THE RIVER SIMALAKATE.

THE history of the assassination of one of the Hottentot followers of Captains Sutton and Moultry, to which allusion was made in a former part of this narrative, is brief.   Like most of his tribe, being unable to keep his hands from picking and stealing, he purloined a musket from the king's kraal; and, presuming also to aspire to the affections of Truëy, Moselekatse's favourite concubine, his body was one morning picked up pierced with assagais. A boy belonging also to one of those gentlemen disappeared about the same time, but his fate and his crime remained equally veiled in obscurity.

The death of the trader Gibson, which formed one of the reasons adduced by the worthy Missionaries at Mosega to dissuade us from prosecuting our journey, was caused by the insalubrious climate of the country bordering on the sea-coast.   It is the invariable policy of all African chiefs, to deter travellers from visiting tribes residing beyond them, by exaggerated representations of peril, hoping by these means to effect a monopoly of traffic.   Gibson had long been engaged in trading speculations, and in hunting elephants, amongst the tribes in the in-

terior; and tempted by the prospect of gain, penetrated, in opposition to the advice of Moselekatse,
amongst the Babariri considerably to the north-
west of Delagoa Bay. There, the whole party, one
Hottentot only excepted, was cut off by fever. The
report of this event reaching Moselekatse, who,
whatever his vices may be, is yet extremely anxious
to produce impressions favourable to himself
amongst the white people, he immediately despatched a commando with directions to bring the
survivor, who had taken refuge with a hostile tribe,
alive—in order that by his testimony he might clear
himself from all suspicion of murder. Ignorant of
the intentions of the commando, and alarmed for his
own safety, the Hottentot resisted, and being slain
in the attack, his head was laid at the feet of the
king. The despot, however, far from being pleased
with the zeal shown by his warriors, ordered four of
the principal of them to be put to death, on the
ground that they had merely brought him a lifeless
head instead of the living person, as he had commanded.

Notwithstanding such acts of cruelty on the part
of the tyrant, the devotion of the Matabili warriors
to his commands almost exceeds belief. No soldier
dares present himself to Moselekatse who has been
wounded in an ignoble part, or has failed to execute
his duty to the very letter. If a lion attacks his
herds, either his death, or that of their guardians
invariably ensues. Armed only with assagais and
shields, they rush in upon the marauder, and gene-

rally at the expense of one or two of their lives, which are held of no account, retire from the conflict, bearing with them his head and feet to their royal master. These are left to decompose within the fence of the imperial kraal, which, as I have already explained, is strewed with the bones of wild animals. War is the prevailing passion of the Matabili; they burn with an insatiate thirst for the blood of their enemies, of whom they cannot even speak without assuming an aspect of vengeance and fury. They are doubtless the stoutest soldiers in Southern Africa, not excepting the most disciplined troops of the Zooloo tyrant, from whom they deserted, and whose invaded armies they have thrice routed in a pitched battle with terrible slaughter.

To be fat is the greatest of all crimes, no person being allowed that privilege but the king. Speaking evil of the king, or alluding to the heir apparent, are considered equivalent to treason, or compassing the death of the Sovereign in Britain. Neglecting his cattle is reckoned a capital crime, the execution following upon the sentence, from which there is no appeal, " quick as the thunderbolt pursues the flash."

It is not permitted to a subject to allude to the elephant in the presence of the despot; "the noble elephant" being one of his titles. When speaking of hunting that animal, Moselekatse frequently urged us to instruct some of his warriors in our method; but as his people can neither ride nor be persuaded to fire a gun, it was impossible to comply

with his request.   Accustomed from childhood to
the use of the assagai, or javelin, without which the
Matabili never quits his home, they are expert in
the destruction of the elephant ; hemming him into
a defile, they attack him with great intrepidity,
and not unfrequently incur the utmost effects of his
rage and fury.   Occasionally, also, they assail the
rhinoceros, but this inert animal is more usually
ensnared in the pitfalls already described, which
are generally provided with a sharp stake at the
bottom, on which he is impaled.

The Matabili possess no horses; all those that
have been from time to time taken from the Griquas
and other tribes, with whom they have been engaged
in war, have been carried off by the *distemper*, as
it is called, a fatal murrain, which sometimes extends
itself to the oxen, over every part of Southern Africa
during the early months of the year.   The ravages
of this disease, which is said to be an affection of
the lungs, are supposed to be occasioned by the
young grass which springs up after the first rain;
and at these seasons, the colonists who can send
their horses into the more elevated districts, are able
generally to preserve them.

The attempts of our friends at equitation drill,
and horsemanship, were ludicrous and awkward in
the extreme.   Although active, muscular, and agile
in a wonderful degree, they tumbled off the horse
as fast as they ascended, notwithstanding that the
saddle, bridle, mane, and even tail were unceremoniously pressed into the service.

Although a soldier of fortune who has gained all his glory and power in the field, Moselekatse has now ceased to lead his armies to battle ; but he still honours with his presence the great hunting expeditions which frequently take place. On these occasions he is attended by a retinue of several thousand men, who extend themselves in a circle, enclosing many miles of country, and gradually converging so as to bring incredible numbers of wild animals within a small focus. Still advancing, the ring at length becomes a thick and continuous line of men, hemming in the game on all sides, which, in desperate efforts to escape, displays the most daring and dangerous exhibition of sport that can be conceived. As the scene closes, the spears of the warriors deal death around them, affording a picture thrilling to the sportsman, and striking in the extreme.

The dexterity of the Matabili in the use of the knob-stick is also wonderful: they rarely miss a partridge or a guinea-fowl on the wing, and knock over hares, cats, and other ground game with equal precision. In a nation such as I have described, it will be readily conceived that agriculture is not in high repute, and accordingly, excepting for the grain used in making beer, I saw little attempt at cultivation. A few melons, rather deserving the name of vegetables, were the only fruit we met with, and these I presume are nurtured chiefly for the gourd, which becomes their calabash, or water flagon. We could hear of no funeral ceremonies amongst them.

High and low, their bodies are thrown forth upon
the plain, soon after life departs, a prey to wild
beasts; the flap of the eagle's wing and the howl
of the hyæna being their only death-note.   In the
Zooloo tribe, however, from which Moselekatse has
sprung, some respect is shown to the memory of
royalty and persons of high distinction; the defunct
dignitary being interred with his head above the
ground, within the hut where he has expired or
been assassinated.   The marriage ceremonies of the
Matabili were exceedingly difficult to understand.
Acceptance or non-acceptance of a snuff-box on
the part of the lady, indicates the success of her
suitor, or the contrary: and it would seem that
marriage has sometimes altogether been prohibited
amongst the Zooloos, or confined to men in advanced life.   We were informed that the *issigoko*,
or ring, so often alluded to, indicated a married
warrior; but to this rule there must be exceptions.
Of the population of Moselekatse's empire, I can
form no correct estimate.   The constant wars in
which he is engaged diminished the number of the
males, but the women are exceedingly prolific.
His standing army of warriors of his own tribe
exceeds five thousand men, but numbers of the
conquered nations swell his followers to a large
amount, and are chiefly employed as guardians of
his cattle during the intervals of peace.

. On the 29th we took the field, accompanied by
the whole of the male inhabitants of three kraals,
in addition to those that had accompanied us from

the Mariqua River. The country here is generally undulating, extensive mimosa groves occupying all the valley, as well as the banks of the Tolaan River, which winds amongst them on its way to join the Mariqua. We had not proceeded many hundred yards before our progress was opposed by a rhinoceros, who looked defiance, but took the hints we gave him to get out of the way. Two fat elands had been pointed out at the edge of the grove the moment before, one of which Richardson disposed of with little difficulty, but the other led me through all the intricacies of the grove to a wide plain on the opposite side, immediately on emerging upon which the fugitive was prostrate at my feet in the middle of a troop of giraffes, who stooped their long necks, astounded at the intrusion, and in another moment were sailing away at their utmost speed. To have followed them upon my jaded horse would have been absurd, and I was afterwards unable to find them. Returning to the camp after killing several elands and rhinoceroses, besides other game, which the savages quickly took charge of, I was furiously charged by a herd of horned cattle, and my horse being much exhausted, I had no small difficulty in escaping their persecution. Objecting, I presume, to my garb or complexion, they pertinaciously pursued me through thickets and over ravines, regardless of the loud whistle of the herdsman, to which they are usually very obedient. During the night, our camp was thrown into disorder by the intrusion of a rhinoceros,

I

which actually stood sometime between the wag-.
gons.

Several hours'diligent search the next day brought
us upon a herd of twelve cameleopards. We pursued them a considerable distance, and repeatedly
wounded the largest, a gigantic male, probably
eighteen feet in height; but our famished horses
falling repeatedly into the numerous holes with
which the ground was covered, we at length became
convinced of the impossibility of humbling the lofty
head of the giraffe, until our steeds should have
improved in condition upon the fine pasturage
which now abounded. The day was sultry and the
glare distressing. To the north-eastward, the distant prospect was bounded by a range of blue
mountains which we visited some weeks afterwards;
the whole of the extensive plain being sprinkled
with huge mokaala trees, mat rushes, and thistles.
Large herds of elands were grazing amongst these,
the host of savages by which we were attended
quickly clearing away the carcases of those we
slew, and then quarrelling for the entrails. I hope
my reader has understood that these barbarians
generally devour the meat raw, although when at
leisure they do not object to its being cooked.
They usually seize a piece of the flesh by the teeth,
cutting a large mouthful of it with the assagai close
to the lips, before masticating it, which they do with
a loud sputter and noise. The meal being finished,
they never failed to wipe their hands on their bodies,
and then being generally gorged, they lay them-

selves down to repose—previously relaxing their leathern girdles, which are so contrived as to be readily expanded according to their girth.

How truly has it been remarked by Captain Owen, that the state of those countries which have had little or no intercourse with civilized nations, is a direct refutation of the theories of poets and philosophers, who would represent the ignorance of the savage as virtuous simplicity—his miserable poverty as frugality and temperance—and his stupid indolence as laudable contempt for wealth; widely different indeed were the facts which came under our observation; and doubtless it will ever be found, that uncultivated man is a compound of treachery, cunning, debauchery, gluttony, and idleness.

As the sun was setting, our friend the rhinoceros imprudently appeared upon the bank of the river within pistol shot. Five balls were immediately lodged in his body, with which he retreated, and was picked up the following morning.

Leaving the Tolaan River, we passed between two ranges of hills, and travelled nearly south-east, over a rugged country, strewed with huge loose masses of stone, and thickly covered with low bush. To the right, extensive stone walls marked the site of a once flourishing Bamaliti town, now destroyed. At noon we unyoked in a well-watered valley, covered with turf and abundantly cultivated. Here 'Unchobe, the captain of an adjacent Matabili kraal, paid us the compliment of climbing into the waggon, and of squatting himself without ceremony upon my

bed, inviting his greasy *vrouw* to do the same.   The
stench of this worthy couple was quite overpowering,
but he was evidently considered by his countrymen
as a person of consequence, being loaded with a
profusion of beads and ornaments, amongst which
we remarked a necklace composed of Spanish dollars, and a medal which had been struck in England
in honour of the abolition of slavery.   His hair,
contrary to the custom of the Matabili, was matted
with grease and *sibilo*, and his consort also was
decorated with beads of various colours, to the
amount of at least thirty pounds weight.   In her
own person this lady possessed a concentration of
ugliness, which would have more than satisfied a
score of ordinary females ; and it might almost be
asserted without fear of contradiction, that a being
of more repulsive exterior never disgraced the fair
form of humanity.   A crowd of women and girls
assembled round the waggon, clamorous for snuff
and tobacco, and afforded us much amusement by
their insatiable curiosity and good humour.   The
looking-glass, that never-failing source of surprise
and delight to uncivilized beings, produced more
than its usual effect upon them.   Forming a group
of merry faces at the end of the waggon, and chattering to each other, they gazed incessantly at their
reflected images, trying, by pressing their hands
behind the mirror, to discover the cause of such a
magical effect ; covering their eyes, and peeping
askance to see if their double selves imitated the
action.   Scarcely a less powerful impression was

produced by some of my drawings of wild animals, which I exhibited to them. In India even educated natives are exceedingly slow in recognizing representations of objects, but these unsophisticated damsels instantly acknowledged the likenesses, by pronouncing the name of the quadruped in an animated manner, drawing the attention of their neighbours to the sight. The Matabili females are neither prepossessing nor engaging; they shave their heads in the manner already described, and wear a short leathern petticoat, which in most cases is their only covering, although they occasionally also have a flap of leather suspended from the neck. Their skin, from being constantly lubricated with grease and fat, acquires a shining appearance, and is of a dark brown colour approaching to copper. Both sexes occasionally employ themselves in sewing skins, an operation which is performed by means of a skewer or awl, by which they pierce a hole, and afterwards introduce a thread composed of an animal's sinew, resembling our fiddle-strings. Of this substance, which is also used to string beads upon, they are generally provided with a large supply suspended from the waist. So far as we remarked, the women appeared little oppressed with sensibility, although affectionate to their children; the latter wander almost in a state of perfect nudity until the age of puberty. All classes are equally devoted to tobacco, taken as snuff; and the plant is so precious that it is never used alone, but invariably adulterated with a due admixture of earth or sand.

Late in the afternoon we halted on the banks of the Simalakate, a deep and tranquil stream, margined by reeds and rushes, affording a ready covert for lions, whose fresh marks were every where visible in the neighbourhood. The day had been very sultry, and our two dogs, nearly blind from thirst, ran down the steep bank to the water's edge, into the jaws of an enormous alligator. One of them returned immediately in a state of great alarm. Suddenly a splash was heard, and bubbles of blood rising a minute after, too truly told what had been the fate of his unfortunate comrade. Not content with depriving us of our valued four-footed companion, the alligators quitted their watery homes during the night, and ate up a portion of the leather of the waggon furniture, besides the shoes of our followers. These scaly monsters are very common in many of the African rivers, and this was not the only occasion on which we suffered from their ravages. We frequently killed some of an immense size.

About sunset an unwieldy white rhinoceros approached the waggons, evidently with hostile intentions. There being neither bush nor hollow to conceal my advance, I crawled towards him amongst the grass, and within forty yards fired two balls into him. He started, looked around for some object on which to wreak his vengeance, and actually charged up, with his eye flashing fire and gore streaming from his mouth, to within an arm's length of me. Crouching low, however, I fortunately eluded his vengeance, and he soon afterwards dropped down dead.

Thus far on our journey we had pursued a partially beaten track, dignified by the Hottentots in colonial phraseology with the name of a road, though since leaving Kurrichane, it had consisted merely of the faint vestiges of the traders' waggons, which "few and far between" had traversed it— and even these could only be discovered by a practised eye. But from our entrance into the hills this morning, all traces had disappeared, nor did we again see the tracks of a waggon for several months, until we had crossed the river Vaal on our return to the colony. Thus left to ourselves, matters resumed a smoother aspect, and the dread of Moselekatse appeared to have forsaken the Hottentots, leaving behind it, like an intermittent fever, an interval of tranquillity, which lasted for some time.

CHAPTER XXI.

MEETING WITH KALIPI'S COMMANDO, AND ARRIVAL AT THE CASHAN MOUNTAINS.

THE morning of the 1st November brought to light several parties of Matabili warriors on the opposite side of the river, escorting large droves of cattle towards Kapain. They appeared purposely avoiding us, but although we were unable to hold any communication with them, we felt convinced that they formed a part of Kalipi's commando. After skirting the deep sedgy channel of the Simalakate several miles, in quest of a ford, we arrived at a point where it takes a sudden bend to the eastward, and, even at this season, falls with considerable violence over a stratum of granite, which forms a rough, but complete pavement. Across this stony drift we effected a passage, though not without sundry violent concussions, that bid fair to dislocate the joints of our heavy vehicles, and rendered necessary the precaution of removing the guns, and all brittle wares, during the *trajet*.

We unyoked for breakfast in an extensive mimosa grove, which rivalled in beauty all that we had hitherto seen. The airy parasol-shaped foliage was intertwined above our heads in such a manner as to be perfectly impervious to the sun's rays, the con-

stant and delicious shade it afforded having induced
the growth of a luxuriant carpet of grass, spangled
with numerous gaudy flowers. Whilst the oxen
were revelling in these sweets, I strolled down the
river with my rifle in search of riet-buck,* of
which some had been seen in the morning. Here
the scenery was beautiful. Three cascades fell
over descents of several feet, within a quarter of a
mile of each other, flanked by stately timber trees,
of splendid growth, and graceful foliage, which
leaning their venerable forms over the limpid stream,
were reflected on its glassy bosom. Huge isolated
masses of rocks reared their stupendous heads at
intervals, as though cast there by some giant hand
in sportive derision of the current which foamed
and bubbled around them. Upon the tops of these
cormorants were sunning themselves in hundreds,
whilst scaly alligators were basking on the lower
tiers amid flowering bushes and evergreens.
Straggling hamlets were scattered along the banks ;
and near the ford I observed one constructed upon
a raised platform, the only instance of attic architecture that occurred during my travels. The
number of huts did not exceed twenty, and they
appeared to have been sometime uninhabited.

We resumed our journey about noon. The route
towards an opening in the mountains led us nearly
due south, through an exceedingly rich and fruitful
part of the country, abounding in verdant savannahs
and hamlets, around which large herds of cattle

* *Redunca Eleotragus.* Delineated in the African Views.

were indulging in luxuriant pasture.   These were
tended by armed herdsmen, and we were at first
surprised to observe the oxen leave their grazing,
and flock around our waggons as they proceeded,
snorting and exhibiting signs of pleasure, as though
in recognition of objects with which they were
familiar.   The appearance shortly afterwards of
several hundred Matabili warriors in their war
costume explained the riddle, and we knew that
these must be some of the cattle taken from the
unfortunate emigrants.   Shortly before this, Mohanycom, our guide, had left the waggons, and
proceeded to a kraal at some distance, for the purpose of communicating to 'Lingap, the subordinate
captain of whom I have before spoken, and who
resided there, the king's orders that he should
attach himself to our suite.   The consequence of
this ill-judged proceeding was, that we were deprived of his services at the very moment when they
were most required.   The warriors not perceiving
any of their own tribe with our party, and having
had their hands so lately imbrued with the blood
of white men, could think of nothing but war and
plunder.   Suspecting, or rather hoping, that we
had found means to enter the country without the
king's knowledge, they closed round the waggons
with every demonstration of hostility, accosting
us with insolence, and peremptorily commanding
the drivers to halt ; several at the same time placing
themselves in front to obstruct the passage.   The
Hottentots looked aghast, and Cœur de Lion, in a

state of extreme agitation, fainted when he saw a
number of wounded warriors borne past on the
shields of their comrades, whilst others groaned
under the weight of accoutrements that had been
stripped from the bodies of the slain.

Our situation was now critical—Andries, whether
from terror, or the disgust excited by his super-
cession at Kapain, showed no disposition to extricate
us by an explanation of the true state of affairs.
No one else understood a word of the language.
The crowd was fast encroaching upon us, and their
pacific intentions becoming momentarily more ques-
tionable.   Some even clambered into the waggons,
overhauling their contents, whilst others cast a
longing eye at the oxen and sheep.   The unhappy
Andries was at length seized by a brawny savage,
an event which proved highly favourable to us, for
in his agony of distress at the supposed approach of
death, he found his tongue, and stuttered out a
brief intimation of our having been the honoured
guests of the king.   The name of Moselekatse acted
like magic on his followers.   The barbarians were
instantly appeased, and, in a few seconds, were
petitioning in an abject tone for snuff, beads, and
tobacco—allowing us to proceed on our way rejoicing.

The warriors were all clad in their full costume,
which was more complete than that I have already
described.   It consisted of a thick fur kilt called
Umcooloobooloo, composed of treble rows of cats' or
monkeys' tails, descending nearly to the knee.   A

tippet, formed of white cows' tails, encircled the shoulders, and covered the upper part of the body, the knees, wrists, elbows, and ankles, being ornamented with a single ox-tail fastened above the joint. Several of their shields bore marks of the recent conflict, being drilled with musket balls, and they carried with them the arms of those who had perished, to place them at the foot of the king— having left the bodies of their comrades, as usual, a prey to vultures and hyænas; for no funeral obsequies ever honour the deeds, or crown the devotion and bravery, of a Matabili warrior.

Nothing could be more savage, wild, and martial, than the appearance presented by this barbarian army returning to their despotic sovereign, wreathed with laurels and laden with spoils. We continued to meet large straggling parties during the whole of the day, and could not have passed fewer than five or six thousand head of captured cattle.

Contrary to the practice of the Kafirs, the Matabili prefer attacking in open ground, rushing in at once upon their foes, striking their shields by way of intimidation, and stabbing with their short spears, of which a bundle of five or six is taken when going to war. So terrible is this mode of combat to the unwarlike Bechuana, that one Matabili champion is a match for fifty of them. In the late affair, however, they received a severe lesson in the superiority of fire-arms, of which, since the signal defeat of Barends' Griquas, in 1831, Moselekatse had entertained a great contempt. Kalipi had

found the emigrant farmers several days' march to
the southward of the position they occupied when
Erasmus's effects were captured.   Being apprized
of the approach of the barbarian horde, they had
drawn up their waggons in a close circle, fortifying
the enclosure with thorn branches, and defending
themselves so stoutly, that they beat off the assailants
with terrible slaughter, wounding Kalipi, and
obliging him to retire from the conflict.   Plunder
is the principal object of all savage warfare, and
although, fortunately for the cause of humanity, he
failed in carrying into effect the orders of his incensed and blood-thirsty master, to massacre the
males without quarter, sparing only the women and
young girls that were calculated to grace the imperial seraglio, Kalipi had yet succeeded in the
more lucrative object of his expedition; he retired
from the field of carnage, sweeping before him the
whole of the flocks and herds of the emigrants, that
were grazing in thousands upon the verdant plains
of the Likwa, leaving the late flourishing camp an
immoveable and shattered wreck in the wilderness.

We soon descended into a fine valley, in which
were situated nine of Moselekatse's principal kraals,
around which countless cattle were grazing.   From
one of these villages, the last Matabili station in
this direction, we were rejoined by Mohanycom,
who brought with him 'Lingap, the captain of our
escort, and a whole host of ladies, who were desirous
of ascertaining the quality of our "Irish blackguard."
They all saluted us with "*Dakha bono, Qui !*"—"I see

you! give me some snuff!" Winding up a little
acclivity, we presently entered a grand and extensive
forest, with occasional open spots, which abounded,
to an incredible degree, with hartebeests, sassaybys,
gnoos, and quaggas. Here, too, we saw the first
traces of the elephant—mimosa trees torn up by
the roots, and sturdy branches, which, rent from the
parent stock, overhung the path. Hundreds of
deep holes, impressed by the feet of these gigantic
quadrupeds during some recent heavy rain, with
heaps of fresh excrement, were every where to be
seen. Andries, who thought every animal less than
an elephant beneath his notice, now became frantic.
Stopping the waggon which he was leading, he
waved his cap aloft, threw a mass of dung into the
air, and huzzaed till he was hoarse.

Arriving at the end of the forest, we again descended, and found ourselves under one of the se-
condary ranges of the Cashan mountains, on the
bank of the Bagobone River, where we halted in a
meadow, having travelled twelve miles. Here again
the scenery was wild and romantic. The mountains
rose on either hand in bold majestic forms, clothed
in parts with luxuriant verdure—their steep rocky
sides besprinkled in others with occasional light
bushes, which enlivened the rich and varied tints
of the broken crags. Rugged cliffs margined the
bubbling river and shut in the lower prospect, whilst
the great range of the Cashan mountains towered
above them in the distance, their spiry blue summits
appearing to us, who had for months seen nothing

larger than an ant-hill, almost to rival the Alps in grandeur.

Whilst the Hottentots were engaged in making a fence for the cattle, I entered one of the nearest groves for the purpose of obtaining food for the people, and presently brought down a water-buck,* a rare and splendid antelope, which is not to be met with until after crossing the Mariqua. The report of my rifle disturbed a lion and lioness from a bush close by, and they instantly slunk into the jungle. Having covered up the carcass with bushes, I returned to the waggons, and found that Piet had already arrived with an abundant supply of gnoo's flesh. He, too, had narrowly escaped stumbling over a lion in long grass. These troublesome beasts appeared to be so numerous, that we made a more substantial fence than usual for the oxen, and had no reason to regret having taken the precaution; as numbers were roaring and prowling round the camp towards morning, endeavouring to effect an entrance.

Over the evening fire,'Lingap favoured us with the particulars that he had been able to collect regarding the attack on the emigrant farmers, extolling Kalipi's bravery to the skies. Himself a warrior of tried courage, he had formed one of the commando that captured Erasmus's waggons. His eyes glistened as he spoke of the pleasure he had derived from feeling his spear enter white flesh. It slipped in, he said, grasping his assagai and suiting the ac-

* *Aigocerus Ellipsiprymnus.* Delineated in the African Views.

tion to the word, so much more satisfactorily than into the tough hide of a black savage, that he preferred sticking a Dutchman to eating the king's beef. When sufficiently sated with roast meat, and primed with snuff, he treated us to a love ditty, in the course of which he looked most killing. Both he and Mohanycom were much elated at Kalipi's success, and as the evening advanced, being joined by a large party of friends, they all struck up a war chorus in praise of the king, which they continued until a late hour, howling and dancing until they were exhausted. We could never arrive at any interpretation of their songs, and of this in particular, beyond what I have already given. Strange though it must appear, it is a fact that, whether from fear or superstition, the devotion of these savages to their tyrannic chieftain amounts to positive adoration. Present or absent he absorbs all their praises, and is the only idol they worship. The following were the words repeated, with occasional transposition, ten thousand times :—

> O Lĭlli bŭkălĕĕ, Bŭnkă Băee
> O nwăng·ă-nĕĕ sŭbŏokană-shee.
> Ai bŭnkă băee—Hibo, hi bo, hi bo bo-shee.

Dancing served in the place of music, and was nothing more than an accompaniment to the song, of which the pathos and feeling were indicated by the contortions of the body, and by the various figures described with the hands, in which they flourished a club of rhinoceros' horn. The feet regulated the time, and imparted the locomotive

effect in which they rejoice.   At first they were
slowly lifted, to descend again with a single or
double stamp; and the sticks being gently clashed
at the same moment, the correspondence was both
diverting and striking.   But as the performers
warmed upon the exercise, their gesticulations became more and more diversified, vehement, and
energetic—leaping, striding, vaulting, and running,
they perpetually crossed each other's orbits, stabbing,
parrying, thrusting, advancing, and retreating,
with so light a foot, and so rigid a muscle, that the
eye could with difficulty follow the velocity of their
motions; now darting to the right, and then as
abruptly recoiling to the left, they brandished their
sticks aloft, increasing in vehemence by each detour;
then vaulting several feet into the air, leaping,
galloping, and charging, in pantomimic conflict,
they made the ground resound under their feet,
and raised a cloud of dust by the eagerness and
rapidity of the exercise—until, foaming and frenzied
by their tortuous movements, they fairly sank beneath the tempest which they had stirred.   To the
bystander this scene conveyed all the reality of the
wildest conflict of savage life; the darkness of the
night, with the peculiar light shed over the features
of the frantic group by the blazing fire, contributing
greatly to heighten the impression it produced.
In consequence of the absence of the warriors, we
had not an opportunity of witnessing any of the
great national dances in which the king himself acts
a prominent part, but the effect of these public *spectacles* may be estimated by what I have described.

CHAPTER XXII.

RHINOCEROS AND WILD BUFFALO HUNTING ALONG THE CASHAN MOUNTAINS.

LEAVING the waggons to proceed to the ground where our operations against the elephants were to commence, I went with 'Lingap to the carcass of the antelope I concealed yesterday, near which I killed two females of the same species. I believe I may with safety assert that I am the only European that ever shot a water-buck. This noble antelope is about the size of an ass, and of somewhat browner colour. The hair is coarse, like that of the Indian Rusa stag, and in texture resembles split whalebone. The appearance of the male animal is stately; the eyes are large and brilliant; the horns ponderous and beetling, three feet in length, white, ringed, and placed almost perpendicularly on the head, the points being curved to the front. A mane encircles the neck, and an elliptical white band the tail, which is tufted at the extremity. The female is similar, but hornless, and rather smaller. The flesh of both is coarse, and so highly ill savoured that even savages are unable to eat it. On cutting off the head, the effluvia literally drove me from the spot. Mr. Steedman had the merit a few years ago of bringing this antelope under the observation of the scientific world, and Dr. Smith brought down other two specimens with the late expedition.

On the bank of the river I observed the perfect skeleton of an elephant. Near to it 'Lingap suddenly stopped, and pointing with his assagai to a bush a few yards off, whispered " *Tao*," and I immediately perceived three lionesses asleep. Ensconcing himself behind his shield, he made signs to me to fire, which I did into the middle of the party, at the same moment springing behind a tree which completely screened me. Thus unceremoniously awakened, the three ladies broke covert, roaring in concert, and dashed into the thick bushes, while we walked as fast as possible in the opposite direction. In the course of a few minutes we heard several discharges of musketry, and an infuriated rhinoceros, streaming with blood, rushed over the brow of the eminence that we were ascending, and was within pistol shot before we were aware of his approach. No bush presenting itself behind which to hide, I threw my cap at him, and 'Lingap striking his shield and shouting with stentorian lungs, the enraged beast turned off. I saluted him from both barrels, and he was immediately afterwards overturned by a running fire from the Hottentots, every one of whom I now saw had left the waggons at the mercy of the oxen, conduct for which we reprimanded them severely, threatening to withhold further supplies of ammunition.

Three hours' travelling between two ranges of the Cashan mountains, brought us to the Ooli river, a

pretty little stream, upon the further bank of which
we halted.   A party of savages joined us, having
feasted heartily upon the gnoo killed yesterday ;
and as we did not require their services, we sent them
to eat up the rhinoceros, with injunctions to return
in the evening.   The banks of the Ooli are precipitous, and clothed with extensive mimosa groves,
abounding with wild buffaloes, pallahs, and guinea-
fowl.* We made a large bag of the latter, and
obtained a supply of ostrich eggs.   In order to
drive the elephants into the plain, preparatory to
hunting them the next day, we set fire to the grass,
and moved the camp to a more secure position,
where the savages, who had returned, assisted in
fortifying our stockade against the lions.

At daybreak the following morning, we crossed
an extensive valley which skirts the mountain range,
passing the ruins of several stone kraals, which in
former times served to confine the cattle of numerous
Bechuana tribes then living in peaceful possession
of the country.   These crumbling memorials now
afford evidence of the extent to which this lovely
spot was populated before the devastating wars of
Moselekatze laid it waste, and indicate also a refinement in the art of building that I had not met with
before.   Our guides eagerly plucked several plants
of tobacco that grew wild about the enclosures, dry-
ing them for the manufacture of snuff.   Soon afterwards we entered a gorge of the mountains, and began to ascend.   The ravages of elephants were here

* *Numida Meleagris.*

still more conspicuous, and footsteps of the preceding day were numerous. We paused on the mountains to admire the stupendous depth and formidable character of the ravines and chasms, which have been scooped out by the mighty torrents of water that roll down during the rainy season, with fury irresistible, uprooting ancient trees, and hurling into the plain below huge masses of rock, which, once put in motion, bound from ledge to ledge until they reach the bottom of the valley. Nearly all the rivers in this part of Africa take their source in the Cashan range. It divides the waters that flow to the eastward into the Mozambique Sea, from those that run to the westward into the Atlantic Ocean; and the country on both sides being abundantly irrigated, is far better calculated both for grazing and cultivation than any part of the district that we found the Matabili occupying. The fear of Dingaan, however, has led them to neglect it, and to establish themselves in a more secure position. A gigantic savage of a subordinate tribe of the Baquaina, a conquered nation to the northward, here accidentally joined us. He was a perfect ogre in dimensions, six feet four inches high, and stout in proportion. From him we learned that there was a large herd of elephants on the opposite side of the mountains, out of which he had speared a young one the day before. We proceeded under his guidance, and threading a pass in the mountains formed by the dry channel of a ravine, through which a waggon might be brought with little difficulty, sat down to breakfast by a refreshing mountain rill.   A large colony of pig-faced baboons * shortly made their appearance above us, some slowly advancing with an inquisitive look, others deliberately seating themselves on the rocks, as though debating on the propriety of our unceremonious trespass on their domains.   Their inhospitable treatment at length obliging us to make an example, we fired two shots among them.   Numbers assembled round the spot where the first had struck, scraping the lead with their nails, and scrutinizing it with ludicrous gestures and grimace. The second, however, knocked over one of their elders, an enormous fellow, who was strutting about erect, laying down the law—and who, judging from his venerable appearance, must have been at least a great-grand-sire.   This national calamity caused incredible consternation, and many affecting domestic scenes.   The party dispersed in all directions, mothers snatching up their infants, and bearing them in their arms out of the reach of danger with an impulse and action perfectly human.

Conducted by an elephant path, we descended through the forest to a secluded dell on the northern side of the range.   Beyond, the whole plain was studded with detached pyramidical stony hills, amongst which we could perceive the extensive remains of cattle enclosures and ruins, similar to those we had passed in the morning, testifying of " cities long gone by."   The tracks of the elephants leading back again to the mountains, we reascended by a

* *Cynocephalus Porcarius.*

steep path considerably to the westward of the defile through which we had come, and, on arriving at the summit, perceived our waggons, like small white specks, in the distant valley.   Bare and sterile rocks occupy the highest elevation of these mountains, commanding an extensive view, and forming a strong contrast with the middle and lower regions, so thickly covered with verdure and forests, the latter chiefly occupying the ravines.   Having reconnoitered the whole country with a telescope, without being able to discern the animals of which we were in quest, we descended by a steep foot-path, the face of the mountain being strewed with round white pebbles. Near the summit grew a venerable mimosa, which completely overshadowed the path, and a little on one side of it we observed a large heap which had been formed by each passenger contributing one of these pebbles as he passed.   Our savages added their mite, simply picking up the nearest, and casting it irreverently towards the hill.   This being the only approach to external worship or religious ceremony that we had seen, we naturally became very inquisitive on the subject, but could elicit no satisfactory information.   Mohanycom said it was "the king," from which very sapient reply we were left at liberty to conclude, either that the hill was a monument of respect to royalty, or that they had been engaged in an idolatrous rite.   The former is the most probable, for, amongst the Matabili, the reigning monarch, whilst he absorbs all their praises, is the only deity.   He it is, in the opinion of this

benighted race, that "maketh the rain to fall and
the grass to grow, that seeth the evil and the good,
and in whose hands are the issues of life and death."
They have no idea of a Creator, so far as we could
learn, or knowledge of a future state ; nor could we
ascertain that by the term "king," they ever referred
to any being beyond the despot who presides over
their mortal destinies.

On reaching the foot of the mountains, we found
a portion of the skull of the elephant's calf that our
colossal savage friend had destroyed the day before.
It was all that the hyænas had left of the little that
he had considered too hard for his own digestion.
The tracks of the drove had gone eastward over
country where we had already hunted, and as it
waxed late, we made the best of our way to the
camp. I shot two quaggas for our savage allies,
who returned during the night laden with flesh, and
bringing with them a wild hog* that they had
buried in the morning in a porcupine's earth, to
which it had been driven by their dogs.

The grass on the opposite side of the mountains
having been burnt, we resolved, by the advice of the
natives, to skirt them on the south side for a day or
two. As soon as it was light, I set out with Mohanycom, and killed a spotted hyæna† that had been
attracted with many others by the smell of the pork
to our camp. I was glad to have my revenge, for
the vagabonds had annoyed our cattle all night long,
moaning funereally in concert with the dismal

* *Sus Larvatus.*   † *Hyæna Crocuta.*

yelling of jackals,* and roaring of lions, with whose melody our only surviving dog never failed to chime in.   The sole of my shoe coming off, during the hot pursuit of a water-buck, whose leg I had fractured, I had the felicity of completing the animal's destruction barefooted, and afterwards running about two miles over sharp flint-stones to overtake the waggons, which had crossed four inconsiderable mountain streams, and were entering a field of tall reed-grass, that waved above the heads of the oxen. An immense white rhinoceros suddenly started from his slumbers, and rushed furiously at the leading waggon, crushing the dry reeds before him, and alarming the cattle by his loud snorting and hostile demonstrations.   A volley, however, cooled his courage, and he retired to a suitable bush, where we despatched him.   Three more rhinoceroses were added to the list on our way to the Massellan river, which flowing through the mountains, joins the Lingkling, a tributary to the Limpopo.

Although said to be very expert in following the tracks of wild animals, the Hottentots are far less skilful than the Asiatics, and I not unfrequently eclipsed them myself.   Piet was the most accomplished in wood-craft, and besides being possessed of considerably more nerve, was the only one of our followers upon whom I could depend for any assistance in the field.   The rest were ready enough to go out, that they might obtain a supply of ammunition, and gain a pretext for evading their other

* *Canis Mesomelas.*

K

duties ; but their natural indolence extending itself even to their recreations, they never hesitated to abandon me at their convenience, in order to divert themselves with the more common species of game, which could be circumvented with little exertion. The savages never accompanied us beyond the carcass of the first large animal slain, upon which having gorged to repletion, they fell fast asleep over the fire.

On the 5th November, we followed the traces of elephants along the side of the mountains for miles, through stupendous forests, all the Hottentots excepting Piet dropping in the rear in succession, either to solace themselves with a pipe, or to expend their ammunition upon ignoble game. Time not permitting us to continue the search, we descended into a valley, bent upon the destruction of a roan antelope,* a large herd of which rare animals were quietly grazing. A pair of white rhinoceroses opposed our descent, and being unwilling to fire at them, we had some trouble in freeing ourselves from their company. A large herd of wilds wine,† or as Indians term it, a *sounder* of hog, carrying their long whip-like tails erect, then passed in order of review, and immediately afterwards two bull buffaloes were observed within pistol shot. It was a perfect panorama of game; I had with great difficulty restrained Piet from firing, and was almost within reach of the bucks, when a Hottentot sud-

---

* *Aigocerus Equina.* Delineated in the African Views.
† *Phascochærus Africanus.*

denly discharging his gun put every thing to flight.
The buffaloes passed me quite close on their way to
the hills. I fractured the hind leg of the largest,
and mounting my horse, closed with him immediately, and after two gallant charges performed upon
three legs, he fell, never to rise again. This was a
noble specimen of the African buffalo, standing
sixteen hands and a half at the shoulder. His
ponderous horns measured four feet from tip to tip,
and like a mass of rock, overshadowing his small
sinister grey eyes, imparted to his countenance the
most cunning, gloomy, and vindictive expression.
The savages instantly set to work upon the carcass
with their teeth and assagais—Piet providing himself with portions of the hide for shoe soles, and of
the flesh, which, though coarse, is a tolerable imitation of beef.

From the summit of a hill which commanded an
extensive prospect over a straggling forest, I shortly
afterwards perceived a large herd of buffaloes, quietly chewing the cud beneath an umbrageous tree.
Creeping close upon them, I killed a bull with a
single ball, but the confused echo reverberating
among the mountains alarming the survivors, about
fifty in number, they dashed panic-stricken from
their concealment, ignorant whence the sound
proceeded ; and every thing yielding to their giant
strength, I narrowly escaped being trampled underfoot in their progress. We moved five miles to the
eastward in the afternoon, stopping to take up the
head of the buffalo, which Andries could with diffi-

culty lift upon the waggon. Myriads of vultures, and the clouds of smoke which arose from the fires of the giant and his associates, directed us to the spot. In commemoration, I presume, of the exploits of Guy Fawkes, they had kindled a bonfire, which bid fair to destroy all the grass in the country, the flames fanned by the wind already beginning to ascend the hills. Nothing can be conceived more horribly disgusting than the appearance presented by the savages who, gorged to the throat, and besmeared with blood, grease, and filth from the entrails, sat nodding torpidly round the remains of the carcass, sucking marrow from the bones, whilst their lean famished curs were regaling themselves upon the garbage. Every bush was garnished with flaps of meat, and every man had turned beef butcher, whilst swollen vultures* were perched upon the adjacent trees, and others yet ungorged were inhaling the odours that arose.

The sun set upon us with every demonstration of rain. The night was dark and gusty. Thunder pealing amongst the mountains, and vivid flashes of forked lightning presaged a coming storm; fortunately, however, it expended its fury in the hills, and only visited us with a few drops. Before going to bed, I had been gazing for hours upon the singular and sublime effect produced by the extensive and rapidly spreading combustion of the grass. A strong south-easterly wind setting towards the hills,

* *Vultus Fulvus,* and *Vultus Auricularis:* White and Black Aas-vogel of the Cape Colonists.

was driving the devouring element, with a loud
crackling noise, up the steep grassy sides, in long
red lines, which extending for miles, swept along
the heights with devastating fury, brilliantly illu-
minating the landscape, and threatening to denude
the whole country of its vegetation.   Suddenly the
storm burst above the scene.   The wind immediately
hushed ; a death-like stillness succeeded to the
crackling of the flames.   Every spark of the conflagration was extinguished in an instant by the
deluge that descended, and the Egyptian-like darkness of the night was unbroken even by a solitary
star.

CHAPTER XXIII.

ELEPHANT HUNTING IN THE CASHAN MOUNTAINS.

BEFORE daybreak the following morning, it was discovered that the oxen, having been alarmed by lions, had made their escape from the pound. A party was despatched in pursuit of them, and we proceeded into the hills to look for buffaloes. The thunder-storm having purified the atmosphere, rendered the weather delightfully cool, and a deep wooded defile which had not been approached by the conflagration of the day before, was filled with game that had fled before the flames. A rhinoceros was killed almost immediately, and before we had reloaded, a noble herd of near one hundred and fifty buffaloes was perceived on a slope overhanging a sedgy stream. Having crept within five-and-twenty yards, we despatched two bulls before the alarm was spread. Crashing through the forest, they overturned decayed trees in their route, and swept along the brow of the opposite hill in fearful confusion, squeezed together in a compact phalanx, and raising an incredible cloud of dust to mark their course. We mounted our horses, and after sticking some time in the treacherous mud of the rivulet, gained the opposite bank, and brought two

more to bay, which were despatched after several
charges. Our savage friends, still torpid from
their yesterday's feast, had not made their appearance ; we therefore despatched Claas, after breakfast was over, to bring in some marrow-bones, in
the act of collecting which delicacies, he was put
to flight by a lion that jumped out of a bush close
to him, and did not leave him time to think of his
gun. After some hours, however, he mustered
courage to proceed with a large party to recover it.

Early in the afternoon the Hottentots returned
with the oxen, and we proceeded without loss of time
to the eastward, following the course of the mountains
through very high grass, and passing between two
conical hills of singular appearance, which stood like
sentinels on either hand ; after crossing six inconsiderable streams, we with some difficulty gained
the vicinity of a remarkably abrupt opening in the
range, which through a telescope appeared to afford
a practicable road to the northward. Both our waggons stuck fast in the Sant river, and were with
difficulty extricated by the united efforts of the
teams. The heat was intense, not a breath stirred,
and heavy black clouds fast collecting bade us prepare for a deluge. We therefore formed the camp
in a sheltered and elevated position, under the lee
of a high stone enclosure, which only required the
entrance to be closed with bushes to make a secure
pound for the cattle. Scarcely were these arrangements completed, when a stream of liquid fire ran
along the ground, and a deafening thunder-clap

exploding close above us, was instantly followed by
a torrent of rain, which "came dancing to the
earth," not in drops, but in continuous streams, and
with indescribable violence, during the greater part
of the night; the thunder now receding and rum-
bling less and less distinctly, but more incessantly
among the distant mountains—now pealing in echoes
over the nearest hills, and now returning to burst
with redoubled violence above our heads.

> ——————————————"Far along
> From peak to peak, the rattling crags among,
> Leapt the wild thunder, not from one lone cloud,
> But every mountain soon had found a tongue."

The horses and oxen were presently standing knee
deep in water; our followers remained sitting all
night in the baggage-waggon, which leaked considerably, but our own, being better covered, fortunately
resisted the pitiless storm. Sleep was however out
of the question, the earth actually threatening to give
way under us, and the lightning being so painfully
vivid that we were glad to hide our heads under the
pillow.

Those only who have witnessed the setting in of
the south-west monsoon in India, are capable of fully
understanding the awful tempest I have attempted
to describe. About an hour before dawn its fury
began to abate, and at sunrise it was perfectly fine,
but the rivers were quite impassable. I proceeded
with some of the Hottentots to reconnoitre the pass,
but found that it was impassable for waggons, being
nothing more than a narrow channel flanked by

perpendicular crags, between which the Sant river
rushes on its way to join the Lingkling, making a
number of very abrupt windings through a most
impracticable country, intersected by a succession
of rocky acclivities.   From the highest peak we saw
several herds of buffaloes, and whilst descending
came upon the tracks of a huge elephant that had
passed about an hour before.   This being the largest
foot-print we had seen, I had the curiosity to measure it, in order to ascertain the animal's height—
twice the circumference of an elephant's foot being,
it is notorious, the exact height at the shoulder.   It
yielded a product of about twelve feet, which, notwithstanding the traditions that have been handed
down, I believe to be the maximum height attained
by the African elephant.*   We followed the trail
across the Sant river, which had now considerably
subsided— and finding that it proceeded eastward
along the mountain chain, returned to our encampment for horses and ammunition.

Leaving the waggons to proceed to a spot agreed
upon, we again took the field about ten o'clock, and
pursued the track indefatigably for eight miles,
over a country presenting every variety of feature.
At one time we crossed bare stony ridges, at another
threaded the intricacies of shady but dilapidated
forests; now struggled through high fields of
waving grass, and again emerged into open downs.
At length we arrived amongst extensive groups of
grassy hillocks, covered with loose stones, inter-

* *Elephas Africanus.*   Delineated in the African Views.

K 5

spersed with streams, and occasional patches of
forest, in which the recent ravages of elephants
were surprising.   Here, to our inexpressible gratification, we descried a large herd of those long-
sought animals, lazily browsing at the head of a
distant valley, our attention having been first directed to it, by the strong and not to be mistaken
effluvia with which the wind was impregnated.
Never having before seen the noble elephant in
his native jungles, we gazed on the sight before us
with intense and indescribable interest.   Our feelings on the occasion even extended to our followers.
As for Andries, he became so agitated that he could
scarcely articulate.   With open eyes and quivering
lips he at length stuttered forth " *Dar stand de
olifant.*"   Mohanycom and 'Lingap were immediately despatched to drive the herd back into the
valley, up which we rode slowly and without noise,
against the wind; and arriving within one hundred
and fifty yards unperceived, we made our horses
fast, and took up a commanding position in an old
stone kraal.   The shouting of the savages, who now
appeared on the height rattling their shields, caused
the huge animals to move unsuspiciously towards us,
and even within ten yards of our ambush.   The
group consisted of nine, all females with large tusks.
We selected the finest, and with perfect deliberation
fired a volley of five balls into her.   She stumbled,
but recovering herself, uttered a shrill note of lamentation, when the whole party threw their trunks
above their heads, and instantly clambered up the

adjacent hill with incredible celerity, their huge fan-like ears flapping in the ratio of their speed. We instantly mounted our horses, and, the sharp loose stones not suiting the feet of the wounded lady, soon closed with her. Streaming with blood, and infuriated with rage, she turned upon us with up-lifted trunk, and it was not until after repeated dis-charges, that a ball took effect in her brain, and threw her lifeless on the earth, which resounded with the fall.

Turning our attention from the exciting scene I have described, we found that a second valley had opened upon us, surrounded by bare stony hills, and traversed by a thinly-wooded ravine. Here a grand and magnificent panorama was before us, which beggars all description. The whole face of the landscape was actually covered with wild elephants. There could not have been fewer than three hundred within the scope of our vision. Every height and green knoll was dotted over with groups of them, whilst the bottom of the glen exhibited a dense and sable living mass—their colossal forms being at one moment partially concealed by the trees which they were disfiguring with giant strength; and at others seen majestically emerging into the open glades, bearing in their trunks the branches of trees with which they indolently protected themselves from the flies. The back-ground was filled by a limited peep of the blue mountainous range, which here as-sumed a remarkably precipitous character, and com-pleted a picture at once soul-stirring and sublime!

Our approach being still against the wind was
unobserved, and created little alarm, until the herd
that we had left behind suddenly showed itself,
recklessly thundering down the side of the hill to
join the main body, and passing so close to us, that
we could not refrain from firing a broadside into
one of them, which however bravely withstood it.
We secured our horses on the summit of a stony
ridge, and then stationing ourselves at an opportune
place on a ledge overlooking the wooded defile, sent
Andries to manœuvre so that as many of the elephants as possible should pass before us in order of
review, that we might ascertain, by a close inspection, whether there was not a male amongst them.
Filing sluggishly along, they occasionally halted
beneath an umbrageous tree within fifteen yards of
us, lazily fanning themselves with their ample ears,
blowing away the flies with their trunks, and uttering the feeble and peculiar cry so familiar to Indians.
They all proved to be ladies, and most of them
mothers, followed by their little old-fashioned calves,
each trudging close to the heels of her dam, and
mimicking all her actions.   Thus situated we might
have killed any number we pleased, their heads
being frequently turned towards us in such a
position, and so close, that a single ball in the brain
would have sufficed for each ; but whilst we were
yet hesitating, a bullet suddenly whizzed past
Richardson's ear, and put the whole herd to immediate flight. We had barely time to recede
behind a tree, before a party of about twenty, with

several little ones in their wake, were upon us, striding at their utmost speed, and trumpeting loudly
with uplifted heads. I rested my rifle against the
tree, and firing behind the shoulder of the leader,
she dropped instantly. Another large detachment
appearing close behind us at the same moment, we
were compelled to retreat, dodging from tree to
tree, stumbling amongst sharp stones, and ever
coming upon fresh parties of the enemy. This
scene of ludicrous confusion did not long continue—
and soon approaching the prostrate lady, we put
an end to her struggles by a shot in the forehead.
Andries now came up in high good humour at his
achievements, and in the most bravado manner discharged his piece into the dead carcass, under the
pretence that the animal was shamming. His object
evidently was to confound the shots—for thrusting
his middle finger into the orifice made by my two-
ounce ball, he with the most modest assurance
declared himself the author of the deed, being
pleased altogether to overlook the fact of the mortal
shot having entered the elephant on the side opposite to that on which he was stationed, and that
his own ball, whether designedly or not, had all but
expended my worthy and esteemed fellow-traveller.

On our way to the camp, of the exact position of
which we were uncertain, in consequence of the late
inundation, we passed three other large herds of
elephants. One of these standing directly in the
route, we attacked it, and pursued the fugitives
about a mile over loose stones. Much has been

said of the attachment of elephants to their young,
but neither on this, nor on any subsequent occasion,
did we perceive them evince the smallest concern
for their safety.   On the contrary, they left them to
shift for themselves, and Mohanycom and 'Lingap,
who were behind us, assagaied one, the tail of
which they brought in.   We slew another old
female as we ascended the brow of an eminence,
and at the same moment perceived our waggons
within a few hundred yards of the spot.   The whole
herd dashed through the camp, causing indescribable consternation amongst cattle and followers,
but fortunately no accident occurred, and after the
fatiguing day's work we had undergone, we were
not sorry to find ourselves at home.

Watery clouds hung about the sun as he set
heavily behind the mountains.   Loud peals of
crashing thunder rent the air, and ere it was dark,
we had a repetition of yesterday's storm, the river
roaring past us with frightful fury.   Troops of elephants flying from the scene of slaughter, passed
close to our waggons during the darkness, their wild
voices echoing amongst the mountains, and sound-
ing like trumpets above the tempest.   It was impossible to keep the fires burning : and the oxen
and sheep were alarmed to such a degree, that they
broke from the kraal, and sought safety in the
wilderness.   Tired as I was, the excitement I had
undergone banished sleep from my eyes.   I rumi-
nated on the spirit-stirring events of the day, and
burned with impatience to renew them.   Heedless

of the withering blast that howled without, I felt that my most sanguine expectations had been realized, and that we had already been amply repaid for the difficulties, privations, and dangers that we had encountered in our toilsome journey towards this fairy land of sport.

CHAPTER XXIV.

ELEPHANT HUNTING CONTINUED; AND LION SHOOTING FROM THE WAGGONS.

IT was still raining heavily when the day gloomily dawned. The mountain torrents having overflown their banks, the valley in which we were encamped had become a continuous pool of water; and those of our followers who had not slung their hammocks beneath the waggons, were partially submerged. High roads had been ploughed through the mire by the passage of the elephants, and whole acres of grass, by which we were surrounded the preceding evening, had been completely trampled down. Soon after sunrise it cleared up, and the cattle having been recovered, we armed a party with hatchets, and proceeded on foot to cut out the teeth of the slain elephants; but walking was exceedingly toilsome, and our feet sinking to the ankles in black mud, were extricated with inconceivable difficulty. Taking advantage of our situation, an irritated rhinoceros sallied from behind an old stone wall; and the damp causing three of the guns to miss fire, he was actually amongst us when my ball fortunately pierced his eye, and he fell dead at our feet.

Not an elephant was to be seen on the ground that was yesterday teeming with them; but on reaching the glen which had been the scene of our exploits during the early part of the action, a calf about three and a half feet high, walked forth from a bush, and saluted us with mournful piping notes. We had observed the unhappy little wretch hovering about its mother after she fell, and having probably been unable to overtake the herd, it had passed a dreary night in the wood. Entwining its little proboscis about our legs, the sagacious creature, after demonstrating its delight at our arrival by a thousand ungainly antics, accompanied the party to the body of its dam; which, swollen to an enormous size, was surrounded by an inquest of vultures. Seated in gaunt array, with their shoulders shrugged, these loathsome fowls were awaiting its decomposition with forced resignation: the tough hide having defied all the efforts of their beaks, with which the eyes and softer parts had been vigourously assailed. The conduct of the quaint little calf now became quite affecting, and elicited the sympathy of every one. It ran round its mother's corse with touching demonstrations of grief, piping sorrowfully, and vainly attempting to raise her with its tiny trunk. I confess that I had felt compunctions in committing the murder the day before, and now half resolved never to assist in another; for in addition to the moving behaviour of the young elephant, I had been unable to divest myself of the idea that I was firing at my old favourite *Mowla-Bukhsh,* from whose gallant back I had vanquished so many of my feline foes in Guzerat—an impression which, however ridiculous it must appear, detracted considerably from the satisfaction I experienced.

The operation of hewing out three pair of tusks occupied several hours, their roots, imbedded in massy sockets, spreading over the greater portion of the face. My Indian friends will marvel when they hear of tusks being extracted from the jaws of a female elephant—but, with very few exceptions, all that we saw had these accessories, measuring from three to four feet in length. I have already stated my belief that the maximum height of the African male is twelve feet; that of the female averages eight and a half—the enormous magnitude of the ears, which not only cover the whole of the shoulder, but overlap each other on the neck, to the complete exclusion of the *mahout*, or driver, constituting another striking feature of difference between the two species. The forehead is remarkably large and prominent, and consists of two walls or tables; between which, a wide cellular space intervening, a ball, hardened with tin or quicksilver, readily penetrates to the brain, and proves instantaneously fatal.

The barbarous tribes that people Southern Africa have never dreamt of the possibility of rendering this lordly quadruped serviceable in a domestic capacity; and even amongst the colonists, there exists an unaccountable superstition that his subjugation is not to be accomplished. His capture, however, might readily be achieved; and, as he appears to possess all the aptitude of his Asiatic relative, the only difficulty that presents itself, is the general absence, within our territories, of sufficient food for his support. Were he once domesticated, and arrayed against the beasts of the forest, Africa would realize the very *beau ideal* of magnificent sport. It is also worthy of remark, that no attempt has ever been made on the part of the colonists to naturalize another most useful animal—the camel, although soil, climate, and productions appear alike to favour its introduction.

We succeeded, after considerable labour, in extracting the ball which Andries pretended to have fired yesterday; and the grooves of my rifle being conspicuous upon it, that worthy, but unabashed, squire was constrained not only to relinquish his claim to the merit of having slain the elephant— but also to forego his fancied right to the ivory. The miniature elephant, finding that its mother heeded not its caresses, voluntarily followed our party to the waggons, where it was received with shouts of welcome from the people, and a band of all sorts of melody from the cattle. It died, however, in spite of every care, in the course of a few days; as did two others, much older, that we subsequently captured.

The day again closed with a thunder-storm, which twice passed off, and twice revisited us in the course of the night. The rivers, which had subsided during the day, became once more agitated, and instead of the trumpet accompaniment from ele-

phants, we were serenaded by a legion of jackals.
An opening shriek from one of these crafty animals,
·resounding during the conflict of the elements, amid
craggy rocks and solitary glens, was the signal for
a general chorus; and, re-answered by a long
protracted scream from a hundred throats, did not
fail in its effect upon our harassed cattle, causing
the sheep to break out of the enclosure, notwithstanding our efforts to control them.

Although the ground was very heavy, we resolved upon shifting the camp a few miles to the
eastward, in order to be within reach of the elephants. All the mountain rills were full, but they
were not of sufficient magnitude to obstruct the
waggons. As we proceeded, several elephants were
observed clambering, with the agility of chamois,
to the very summit of the chain, until at length
they stood out in bold relief against the blue sky.
Shortly after we had halted, I went out alone, and
ascending by a narrow path trodden by wild animals,
entered a strip of forest occupying an extensive
ravine. On the outside of this, stood a mighty bull
elephant, his trunk entwined around his tusk, and,
but for the flapping of his huge ears, motionless as
a statue. Securing my mare to a tree, I crept
silently behind a block of stone, and levelled my
rifle at his ample forehead. The earth trembled
under the weight of the enormous brute as he
dropped heavily, uttering one deep groan, and
expiring without a struggle. His height at the
shoulder was eleven feet and a half, and his tusks

measured more than seven in length.　The echo of
the shot, reverberating through hill and dale, caused
the mare to break her tether and abscond, and
brought large tribes of pig-faced baboons from their
sylvan haunts, to afford me anything but sympathy.
Their ridiculous grimaces, however, could not fail
to elicit my mirth, whatever might have been my
humour.　It was long before I recovered my horse,
and I did not regain the waggons until after night-
fall.　The new moon brought, if possible, a more
abundant supply of rain than usual; nor did the lions
fail to take advantage of the nocturnal tempest, having twice endeavoured to effect an entrance into the
cattle-fold.　It continued until nine o'clock the next
morning, to pour with such violence, that we were
unable to open the canvas curtains of the waggon.
Peeping out, however, to ascertain if there was any
prospect of its clearing up, we perceived three lions
squatted within a hundred yards, in the open plan,
attentively watching the oxen.　Our rifles were
hastily seized, but the dampness of the atmosphere
prevented their exploding.　One after another, too,
the Hottentots sprang out of the pack-waggon, and
snapped their guns at the unwelcome intruders, as
they trotted sulkily away, and took up their position
on a stony eminence at no great distance.　Fresh
caps and priming were applied, and a broadside
was followed by the instantaneous demise of the
largest, whose cranium was perforated by two
bullets at the same instant.　Swinging their tails
over their backs, the survivors took warning by the

fate of their companion, and dashed into the thicket with a roar. ˙ In another half-hour, the voice of *Leo* was again heard at the foot of the mountains, about a quarter of a mile from the camp; and from the waggon-top we could perceive a savage monster rampant, with his tail hoisted and whirling in a circle—charging furiously along the base of the range—and in desperate wrath, making towards John April, who was tending the sheep. Every one instinctively grasped his weapon, and rushed to the rescue, calling loudly to warn the expected victim of his danger. Without taking the smallest notice of him, however, the infuriated monster dashed past, roaring and lashing his sides until concealed in the mist. Those who have seen the monarch of the forest in crippling captivity only, immured in a cage barely double his own length, with his sinews relaxed by confinement, have seen but the shadow of that animal which " clears the desert with his rolling eye."

The reader is aware that the tiger is not a denizen of Africa. Both the leopard, and the hunting-leopard occur, but differ in no respect from those found in India; neither does the South African lion differ in any material points from those found in Guzerat, in Western India, measuring between ten and eleven feet in extreme length, but generally possessing a finer. mane, a peculiarity which is attributable to the less jungly character of the country that he infests, and to the more advanced age which he is suffered to attain.

Amongst the Cape Colonists it is a fashionable belief, that there are two distinct species of the African lion—the yellow, and the black—and that the one is infinitely less ferocious than the other. But I need scarcely inform the well-instructed reader, that both the colour and the size depend chiefly upon the animal's age; the development of the physical powers, and of the mane also, being principally influenced by a like contingency. That which has been designated the "maneless lion of Guzerat," is nothing more than a young lion whose mane has not shot forth; and I give this opinion with less hesitation, having slain the "king of beasts" in every stage from whelphood to imbecility.

CHAPTER XXV.

SHOOTING THE HIPPOPOTAMUS, AND HUNTING IN THE VALLEY OF THE LIMPOPO.

It was unfortunately requisite, during the greater part of our journey, to furnish the Hottentots with ammunition for their protection whilst tending the cattle; and their incessant firing, which no remonstrance could control, soon disturbing the whole of the game in our neighbourhood, we found it useless to remain more than one day at any place. Compared with the quantity of powder expended by these men, the number of animals they killed was exceedingly limited—the supply of meat for the camp generally depending upon my success; but the beasts of the forest having been unmolested all their lives, and unaccustomed to the report of the gun, fled before their attacks in consternation, so that within a few hours after the formation of the camp in a spot abounding with game, not a living quadruped was to be seen.

The country through which we travelled being chiefly characterized by open plains or straggling forests with little undergrowth, it will readily be conceived that *wood-craft* availed little in the destruction of game. Many of the species that occur are naturally slow and heavy; and the gregarious habits of the fleeter rendering them easy of approach on horseback, almost every animal, from the mighty elephant to the most diminutive antelope, must be pursued in the saddle.   Not only, however, does the success of a hunting party mainly depend upon the number and condition of the horses—which are almost daily required also for the recovery of straying cattle, and, owing to some peculiarity in the Hottentot conformation, which ill adapts him for equestrian excellence, are invariably brought home with galled backs—but its safety, in event of an attack from the savage tribes, is equally involved. We could, therefore, have found ample employment for forty, instead of sixteen, half-starved, shoeless Rozinantes, with nothing but grass to eat, and not so much even as a cloth to protect them from the cold and wet during a succession of inclement nights. But whilst none of our many trading advisers, who had doubtless experienced the difficulty of destroying on foot sufficient game for the subsistence of their followers, had suggested our going better provided, they had unfortunately succeeded in dissuading us from carrying a supply of shoes or grain, the absence of both of which essentials we never ceased to deplore.   The anxiety may be estimated with which we watched the now daily improving condition of our meagre steeds, and assiduously endeavoured to free them from the clusters of bursting ticks, which, having been contracted amongst the bushes, threatened to relieve them of the little blood they possessed.   A sturdy stall-fed Arab would have now

L

been worth his weight in gold; but ragged as the
Cape horses undoubtedly are, it is but justice to
their manifold merits to declare that they only require
feeding to render them most useful allies during an
African campaign.   Hardy, docile, and enduring,
any number may be driven on the line of march
by a single Hottentot; and they are soon habituated
to graze unattended within sight of the waggons,
wherever grass is abundant.   In the chase, the most
formidable animal does not inspire them with the
slightest alarm; and the bridle being thrown over
their heads, they may generally be left standing in
the wilderness for hours together, without attempting to stir from the spot.

Our next movement brought us to the source of
the Oori or Limpopo—the Gareep of Moselekatse's
dominions.   Fed by many fine streams from the
Cashan range, this enchanting river springs into
existence as if by magic; and rolling its deep and
tranquil waters between tiers of weeping willows,
through a passage in the mountain barrier, takes
its course to the northward.   Here we enjoyed the
novel diversion of hippopotamus* shooting—that
animal abounding in the Limpopo, and dividing the
empire with its amphibious neighbour the crocodile.
Throughout the night, the unwieldy monsters might
be heard snorting and blowing during their aquatic
gambols, and we not unfrequently detected them in
the act of sallying from their reed-grown coverts to
graze by the serene light of the moon; never, how-

* *Hippopotamus Amphibius.*   Delineated in the African Views.

ever, venturing to any distance from the river, the
stronghold to which they betake themselves on the
smallest alarm.   Occasionally during the day they
were to be seen basking on the shore amid ooze and
mud; but shots were more constantly to be had at
their uncouth heads, when protruded from the water
to draw breath, and if killed, the body rose to the
surface.   Vulnerable only behind the ear, however,
or in the eye, which is placed in a prominence, so as
to resemble the garret-window of a Dutch house,
they require the perfection of rifle practice, and after
a few shots become exceedingly shy, exhibiting the
snout only, and as instantly withdrawing it.   The
flesh is delicious, resembling pork in flavour, and
abounding in fat, which in the colony is deservedly
esteemed the greatest of delicacies.   The hide is
upwards of an inch and a half in thickness, and
being scarcely flexible, may be dragged from the
ribs in strips like the planks from a ship's side.   Of
these are manufactured a superior description of
sjambok, the elastic whip already noticed as being
an indispensable piece of furniture to every boor
proceeding on a journey.   Our followers encumbered
the waggons with a large investment of them, and
of the canine teeth, the ivory of which is extremely
profitable.

Of all the mammalia, whose portraits, drawn
from ill-stuffed specimens, have been foisted upon
the world, the *Behemoth* has perhaps been the most
ludicrously misrepresented.   I sought in vain for
that colossal head—for those cavern-like jaws, gar-

L 2

nished with elephantine tusks—or those ponderous
feet with which "the formidable and ferocious quadruped" is wont "to trample down whole fields of
corn during a single night." Defenceless and in-
offensive, his shapeless carcass is but feebly supported upon short and disproportioned legs, and
his belly almost trailing upon the ground, he may
not inaptly be likened to an overgrown "prize pig."
The colour is pinkish brown, clouded and freckled
with a darker tint. Of many that we shot, the
largest measured less than five feet at the shoulder;
and the reality falling so lamentably short of the
monstrous conception I had formed, the " river
horse," or " sea cow,"* was the first and indeed
the only South African quadruped in which I felt
disappointed.

The country now literally presented the appearance of a menagerie; the host of rhinoceroses in
particular, that daily exhibited themselves, almost
exceeding belief. Whilst the camp was being
formed, an ugly head might be seen protruded from
every bush, and the possession of the ground was
often stoutly disputed. In the field, these animals
lost no opportunity of rendering themselves obnoxious—frequently charging at my elbow, when
in the act of drawing the trigger at some other
object—and pursuing our horses with indefatigable
and ludicrous industry, carrying their noses close

* The Hippopotamus is termed by the colonists *Zekoe*, or Sea
Cow, the least applicable designation perhaps, not excepting that
of the *River Horse*, that could have been conferred.

to the ground, moving with a mincing gait, which ill-beseemed so ungainly and ponderous a quadruped, and uttering, the while, a sound between a grunt and a smothered whistle. In removing the horn with an axe, the brain was discovered, seated in a cavity below it, at the very extremity of the snout— a phenomenon in the idiosyncrasy of this animal, which may in some measure account for its want of intelligence and piggish obstinacy; as well as for the extraordinary acuteness of smell with which it is endowed. Irascible beyond all other quadrupeds, the African rhinoceros appears subject even to unprovoked paroxysms of reckless fury; but the sphere of vision is so exceedingly limited, that its attacks, although sudden and impetuous, are easily eluded, and a shot behind the shoulder, discharged from the distance of twenty or thirty yards, generally proves fatal.

On our way from the waggons to a hill, not half a mile distant, we counted no less than twenty-two of the white species of rhinoceros, and were compelled in self-defence to slaughter four. On another occasion, I was besieged in a bush by three at once, and had no little difficulty in beating off the assailants. Wild buffaloes, too, might often be seen from the waggons. Riding up a narrow defile, flanked by steep banks, I one morning found myself suddenly confronted with the van of a vast troop of these formidable animals, which were ascending from the opposite side—their malevolent grey eyes scowling beneath a threatening brow. Unable to

turn, they must have charged over me, had my
horse not contrived to scramble up the bank ; from
the top of which I fired both barrels into the leader,
a ponderous bull, whose appearance stamped him
father of the herd. Falling on his knees, the
patriarch was instantly trampled underfoot by his
followers as they charged, bellowing, in close squad-
ron, down the declivity, with the fury of a passing
whirlwind, and making the woods re-echo to the
clatter of their hoofs.

In the vegetable world, a great variety of novel
and interesting forms grace the banks of the Limpopo, but the airy acacia is still pre-eminently beautiful. Green and shady belts, bedizened with golden
blossoms and purple pods, or fringed with the cradle
nests of the pensile grosbeak, extend on either side—
their mazes being intersected by paths worn by hippopotami during their nocturnal rambles. The
recesses of these fairy groves, ringing with " wood-
notes wild," are the favourite haunts of many forest-
loving antelopes. The graceful pallah, with knotted
and eccentrically inflected horns of extraordinary
proportions, is found in large families. Shy and
capricious in its habits, the elegance of its form,
and the delicate finish of its limbs, are unrivalled.
The usual succentorial hoofs are wanting, but the
hind legs are furnished with remarkable cushions
of wiry hair, which occur in no other species, and
remind us of the heels of a Mercury. This favoured spot, too, is a chosen resort of the majestic
water-buck, which I now found might be ridden

down with facility ; a discovery that enabled me to
obtain many splendid specimens.   This rare and
remarkable animal, which has been already described, is never found at a distance from the banks
of tropical rivers, in the waters of which he delights
to plunge.

Another rare species—the roan antelope, or
bastard gemsbok—is an inhabitant of the elevated
downs and ridges about the source of this river, and,
being utterly destitute of speed, may be ridden to
a stand-still without difficulty.   This most imposing animal, which charges viciously when unable
to continue its flight, is the size of a large horse ;
and, excepting the head and tail, which are jet black,
is uniformly of a delicate roan colour.   It is heavily
built, and has an upright mane, long asinine ears,
and robust scimitar-shaped recurved horns.   Here,
too, I first met with, and slew, the koodoo.*   Majestic in its carriage, and brilliant in its colour, this
species may with propriety be styled the king of
the tribe.   Other antelopes are stately, elegant, or
curious—but the solitude-seeking koodoo is abso-
lutely regal!   The ground colour is a lively French
grey approaching to blue, with several transverse
white bands passing over the back and loins; a
copious mane, and deeply fringed, tricoloured dewlap, setting off a pair of ponderous, yet symmetrical,
horns, spirally twisted, and exceeding three feet in
length.   These are thrown along the back, as the
stately wearer dashes through the mazes of the

* *Strepsiceros Koodoo.* Delineated in the African Views.

forest, or clambers the mountain side. The old
bulls are invariably found apart from the females,
which herd together in small troops, and are destitute of horns.

Every open glade abounds with the more common
species of game, such as the brindled gnoo, hartebeest, sassayby, and quagga, together with the
ostrich and wild hog; the tusks of this latter most
hideous animal attaining in some instances to an
enormous size, although its stature is insignificant.
Among the sedge-grown rivulets, the riet-buck is
common; and the mountain range and its grassy
environs, are the resort of six smaller species of
antelope, hitherto unnoticed in these pages; viz.,
the klipspringer, rheebuck, rooe rheebuck, or nagor,
ourebi, steenbuck, and duiker,* of each of which I
obtained several specimens. Although described
in the Appendix, the remarkable character of the
two first demand further notice; the klipspringer,
which is closely allied to the chamois of Europe,
and coney-like, has its house on the mountain-top,
being furnished with singularly coarse hair, imparting the appearance of a hedgehog; whilst the fur
of the rheebuck again, is of a curly woolly nature,
resembling that of the wild rabbit.

Excepting the garrulous guinea-fowl, which usually
abounded in the vicinity of wood and water, and
whose grating cackle might here be nightly heard
as it ascended the trees to roost, feathered game

* *Oreotragus Saltatrix, Redunca Capreolus, R. Lalandii, R.
Scoparia, Tragulus Rupestris,* and *Cephalopus Mergens.*

was comparatively scarce throughout our journey. Occasionally, however, and here in particular, we found two species of the bustard, or *paow* of the colonists—two of the florican or *koraan*—with four distinct kinds of partridge. To these, however, I had little leisure to attend, my time being fully occupied from dawn until dark, in the pursuit of, to me, far more attractive objects.

In the extensive and romantic valley of the Limpopo, which strongly contrasts with its own solitude, and with the arid lands which must be traversed to arrive within its limits, Dame Nature has doubtless been unusually lavish of her gifts. A bold mountain landscape is chequered by innumerable rivulets abounding in fish, and watering a soil rich in luxuriant vegetation. Forests, producing timber of the finest growth, are tenanted by a multitude of birds, which, if not universally musical, are all gorgeously attired; and the meadows throughout are decked with blossoming geraniums, and with an endless profusion of the gayest flowers, fancifully distributed in almost artificial parterres. Let the fore-ground of this picture, which is by no means extravagantly drawn, be filled in by the animal creation roaming in a state of undisturbed freedom, such as I have attempted to describe, and this hunter's paradise will surely not require to be coloured by the feelings of an enthusiastic sportsman, to stand out in prominent relief from amongst the loveliest spots in the universe.

CHAPTER XXVI.

EXCURSION TO THE EASTWARD OF THE LIMPOPO, AND JOURNEY ACROSS THE CASHAN MOUNTAINS TO THE NORTHWARD.

THE perils of waggon-travelling were now so materially increased by the rugged character of the country, that in order to follow a retreating herd of elephants, it was found necessary to leave the camp standing—a measure to which we were further driven by a positive refusal on the part of the guides to accompany us to the eastward of the Limpopo; alleging their apprehension of hostilities from Dingaan as a reason for their non-compliance in this instance with the king's orders to escort us wherever we pleased. Crossing the river, therefore, we skirted the mountain range on horseback, arriving, at the close of the second day's hunting, below its highest point; the sources of the Bekane and Umpeban here marking the site of the last great battle fought between the armies of Moselekatse and Dingaan, in which that of the former was completely routed. These rivers speedily become confluent; and after describing a nearly semicircular course, join the Limpopo a considerable distance to the northward of the range, where the country assumes a more rugged character than ever, being intersected by detached stony hills and mountain chains of barren and forbidding aspect. To the southward it becomes very open and level, with occasional clumps of forest; but although the black soil continued, the vegetation was becoming visibly less and less abundant.

Although unquestionably the highest part of southern Africa, if measured from the level of the sea, yet the actual altitude of the Cashan mountains, jutting up as they do, from an elevated base, is not so great as might be expected. From one point which we ascended, the extraordinary refraction of the atmosphere enabled us to obtain a glimpse, in the direction of Delagoa, of a very distant range stretching north and south, and said to form the boundary of Moselekatse's conquests in that direction, during his progress from the Zooloo country to that he at present occupies. It is in this tract of country, to the eastward of the beautiful but unhealthy slopes in which the Vaal river takes its origin, that Louis Triechard, the leader of the first party of colonial emigrants, has long been located, on the banks of what appears to be a very large river, reported by the natives to be tributary to the Limpopo; but of which the source and course remain unexplored. The first accounts of its existence were brought to the colony by Robert Scoon, the trader to whose name I have before alluded. Coming accidentally upon it whilst hunting elephants, he followed the banks for several days without being able to discover a ford, and such is

the sluggish character of the stream, that it was some
time before he could even determine the course;
pieces of wood which were thrown in remaining
almost stationary on the surface. An exploring
party of the emigrants, under a boor named Bronkhorst, subsequently visited this water from Triechard's
camp, and described its breadth to be more than a
mile, from which circumstance, combined with its
proximity to the head of the Vaal River, it is probably merely a lagoon.*

I shall not tax the patience of those of my readers, who may not be votaries of the chase, by a
repetition of hunting scenes. We returned to our
camp on the 14th, laden with spoils, having also
fully established the possibility of dispensing,
even to cooking apparatus, with every article of
baggage. Carrying nothing but the raiment on
our backs, the saddle served for a pillow, and the
horse-rug for a blanket. Our tent was the starry
canopy of heaven; we drank of the waters of the
crystal stream, and our viands were the produce
of our trusty rifles. It is said that the epicures of
Rome esteemed the trunk of an elephant an extraordinary luxury; and descending to more modern

* In Isaac's Travels in Eastern Africa, vol. i. p. 219, the
author, speaking of a party of Chaka's warriors who had just
returned from a foray, says, "In this expedition the Zooloos
penetrated north-west of Delagoa Bay. They arrived at an immense river, or lake, and travelled on its banks for a fortnight, in
an easterly direction, with a river to cross, but could not find any
thing like a fording place. They met with some yellow people
on horses, who compelled them to return."

times, we find our brother traveller, Le Vaillant, feasting upon the foot with extraordinary relish. To the attention of the city aldermen, however, I must be allowed to recommend the slice round the eye, which appears to have been hitherto overlooked by *bon vivans*. Upon this dainty morsel, roasted upon a stick before a blazing fire, or singed among the embers, so as to come under the Hottentot denomination of *carbonaadtje*, or devilled-grill, we frequently feasted; and I can aver, without the smallest fear of contradiction, that the dish rather resembled the fragment of a shoe, picked up after a conflagration, than meat which could boast of having been subjected to a culinary process.

Nothing momentous had transpired during our absence, Cœur de Lion, our deputy, having proved himself a bold and vigilant commander. The merciless inroads of the lions, and the trouble that their attacks involved, had at length taught our followers the necessity of keeping up constant watch-fires; and whenever the night was fine—which, " by the king's orders," was sometimes the case—the guides howled forth his praises, glutted themselves, and took snuff by turns. The wild wood rang with their shrill herdsman's whistle, and reiterated chorus of " *Hi-bo-bo*;" and when the night was spent, they leisurely fetched a large stone, upon which downy pillow, having first refreshed the edges of their weapons, they placed their woolly heads by the fire-side.

In these regions, where the heavenly bodies are seen through the clearest of mediums, a star-lit firmament is remarkably brilliant and beautiful. We frequently sat for some hours, over unadulterated "tea-water," witnessing Mohanycom's ludicrous imitations of the dancing of our country-women at the Cape, or listening to tales of the success of the king's arms. One favourite theme was the defeat of Sobiqua, king of the Wangkets, in accomplishing whose downfall 'Lingap had aided and abetted. Like many other African potentates, he had been found guilty of possessing too many cattle, and was presently compelled to fly to the Kalahari desert, with the wreck of his tribe. Conjecture, too, was alive, as to the fate of a commando, that had four years before been despatched for the subjugation of the *Damaras*, but of which no tidings had ever been received ; and the proceedings of a Dutch trader were not unfrequently brought on the *tapis*. It appeared that this wretch had undertaken, in return for a quantity of ivory, to add a white female to the beauties of the king's seraglio; and had actually succeeded in enticing a farmer, with his fair *vrouw*, to the very borders of the country, within which a commando was in readiness to seize the lady. The diabolical scheme being suspected, however, his designs were frustrated ; and a fear of Moselekatse's implacable revenge has obliged him to relinquish all trade with the savages, whilst the colonists, on the other hand, have placed the delinquent beyond the pale of society.

Our horses having now greatly improved in condition, we resolved to proceed immediately to the country of the Bakone, or Baquaina, where cameleopards were reported by the savages to be very abundant; and accordingly, on the 15th November, having previously cleared away several of the trees, we crossed over to the north side of the Cashan mountains, by a perilous and barely practicable path. The waggons were several times only prevented from being dashed to pieces by means of guy-ropes, which fortunately preserved their equilibrium, and we were enabled to encamp on the western banks of the Limpopo, some distance below the point where it winds through the bowels of the mountains, which rise on either hand in abrupt precipices, as though torn asunder by some mighty convulsion of nature. Here the country again assumes a more level character, but is broken to the eastward by detached hills and low ridges, imperceptibly increasing in importance, until they grow into a great range of mountains, known to the natives as the Mural. These may be said to take their origin about one degree north of the parallel of Delagoa, assuming a nearly northerly direction, and dividing the tracts occupied by the Baquaina and Babariri. During the rainy season especially, they are infested by a large species of gad-fly, nearly the size of a honey-bee, the bite of which, like that of a similar pest in Abyssinia, proves fatal to cattle. A desire to escape the officious visits of these destructive insects, whose persecutions relieved us of two of our oxen, soon obliged us to abandon the willow-fringed river, which threads the mountains for a considerable distance; and, after crossing the

Lingkling, the embouchure of which is not many miles above that of the Umpeban, our difficulties were not a little increased by the broken and stony character of the country.

On the 17th, whilst crossing a nameless and insignificant stream, the treacherous appearance of which had induced us to follow a path ploughed by hippopotami, the pack-waggon became suddenly ingulfed in a quagmire. The *trektouw*, or leathern trace, having been nibbled by alligators, twice snapped in the attempt to extricate it by double purchase; and all other resources failing, we were at length actually compelled to dig it out! This subsequently unfortunate vehicle was shortly afterwards upset for the first time during our journey, by the carelessness of Frederick, who had been appointed to the post of leader of the team, *vice* April, removed. With one hind wheel on the slope of a steep bank, and the other in a deep hollow, it vibrated for some seconds, as though the turn of a hair were to decide whether it should stand or fall. "It's over "—" now it's safe "—" No, gone by heavens!" burst from half a dozen mouths at once; and just sufficient time having elapsed to admit of the inmates effecting their escape, down it went with an appalling crash, the wheels appearing uppermost, and the motley contents displaying themselves in admirable disorder. Peltry, merchandize, and hunting trophies—camp furniture, tinman's wares, and oilman's stores, were speedily strewed upon the plain; whilst ten thousand leaden bullets, having been liberated by the sudden shock from the sacks in which they were put up, might be seen emulating each other in a race to arrive at the lower ground. To a spectator unacquainted with the construction of a Cape waggon, no one component part of which is attached to another, this would have appeared an irrecoverable and total wreck. In the course of two hours, however, every thing was in its proper place again, and the vehicle in motion, a trifling distortion of the awning being the only trace left to remind us of the catastrophe. It served as a lesson, nevertheless, to trim the waggons with greater care; and as we had now eaten some way into the stores, the hunting trophies were removed from the awning, to which they had hitherto been lashed, and stowed away in the hold as pig ballast. Yet even this precaution did not exempt us from further misfortune— the same ill-fated van was again overthrown in a few days with most alarming detriment to its contents—the portable sextant, amongst other things, being flattened in one of the side pockets, whilst the mercury of Fahrenheit's thermometer was scattered to the four winds of heaven.

The third day after crossing the mountains, we encamped on the Machachochan river, near the scene of the signal defeat of Barend Barend's Griquas in 1831, an event to which I have before had occasion to allude. A conical mountain, seen from a considerable distance in every direction, points to the spot; and its base is a perfect Golgotha, thickly strewed with the whitened bones of men and horses,

broken guns, and tattered furniture. Taking advantage of the absence of Moselekatse's army, on
an expedition against a tribe to the northward, a
thousand mounted Bastaards dashed across the
River Vaal, and obtained possession of vast herds
of cattle without opposition. Elated by success,
they were encamped, on their return, in straggling
detachments; and whilst slumbering in that ill-timed
security for which the tribe is remarkable, were surprised about an hour before daylight—the approved
opportunity in savage warfare—by a band of un-
practised soldiers, who had been hastily called together to meet the emergency. Such was the panic
created, that many fell by the guns of their comrades, and few indeed escaped to tell the fate of the
less fortunate. Dowd, the chief whom we met at
Daniel's-kuil, and Hendrik Hendrik, a Griqua captain residing at Phillipolis, state themselves to be the
only survivors of that disastrous day. Ensconced in
a thick bush, they kept up an incessant fire while
their ammunition lasted; jumping on the first
horses they could catch, and riding for their lives,
the instant the dawn appeared. The scene of carnage was visited by Moselekatse, and as he viewed
the carcases of his foes "strewing the earth like
broken glass," his exultation knew no bounds; the
contempt he had entertained for fire-arms being fully
confirmed by this signal defeat. Barend Barends,
who was infirm in years, had not accompanied the
invading army beyond the Vaal River, but died
shortly after the destruction of his clan.

CHAPTER XXVII.

HUNTING THE CAMELEOPARD, OR GIRAFFE.

To the sportsman, the most thrilling passage in my adventures is now to be recounted. In my own breast, it awakens a renewal of past impressions, more lively than any written description can render intelligible; and far abler pens than mine, dipped in more glowing tints, would still fall short of the reality, and leave much to be supplied by the imagination. Three hundred gigantic elephants, browsing in majestic tranquillity amidst the wild magnificence of an African landscape, and a wide stretching plain, darkened, far as the eye can reach, with a moving phalanx of gnoos and quaggas, whose numbers literally baffle computation, are sights but rarely to be witnessed; but who amongst our brother Nimrods shall hear of riding familiarly by the side of a troop of colossal giraffes, and not feel his spirit stirred within him? He that would behold so marvellous a sight must leave the haunts of man, and dive, as we did, into pathless wilds, traversed only by the brute creation—into wide wastes, where the grim lion prowls, monarch of all he surveys, and where the gaunt hyæna and wild dog fearlessly pursue their prey.

Many days had now elapsed since we had even seen the cameleopard—and then only in small num-

bers, and under the most unfavourable circumstances.
The blood coursed through my veins like quicksilver,
therefore, as ou the morning of the 19th, from the
back of *Breslar*, my most trusty steed, with a firm
wooded plain before me, I counted thirty-two of these
animals, industriously stretching their peacock necks
to crop the tiny leaves which fluttered above their
heads, in a mimosa grove that beautified the scenery.
They were within a hundred yards of me, but
having previously determined to try the *boarding*
system, I reserved my fire.   Although I had taken
the field expressly to look for giraffes, and had put
four of the Hottentots. on horseback, all excepting
Piet had as usual slipped off unperceived in pursuit
of a troop of koodoos. Our stealthy approach
was soon opposed by an ill-tempered rhinoceros,
which, with her ugly calf, stood directly in the path ;
and the twinkling of her bright little eyes, accompanied by a restless rolling of the body, giving
earnest of her intention to charge, I directed Piet
to salute her with a broadside, at the same moment
putting spurs to my horse. At the report of the
gun, and the sudden clattering of hoofs, away
bounded the giraffes in grotesque confusion, clearing the ground by a succession of frog-like hops,
and soon leaving me far in the rear. Twice were
their towering forms concealed from view by a park
of trees, which we entered almost at the same
instant ; and twice, on emerging from the labyrinth,
did I perceive them tilting over an eminence immeasurably in advance. A white turban, that I

wore round my hunting cap, being dragged off by a
projecting bough, was instantly charged by three
rhinoceroses; and looking over my shoulder, I could
see them long afterwards fagging themselves to
overtake me. In the course of five minutes, the
fugitives arrived at a small river, the treacherous
sands of which receiving their long legs, their flight
was greatly retarded; and after floundering to the
opposite side, and scrambling to the top of the bank,
I perceived that their race was run. Patting the
steaming neck of my good steed, I urged him again
to his utmost, and instantly found myself by the side
of the herd. The stately bull, being readily distinguishable from the rest by his dark chesnut robe,
and superior stature, I applied the muzzle of my
rifle behind his dappled shoulder, with the right
hand, and drew both triggers; but he still continued
to shuffle along, and being afraid of losing him,
should I dismount, among the extensive mimosa
groves, with which the landscape was now obscured,
I sat in my saddle, loading and firing behind the
elbow, and then placing myself across his path,
until, the tears trickling from his full brilliant eye,
his lofty frame began to totter, and at the seven-
teenth discharge from the deadly grooved bore,
bowing his graceful head from the skies, his
proud form was prostrate in the dust. Never
shall I forget the tingling excitement of that
moment! Alone, in the wild wood, I hurraed with
bursting exultation, and unsaddling my steed,
sank exhausted beside the noble prize I had won.

When I leisurely contemplated the massive frame before me, seeming as though it had been cast in a mould of brass, and protected by a hide of an inch and a half in thickness, it was no longer matter of astonishment that a bullet discharged from a distance of eighty or ninety yards should have been attended with little effect upon such amazing strength. The extreme height from the crown of the elegantly moulded head to the hoof of this magnificent animal, was eighteen feet; the whole being equally divided into neck, body, and leg. Two hours were passed in completing a drawing; and Piet still not making his appearance, I cut off the tail, which exceeded five feet in length, and was measurelessly the most estimable trophy I had gained; but proceeding to saddle my horse, which I had left quietly grazing by the side of a running brook, my chagrin may be conceived, when I discovered that he had taken advantage of my occupation to free himself from his halter, and abscond. Being ten miles from the waggons, and in a perfectly strange country, I felt convinced that the only chance of recovering my pet, was by following the trail, whilst doing which with infinite difficulty, the ground scarcely deigning to receive a foot-print, I had the satisfaction of meeting Piet and Mohanycom, who had fortunately seen and re-captured the truant. Returning to the giraffe, we all feasted heartily upon the flesh, which, although highly scented at this season with the rank mokaala blossoms, was far from despicable; and after losing our way in

HUNTING THE GIRAFFE.

HUNTING THE OSTRICH.

consequence of the twin-like resemblance of two
scarped hills, we regained the waggons after sunset.

The spell was now broken, and the secret of
cameleopard hunting discovered. The next day
Richardson and myself killed three; one a female,
slipping upon muddy ground, and falling with
great violence, before she had been wounded, a
shot in the head despatched her as she lay. From
this time we could reckon confidently upon two
out of each troop that we were fortunate enough to
find, always approaching as near as possible, in
order to ensure a good start, galloping into the
middle of them, *boarding* the largest, and riding
with him until he fell. The rapidity with which
these awkwardly formed animals can move, is
beyond all things surprising, our best horses being
unable to close with them under two miles. Their
gallop is a succession of jumping strides, the fore
and hind leg on the same side moving together
instead of diagonally, as in most other quadrupeds,
the former being kept close together, and the latter
so wide apart, that in riding by the animal's side,
the hoof may be seen striking on the outside of the
horse, momentarily threatening to overthrow him.
Their motion, altogether, reminded me rather of
the pitching of a ship, or rolling of a rocking-horse,
than of any thing living; and the remarkable gait
is rendered still more automaton-like, by the switching, at regular intervals, of the long black tail,
which is invariably curled above the back, and by
the corresponding action of the neck, swinging as it

does, like a pendulum, and literally imparting to the animal the appearance of a piece of machinery in motion. Naturally gentle, timid, and peaceable, the unfortunate giraffe has no means of protecting itself but with its heels; but even when hemmed into a corner, it seldom resorted to this mode of defence. I have before noticed the courage evinced by our horses, in the pursuit of game. Even when brought into actual contact with these almost unearthly quadrupeds, they evinced no symptom of alarm, a circumstance which may possibly be traced to their meagre diet.

The colossal height, and apparent disproportions of this extraordinary animal, long classed it with the unicorn and the sphinx of the ancients, and induced a belief that it belonged rather to the group of chimeras with which the regions of imagination are tenanted, than existed amongst the actual works of nature. Of its form and habits, no very precise notions were obtained until within the last forty years; and even now, the extant delineations are far from the truth, having been taken from crippled prisoners instead of from specimens free in their native deserts. The giraffe is by no means a common animal, even at its head-quarters. We seldom found them without having followed the trail, and never saw more than five-and-thirty in a day.* The senses of sight, hearing, and smell, are acute

* A traveller whom I met in the Cape Colony, assured me, before I visited the interior, that he had himself counted eight hundred giraffes in a single day; and during his travels, had

and delicate; the eyes, which are soft and gentle, eclipsing those of the oft-sung gazelle of the East, and being so constructed that, without turning the head, the animal can see both before and behind it at the same time.   On the forehead there is a remarkable prominence; and the tongue has the power of mobility increased to an extraordinary degree, accompanied with the faculty of extension, which enables it, in miniature, to perform the office of the elephant's proboscis.   The lofty maned neck, possessing only seven joints, appears to move on a pivot, instead of being flexible like that of the swan or peacock, to which, from its length, it has been likened.

The giraffe utters no cry whatever.   Both sexes have horns, covered with hair, and are similarly marked with an angular and somewhat symmetrical pattern.   The male increases in depth of colour according to the age, and in some specimens is nearly black; but the female is smaller in stature, and of a lighter colour, approaching to yellow.   Although very extensive, the range of its *habitat* is exclusively confined to those regions in which the species of mimosa termed mokaala, or *kameel-doorn*, is abundant, the leaves, shoots, and blossoms of that tree being its ordinary food.

On the 22nd, being encamped on the banks of a

ridden down *hundreds*.   On my return, however, after a little cross-examination, the number destroyed dwindled gradually down to *one*; which solitary individual appeared, upon further investigation, to have been taken in a pit-fall!

M

small stream, a cameleopard was killed by a lion, whilst in the act of drinking, at no great distance from the waggons.   It was a noisy affair, but an inspection of the scene on which it occurred, proved that the giant strength of the victim had been paralysed in an instant.   Authors have asserted that the king of beasts is sometimes carried fifteen or twenty miles, " riding proudly" on the back of the giraffe; but notwithstanding the amazing and acknowledged power of this superb animal, I am greatly disposed to question his ability to maintain so long a race under such merciless jockeyship!

CHAPTER XXVIII.

RETURN TO THE SOUTHWARD FROM THE TROPIC OF CAPRICORN.

ALTHOUGH hunting the cameleopard we continued
to advance to the northward, by marches of ten and
fifteen miles a day, over extensive rugged tracts,
strewed with numerous stone walls, once thronged
by thousands, but now presenting no vestige of inhabitants. Wherever we turned, the hand of the
destroyer was apparent:

> ———————" The locusts' wasting swarm,
> Which mightiest nations dread,"

is not more destructive to vegetation than he has
been to the population of this section of Southern
Africa. We frequently travelled for days without
meeting a solitary human being—occasionally only
falling in with the small and starving remnant of
some pastoral tribe of Bechuana, that had been
plundered by Moselekatse's warriors. These famished wretches, some of whom had been herding
the king's cattle during the absence of Kalipi's
commando, hovered around us, disputing with
vultures and hyænas the carcases we left, which
they devoured with such brutish avidity as scarcely
to leave a bone to attest the slaughter.

The moon was full on the night of the 23rd, and

M 2

a spotted, or "laughing" hyæna, superior in size to the largest mastiff, was shot through the head, by the clear light it afforded, as he was in the act of skulking under the sheep-pen. The great muscular power of this animal, which is called by the colonists "the wolf," renders it exceedingly formidable; the difficulty of determining the sex being the most remarkable feature it possesses. On the 27th we again encamped on the banks of the Limpopo, in which a buffalo was shot as it was swimming across. Few other sporting incidents occurred of an extraordinary character, except the death of a very large black rhinoceros, which, being pent up in an old stone enclosure, forming a *cul de sac,* the entrance to which I closed up, received no less than twenty-seven shots before it fell. A troop of brindled gnoos, being pursued by another of these animals, dashed into a narrow defile in the hills, at the outlet of which, having stationed myself, I disposed of two with each barrel.

As we approached the junction of the Mariqua with the Limpopo, in about latitude 24° 10′, bushes usurped the place of trees; the country daily became less inviting, and the game in consequence less and less abundant, although a supply was still always to be obtained. The few inhabitants that we now met with refused to hold any communication with our escort—seating themselves at a distance, and declining the proferred snuff-box. These men were the wreck of the Bakone or Baquaina, once the most powerful and prosperous of the Bechuana

nations.   Conquered by Moselekatse, however
and. Caama,* their king, having been slain, they
fled to this part of the country, and are now reduced
to an extremity of misery and want, little short of
actual starvation—the emaciated forms of many too
plainly testifying to their precarious means of subsistence.

The obtaining of information relative to the country and inhabitants had uniformly been attended
with much difficulty; but our guides, who had
evidently received instructions from the king to
entice us as far as possible from the scene of con-
tention with the emigrant boors, in the hope of
eventually inducing us to return by Kapain, instead
of by the Likwa, being now apprized of our intention
of discontinuing our journey northward, brought
seven savages who volunteered information regarding
the *great inland lake,* and even proposed, for a
suitable remuneration in beads, to accompany us
thither as guides.   They stated that this vast fresh-
water sea, towards the discovery of which geographical attention has long been directed, and the existence of which was first fully established by Dr.
Smith's expedition, might easily be reached from
our present position in *two moons,* through the
country of the Bukaws; a small intervening desert
tract being passable at this season, the recent
heavy rains having filled the pools upon which the
supply of water depends.   Nothing could be more
tantalizing than this proposal, made at a time when

* King Hartebeest!

our oxen were in superb condition, our supplies abundant, and our followers in better heart than usual; but knowing from experience how little reliance can be placed upon a savage's estimate of distance, we were not without reasonable apprehensions of being detained beyond the Bukaws until after next rains, and thus exceeding our leave. All circumstances but this, conspiring to favour both the successful continuance of our journey, and the discovery of the " great water,"—it was with feelings of no ordinary regret and disappointment, that we felt ourselves thus compelled to return, at the very moment when a prize of such value appeared actually within our grasp.

Although not more than fifty miles to the south of the tropic of Capricorn, we did not find the heat by any means oppressive; a circumstance which was of course in a great measure to be attributed to the prevalence of rain. After the thunder-storm which usually ushered in the night, the mornings had been always remarkably cool; and even during the middle of the day the range of the thermometer in the waggons had rarely exceeded 85°. Before turning to the southward, we crossed the Limpopo, and made an excursion of forty miles to the northeastward, on horseback, with a design of determining the course assumed by this interesting feature in the geography of Southern Africa. So far as it was possible to comprehend the descriptions given by savages, which are not the clearest in the world, this river, after being joined by another, called the

Clabatz, or Balapatse, which rises in the Mural
mountains, turns suddenly through that chain, and
flows into the unexplored country of the Babariri,
towards Delagoa, distant probably about three
hundred and fifty miles. This account is in a great
measure confirmed by information given me by
David Hume, an exceedingly clear-headed, observing traveller, who has made several enterprising
journeys into the interior, in quest of the gold-mines
said to exist in the country of the Bakalaka. By
whomsoever it may eventually be traced, therefore,
the Limpopo will in all probability be found identical
with the *Manice*, the river which was surveyed by
Captain Owen, from its embouchure in Delagoa
Bay, as far as latitude 25° 21' south, and longitude
32° 52' east.

For the satisfaction of those of my readers who
take an interest in the geography of the African
quarter of the globe, it may be proper here to state,
that with a view of ascertaining our position on the
map, I adopted the very simple, but excellent
method pursued by Burchell, during his travels.
The exact distance passed over each day was calculated by a table, computed from the circumference
of the larger waggon-wheel, multiplied by the
number of revolutions performed per minute; the
time that the vehicle was actually in motion being
carefully noted by an inside passenger, as well as
the course by compass. This plan, with occasional
correction from the now broken pocket sextant, used
on a sheet of pasteboard by way of false horizon, had

determined our position in so level a country with sufficient accuracy. Rude as it may appear, few inland portions of this vast continent have been surveyed by a more scientific process; and during the early part of our journey, especially while travelling between known points, I had frequent opportunities of satisfying myself of its practical correctness.

Judging, therefore, from a minute daily register kept throughout our journey, we must now have been about the tropic, our distance to the north of the known latitude of Mosega being upwards of one hundred and fifty miles. We retraced our steps on the 1st December, the previous night having been passed at a kraal of starving Baquaina, for whom we had killed a rhinoceros. Fearful indeed was the uproar that attended the division of the carcass —a large party of ladies, possessing remarkably slender wardrobes, rushing forth like witches, and leaving nothing in the course of a few hours but a pool of blood.

Thus far we had been treated by the guides with tolerable civility. No sooner, however, had we turned to the southward than they began to evince the greatest impatience at their detention, complaining loudly of their limited rations of snuff and bread, and insolently urging our return to the Cashan mountains with all expedition, upon the plea that the king would be displeased at our making so long a stay; his Majesty having, they said, instructed them that we were only to hunt during one moon.

Knowing this to be false, we continued hunting giraffes, and paid little attention to their remonstrances; but on arriving opposite the scene of the Griqua defeat, we were joined, on the 6th, by four Matabili warriors from Kapain, who stated that they had been following our waggon tracks, by command of the king, for ten days past, in order peremptorily to direct our return to the Cashan mountains, where we should be met by our friend Um'Nombate, who had a further message to communicate. This mysterious intimation had the effect of conjuring back the dormant apprehensions of the Hottentots: Andries, as usual, gloomily persisting that the king had never intended to let us go through by the Vaal River, and was now about to recal the permission we had extorted. Although we stoutly combated these dismal forebodings, there really appeared to be some grounds for entertaining them—it being impossible to imagine why else the minister should have been sent. The result of our deliberations, however, was, that nothing short of main force should induce us to relinquish the permission we had purchased; and that having successfully struggled thus far with difficulties and annoyances, we would now

—————————"Not bate a jot
Of heart or hope, but still bear up and steer
Right onwards."

With this determination we hurried our advance towards a large Matabili kraal, which, situated to the north of the Cashan range, among a group of

M 5

pyramidical hills, had been selected as the point of
rendezvous with the ambassador.   On arriving
there, however, crowds of both sexes issuing forth,
we were informed that he was still a day's journey
in advance; and were thus provokingly hurried
from place to place, until late on the evening of the
8th, when we reached a small collection of deserted
wigwams, on the Sant river, immediately under the
mountains.   But even here we were destined to
experience further disappointment and suspense—
the catiff guides declaring that the object of our
search, who was still not forthcoming, must have
been *asleep* in one of the kraals that we had passed
in the morning! Suspecting the story of his advent
to be a hoax, invented merely to annoy us, we
now distinctly intimated to the messengers, that if
the minister did not make his appearance in the
course of the following forenoon, we should not wait
for him; and with this understanding they left the
waggons, accompanied by the guides, faithfully
promising to return with the great man in the
morning.

CHAPTER XXIX.

INTERVIEW WITH UM'NOMBATE, AND JOURNEY THROUGH THE CASHAN MOUNTAINS TO THE SOUTH-EASTWARD.

CONTRARY to our expectations, Um'Nombate was actually descried at an early hour the next morning approaching our waggons with a large retinue and three wretched oxen. The important preliminary of snuff-taking having been duly concluded, the crafty old courtier, without making the slightest allusion to the object of his visit, delivered abundant compliments on the part of his Majesty, regarding whose august health we made befitting inquiries. The table having, in the mean time, been spread with dainty viands, amongst the most inviting of which I may be permitted to notice a pile of rhinoceros' steaks, we proceeded to breakfast, and were not a little diverted by the grand vizier's uncouth attempts at the use of the knife and fork. Copying the polished example set by Mrs. John Smith, of Somerset, he presently cut the corner of his mouth, repeatedly placing his sight in imminent jeopardy by bringing his hand to the bleeding orifice instead of the point of the fork, which, loaded with meat, appeared above his head. His son, a fine young savage, to whom we were formally introduced, sat

upon a tar-barrel at the head of the table, but wisely
preferred making use of his nails and assagai; whilst
the retinue, squatting themselves behind the old
man's chair, quarrelled like dogs for the scraps
which he was pleased from time to time to throw to
them. The mass of meat disappearing like magic
before their reiterated attacks, in the course of a
few minutes the board was swept of its smoking load,
and tea having been baled out of a large kettle to
the whole party, the repast was concluded by the
greedy consumption of half a pound of snuff.

After a long and mysterious conference with the
guides, which was conducted at a distance, in an
under tone of voice and with great earnestness,
Um'Nombate proceeded with an air of cold reserve
to open the business of his embassy by presenting
to each of us first, and then to Andries, a leopard's
skin, a bag of Kafir corn, and a scrubby ox. The
animal sent expressly for Andries, besides being
hornless, was wall-eyed on the dexter side—a peculiarity which elicited many personal jokes at the
expense of our trusty follower, whom his Majesty,
when in merry mood, was in the habit of addressing
by the familiar soubriquet of *Mutlee,* or cock-eye.
The pleasantry of the conceit being fully appre-
ciated, that designation was immediately bestowed
upon the ox; and we learned shortly afterwards
that Andries had engaged to return from the colony
and enter the despot's service, upon condition of being
rewarded by the hand of Truëy, the Griqua captive.

After a few unimportant remarks relative to the

country we had visited, the game, and the liberal
supply of rain which it had been the king's gracious
pleasure to send us, the ambassador proceeded,
without further preamble, to disclose his important
errand, by acquainting us with his Majesty's sudden
determination to become the proprietor of a fowling-
piece upon the detonating principle; at the same
time declaring his own readiness immediately to
receive charge of the weapon, together with any
other trifling presents that we might be desirous
of sending. We evaded compliance with the first
part of this very modest demand by promising,
when the elephant-hunting should be concluded, to
send a gun by our escort party on its return *from
the Vaal River;* at the same time meeting the
spirit of the request by producing another coil of
the identical brass-wire which had proved so attractive at Kapain—several articles of crockery ware
—a gross of gilt regimental buttons, and a brown
jug, with raised representations of Toby Philpot in
five different stages of intoxication—from which
most appropriate vessel we begged that his Majesty
would be pleased to quaff his beer in future.

The mention of the Vaal River passing off without
any remark, our anxiety on that score was relieved;
and the jug having been duly admired, we proceeded
to complain of the mutinous behaviour of the guides,
who we requested might be exchanged for others.
Mohanycom being the channel through which this
communication must pass, had an opportunity of
distorting it as he pleased, and delivered a smooth

honied speech in reply, the substance of which was, that no further difficulties would be made.   A warrior, answering to the name of *Maphook*, was then directed by the ambassador to reinforce our escort: and having duly enlisted himself under our banner, they all received injunctions to accompany us, by any route we fancied, to the Vaal River, but on no account to return thence without the percussion gun.

Having requested Um'Nombate to express to his royal master the gratification that we had derived from our visit to his extensive preserves, I proceeded to the exhibition of the drawings I had made of the different game animals, which was attended with the usual theatric effect.   The production of "the noble elephant" caused an involuntary elevation of the eyelids, although no remark was made.   On seeing the giraffe, every one exclaimed "*'Intootla!* *'Intootla!* *'Intootla!*" at the same time standing on tiptoe, and stretching his neck to the utmost extent.   *Tao*, or the lion, caused a general flourish of weapons and beating of shields; and *'Imfooboo*, the hippopotamus, whilst it nearly threw the old man into fits, elicited the observation that I " undoubtedly took *very strong medicine!*"   After some other equally sapient remarks, the peer arose, and reminding us of his sovereign's caution to return by Kuruman if we visited him again, which he trusted we would, took leave of us in the usual manner, and set out on his return, carrying the brown jug in his own hand.

We forthwith continued our journey to the southeastward with renewed spirits, passing through the

mountains by the opening described in a former
chapter, and arriving, with some hair-breadth
escapes, at one of our former stations, on the south
side of the range.   The next day, our route lying
across a belt of hillocks, with many steep acclivities,
over which the unweildy waggons toiled with infinite difficulty, our progress was repeatedly delayed
by the breaking of one of the tow-ropes; the half-
starved dogs of the savages, which not unfrequently
devoured the *veldtscoen*, or untanned leather shoes
of our followers, having, at our last station, gnawed
through some of the strands.   A large herd of wild
buffaloes being observed at a little distance, my
companion and myself mounted our horses, and
soon despatched a splendid bull.   Whilst several
of the followers were employed in flaying the
animal, we returned to the waggons, and sent
Andries with a pack-horse for the hide, of which a
new *trek-touw* was to be manufactured.   He presently returned at speed, to acquaint us that Piet
had been badly wounded in the leg by the accidental
discharge of a gun; and 'Lingap, who accompanied
him, after pointing with breathless dismay to a hole
perforated by the same bullet through his own
shield, proceeded to a minute practical illustration
of the affair, by placing Andries' clumsy piece
against a tree in such a way, that it also fell down,
and was discharged, but, fortunately, without doing
further mischief.   The unhappy Piet was brought
in shortly afterwards, when our nervous anxiety
respecting him was not a little relieved by an in-

spection of the limb, which, although dreadfully burnt and lacerated, was providentially unbroken. Our skill in surgery being exercised with good effect, the wound healed rapidly; and I, feeling obliged to the patient for the little assistance he had occasionally afforded me in the field, again resigned my cot to him during the day; a piece of kindness which, like the rest of his unthankful tribe, he mistook for weakness, repaying me in the end by the grossest ingratitude.

Every feature of this part of the country was beautiful beyond description. Grassy meads, spangled with brilliant flowers, extended between rich masses of grove and forest. Stately trees were festooned with clambering vines, or scented creepers. Here the gorgeous aloe reared its coral tufts above the olive brake—and there the meadows were flushed with the crimson or lilac hues of the poppy and amaryllis. Amongst a variety of animals, a herd of elephants was visible from the waggons; and, the next day, from the top of a commanding eminence, we again saw the face of the highly picturesque landscape covered with these stately beasts, browsing in indolent security, and bathing in the pellucid stream. Upon being attacked, one hundred at least,

"Trampling their path through wood and brake,
   And canes which, crackling, fell before their way,"

rushed franticly down a ravine, with upraised ears, and tossing trunks, screaming wildly, and levelling every thing before them. A shot, fired from the bank, while it sealed the fate of the leader, turned the rest back again, and this persecution was repeated until they became fairly stupified. On one occasion they attempted to retrieve the day by a headlong charge from several quarters at the same moment, and we were often so surrounded by small detachments, that it appeared doubtful which party would be obliged to quit the field. The sound of our voices, however, uniformly turned the scale, and declared man the victor. Among several hundred females and calves, we could find but one bull ; and, as we were tracking him on horseback through a heavy forest, by his life-blood welling from fifty wounds, a savage rhinoceros dashed out of a bush into the very middle of our party, overthrowing several, but injuring none. Andries, though he was ever thrusting upon us his code of sage laws regarding elephant hunting, was always the first to infringe it ; and wantonly firing at a peaceably disposed rhinoceros, while we were upon the hot trail of elephants in the early part of the day, his horse got away, and he was knocked over; the damage sustained by the hinder part of his leathern trowsers, which were rent by the animal's horn, proving how nearly we had been bereft, for ever, of his valuable services.

Both our vehicles were now so crammed with *spolia*, that, being unable to find room for any more ivory, we were reluctantly compelled to leave the ground strewed with that valuable commodity. Great difficulty was experienced in getting our heavily laden waggons clear of the formidable belt of wooded hillocks which, intersected by deep ravines, form the *suburbs* of the Cashan range. In some places, the paths worn by the huge tenants of this almost trackless region being too narrow, it was found necessary to send a party of pioneers to widen them—thus literally cutting our way through the country, and making the aged, and hitherto silent, forest ring to the unwonted sound of the axe.

Scarcely a day passed without our seeing two or three lions, but, like the rest of the animal creation, they uniformly retreated when disturbed by the approach of man.   However troublesome we found the intrusions of the feline race during the night, they seldom, at any other time, showed the least disposition to molest us, unless we commenced hostilities ; and this, owing to the badness of the horses, we rarely felt disposed to do.   Returning one afternoon with Maphook to a koodoo that I had shot, in order to take up the head, which I had concealed in a bush, I was surprised to find an enormous lion * feasting upon the carcass; an odious assemblage of eager vultures, as usual, garrisoning the trees, and waiting their turn when the gorged monarch should make way for them.   Immediately upon my appearance, he walked heavily off, expressing, by a stifled growl, his displeasure at being thus unceremoniously disturbed at dinner.   It was not destined, however, that our acquaintance should cease here; for passing the scene of this introductory

* *Felis Leo.*   Delineated in the African Views.

BECHUANA HUNTING A LION.

interview the following morning, Richardson and
myself were suddenly made aware of the monster's
presence by perceiving a pair of gooseberry eyes
glaring upon us from beneath a shady bush; and
instantly upon reining up our horses, the grim
savage bolted out with a roar, like thunder, and
bounded across the plain with the agility of a greyhound. The luxuriant beauty of his shaggy black
mane, which almost swept the ground, tempted us,
contrary to established rule, to give him battle, with
the design of obtaining possession of his spoils; and
he no sooner felt himself hotly pursued than he
faced about, and stood at bay in a mimosa grove,
measuring the strength of his assailants with a port
the most noble and imposing. Disliking our appearance, however, and not relishing the smell of
gunpowder, he soon abandoned the grove, and took
up his position on the summit of an adjacent stony
hill, the base of which being thickly clothed with
thorn trees, we could only obtain a view of him from
the distance of three hundred yards. Crouched on
this fortified pinnacle, like the sculptured figure at
the entrance of a nobleman's park, the enemy dis-
dainfully surveyed us for several minutes, daring us
to approach with an air of conscious power and pride,
which well beseemed his grizzled form. As the rifle
balls struck the ground nearer and nearer at each
discharge, his wrath, as indicated by his glistening
eyes, increased roar, and impatient switching of the
tail, was clearly getting the mastery over his prudence. Presently a shot broke his leg. Down he

came upon the other three with reckless impetuosity, his tail straight out and whirling on its axis, his mane bristling on end, and his eye-balls flashing rage and vengeance.   Unable, however, to overtake our horses, he shortly retreated under a heavy fire, limping and discomfited to his strong hold.   Again we bombarded him, and, again exasperated, he rushed into the plain with headlong fury—the blood now streaming from his open jaws, and dyeing his mane with crimson.   It was a gallant charge, but it was to be his last.   A well-directed shot arresting him in full career, he pitched with violence upon his skull, and throwing a complete somerset, sub-sided amid a cloud of dust.

CHAPTER XXX.

DISCOVERY OF A NEW ANTELOPE, AND FINAL
DEPARTURE FROM THE CASHAN MOUNTAINS,
TOWARDS THE RIVER VAAL.

THE list of large animals killed during the campaign, now exceeded four hundred head of various sorts and sizes. Of these the minimum height at the shoulder had been three feet, and not a few had measured ten and twelve. Within the last few days, I had obtained several superb specimens, especially of the koodoo and bastard gemsbok; and excepting some of the smaller antelopes, which only occur in parts of the country that we were subsequently to visit, my collection of horns and *exuviæ* had by this time extended itself to every known species of game quadruped in Southern Africa. But a still prouder trophy than all was yet in abeyance, and before leaving this hunters' Elysium, my researches were to be crowned by a truly splendid addition to the catalogue of Mammalia.

My double-barrelled rifle having again suffered in a fall with my horse, I took the field on the 13th December with a heavy weapon constructed upon the primitive principle of flint and steel, which, as a *pis-aller*, I had obtained from Mr. Moffat. Our

party were in full pursuit of a wounded elephant,
when a herd of unusually dark-looking antelopes
attracted observation in an adjacent valley. Re-
conuoitring them through a pocket telescope from
the acclivity on which we stood, I at once exclaimed
that they were perfectly new to science; and having
announced my determination of pursuing them, if
requisite, to the world's end, I dashed down the
slope, followed by the derision of the Hottentots,
for my unsportsman-like attention to an "ugly buck,"
one specimen of which, however, I assured them
I would rather have possessed than all the elephants
in Africa! In an instant I was in the middle of
the herd, which was then crossing the valley—nine
chesnut-coloured does leading, and two magnificent
coal-black bucks—all with scimitar-shaped horns
—bringing up the rear. Hastily dismounting, I
was delighted to observe them stand for a few
seconds within fifty yards, and stare at me with
amazement. In vain was it, however, that I pulled
the trigger of my rifle; three several times the heavy
machinery of the lock descended with alarming
vehemence, but no report followed the concussion;
and the herd having in the mean time ascended a
steep hill, I fairly rode my horse to a stand in the
attempt to overtake them. Cursing my hard fortune, as I dashed the hateful weapon to the ground,
I hastened to the camp, to repair my broken rifle;
armed with which, and mounted on a fresh steed, I
returned with my companion to the spot; where,
having taken up the foot-marks, we followed them,

with unwearied perseverance, among the hills, during the whole of that and the following day, without attaining even a glimpse of the objects of our quest. At noon of the third day, however, peeping cautiously over a bank, our laudable assiduity was rewarded by the gratifying sight of the two bucks grazing by themselves, unconscious of our approach, in a stony valley. Having disposed our forces, after a moment's consultation, so as to intercept the game from a tangled labyrinth of ravines, the attack was made. The hind leg of the handsomer of the two was dangling in an instant, and in another he was sprawling on the earth. Quickly recovering himself, however, he led me more than a mile over the sharp stones ere he was brought to bay, when twice charging gallantly he was at length overthrown and slain.

It were vain to attempt a description of the sensations I experienced, when thus, after three days of toilsome tracking, and feverish anxiety, unalleviated by any incident that could inspire the smallest hope of ultimate success, I at length found myself in actual possession of so brilliant an addition to the riches of natural history. The prize evidently belonged to the Aigocerine group, and was equal in stature to a large galloway. The horns, which were flat, and upwards of three feet in length, swept gracefully over the back in the form of a crescent. A bushy black mane extended from the lively chesnut-coloured ears, to the middle of the back; the tail was long and tufted; and the glossy

jet-black hue of the greater portion of the body
contrasted beautifully with a snow-white face and
belly.* We thought we could never have looked
at, or admired it sufficiently ; my companion observing, after a long pause, "that the sable antelope
would doubtless become the admiration of the
world." A drawing and description having been
completed on the spot, the skin was carefully removed, and conveyed upon a pack-horse in triumph
to the camp; and it may possibly interest those of
my readers, who shall have followed me during the
last three days, to learn, that I succeeded, with
infinite difficulty, in bringing this unique and interesting specimen of African zoology, in a state of

* The following were the dimensions of this singular and
beautiful antelope, which is faithfully depicted in the African
Views.

	Inches.		Inches.
Height at the wither	54	Hock to foot	18¼
Length of body	44	Breadth of fore-arm	6
Ditto neck	17	Ditto thigh	6
Ditto head	19	Ditto fore-leg	2¼
Ditto tail	25	Ditto hind-leg	3
Ditto hind quarter	19	Ditto neck	16
Depth of chest	30	Length of horns	37
Length of fore-arm	16	Asunder at base	1
Fore-knee to foot	15	Ditto tips	9¼
Height of mane	6¼	Length of ears	10
Croup to hock	36		

During the first day, I had opportunities of distinctly remarking that the females were all furnished with crescent-shaped horns;
and although of smaller stature than the males, were similarly
marked—a deep chesnut-brown taking the place of jet black.
The species was evidently not recognized by the natives, although,
to conceal their ignorance, they pronounced it to be *kookaam*,
which signifies the oryx, an animal of such extremely rare occurrence in Moselekatse's country, that they had in all probability
never seen it.

high preservation to Cape Town ; where, in October last, it was elegantly set up by Monsieur Verreaux, the French naturalist, and obligingly taken to England by my well-known friend Captain Alexander, 42nd Royal Highlanders.

Notwithstanding the arrangements made by Um-'Nombate, our escort was daily becoming more unruly and impatient ; and upon our attempting to move some miles further to the eastward, in order, if possible, to obtain a female specimen of the new species, they positively refused to accompany us in any direction but that of the Vaal River. The most tempting bribes failed to shake their resolution ; and upon our threatening to send an express to the king, for which duty Andries eagerly volunteered, they sat sullenly grinding tobacco with the most calm and provoking indifference. The murrain having attacked our oxen, and the horses, moreover, being so galled and reduced in condition that many were unfit for further work, it was resolved, that since the objects of our expedition had been thus far fully accomplished, we should at once set out on our return to the Colony by the unexplored route.

Right joyfully was this announcement received by our followers. Ever discontented with their present lot, the Hottentots had long impatiently sighed for the drunken brawls of the canteen, and the bewitching smiles of their absent sweethearts. Cœur de Lion could instantly perceive in dim perspective the auspicious termination of *his* perils by sea and land ; nor was the worshipper of the cow,

N

in his turn, less pleased at the increased prospect
of escape from a land so little suited to the prejudices of his *caste*.   The bovine appearance of most
of the African animals having precluded this faith-
ful follower from partaking of their flesh, he had
suffered greater privations than any one, and had
not unfrequently been compelled to observe a fast.
Without a moment's loss of time, Kobus repaired
his dilapidated violin, which in a fit of passion he
had broken over a comrade's head; and a wild-
peppermint tea-party, with dancing to its discordant
notes round our gipsy fire, celebrated the approaching termination of the campaign.

At noon on the 16th of December, then, bidding
a final adieu to the enchanting forests of Cashan,
we turned our faces to the southward, and having
crossed a small range of hills, which were all that
divided us from the vast plains of the Vaal River,
entered at once upon a new region, totally different
in character from all that we had hitherto traversed.
Such had been the recent abundance of water, that
our people had for some time past allowed the
wholesome practice of filling the water-flagons to
fall into desuetude; and we had in consequence the
felicity of passing the night without any of that
necessary, although we travelled until dark in the
hope of finding it.   A ponderous bull eland, with
only one horn, being observed in the neighbourhood, Richardson and myself drove him up to the
caravan, where his blood was eagerly quaffed both
by the savages and Hottentots.

In the total absence of materials for the construction of a pound, the cattle became so restless during the night, that we were glad to resume our journey two hours before dawn.   Numerous hartebeests and quaggas were disturbed by our advance; and the white-tailed gnoo, which now occurred for the first time since passing Kuruman, startled at the approach of our waggons, was again bellowing, stamping, and tossing its eccentric head.   As the day broke, boundless meads kept extending to the eye, covered with luxuriant herbage, and enamelled with rich parterres of brilliant flowers.   These were animated by droves of portly elands, moving in long procession across the silent and treeless landscape.   The rank odour of these animals, resembling the exhalation from a cattle close, could be winded from a great distance; and it is a singular fact that their bodies are infested by the ticks and parasitic flies commonly found in such places.

Pursuing a herd of many hundred elands, which literally resembled a vast drove of stall-fed oxen, we were joined in the chase by the prettily-striped foal of a quagga, which neighed and frisked by the side of our horses for a considerable time, before it discovered its mistake.   The lighter-bodied cows skipped nimbly over each other's heads, while their unweildy lords laboured in the rear, their sleek sides shaking with fat, and frothing with perspiration.   Two minutes were sufficient to reduce them all to a walk, and although some turned in desperation upon their pursuers, these enormous creatures are so

N 2

easily disposed of that the whole herd might have
been slaughtered.   Their flesh being so greatly
superior to that of any other animal, was always
eagerly sought after ; and on this occasion, we killed
a sufficient number to afford a stock of tongues and
briskets for salting, in case the country in advance,
of which every one was equally ignorant, should
not afford a supply of game.   Leaving the carcases
a banquet for the vultures, we placed these delicacies on our meagre steeds, and rejoined the *cafila* in
the afternoon.   Weary and exhausted for want of
water, we were not a little rejoiced on our arrival to
find it drawn up on the banks of the beautiful
Chonapas, a deep gurgling stream tenanted by
hippopotami, and meandering amid clusters of
sighing reeds.   Some of our people were busily engaged in the manufacture of a buffalo hide drag-rope
for the approaching journey, and others had gone
in search of fire-wood.   Not a dry twig was to be
obtained, however, in the whole country, and it was
found necessary to break up one of our boxes in order
to boil the water and dress some fish that had been
taken.   The savages had always evinced the strongest
antipathy to the finny tribe, flying in dismay if one
were suddenly exhibited ; and Andries here attempting some ill-timed practical joke of the kind upon
Maphook, the savage sprang tiger-like upon his back,
and throwing him to the ground, handled him so
roughly, that our crest-fallen hero, whose short thick
figure and bull neck betokened incalculable strength,
was nevertheless fain to sue for quarter,

From our present position, the Vaal River was stated by the guides to be only two days' journey to the southward, the range of mountains in which it rises being indistinctly visible to the south-east. Having conducted us thus far on our journey, they now declared their intention of returning immediately to the king, for whom they had the impudence to demand the gun, as well as the promised wages of their own services; adding, in reply to our remonstrances, that as we were now standing on the ground where the emigrants had been routed, they found it impossible to proceed farther, or to overcome the dread they entertained of their enemies the Dutchmen.   An intimate acquaintance with the lying propensities of the savages, combined with other circumstances, satisfied us that the unusual appearance of sheep-droppings, to which they referred in support of their assertions, had been occasioned during Kalipi's return with the booty.   Feeling confident, therefore, that they had no cause for alarm, and having every reason to be apprehensive for our own safety, should they desert us under existing circumstances, we steadily refused to comply with their demand.   Upon this they assumed a tone of ultra insolence, and in the end menaced us with an attack from a neighbouring Matabili outpost, if we longer withheld the presents.

Without any just grounds for doubting the good faith of the king, we had been a little suspicious of the real object of Um'Nombate's visit, and after this threat, felt doubtful to what extent the guides

might be acting under the royal instructions, with
a design of deterring us from proceeding.   Personal considerations would have justified, if they
did not demand, our putting the caitiffs to death
upon the spot; but after some deliberation, it was
resolved, after adopting precautionary measures
against a night surprise, that we should see whether
the morrow's dawn might not find them in a more
accommodating humour.   Ammunition was accordingly served out, and a place allotted to every one
in case of an attack—the horses being secured to
the front of our own waggon, lest the weak nerves
of the Hottentots should induce them to jump upon
their backs on the first appearance of danger.   As
a last arrangement before going to bed, Ethaldur—
whose nights, if passed at a distance from the
"licensed retailer of wine and brandy," were usually
restless—was selected to perform the important
part of *Cerberus*, in which duty he was voluntarily
assisted by Cœur de Lion, who declared his utter
inability to close his eyes.   "Did I not tell you,"
croaked the former of these bold spirits to his
companion, as, pipe in mouth, he proceeded to
mount guard—" Did I not tell you that we should
all have our throats cut, so sure as we came out by
the Vaal Rivière!"

CHAPTER XXXI.

DESERTION OF OUR ESCORT, AND ARRIVAL AT THE RIVER VAAL.

AWAKING as the bright morning star shot above the eastern horizon, I perceived four elands standing within a few yards of the camp, undetected by the vigilance of the sentinels, whose eyes nevertheless were wide open.   Directions for yoking the oxen were no sooner given, than the guides commenced packing their goods and chattels, and otherwise preparing for their return to the king.   Seeing the impossibility of inducing them to accompany us farther on our journey, and apprehensive of their resentment if the rewards were withheld, we made a merit of necessity, and attempted to restore them to good humour, by presenting each in his turn with a red woollen night-cap, and a complete suit of European clothing, together with some beads which had been expressly reserved for their use.   The only remaining coil of brass wire was likewise handed over, with a box of lucifers and a few mould candles, as a farewell offering to his Majesty, to whom we desired a complimentary message, expressive of our regret at having been deprived of the means of sending him the gun from the Vaal River.   Hereupon, spurning the proferred treasures

from them, the savages indignantly demanded if
such rubbish could be considered a suitable recom-
pense for their long and meritorious services, feigning
at the same time as if about to retire.   After some
consultation, however, they carefully scraped together the scattered beads; and hanging each a hoop
of wire about his neck, and placing their shields and
bundles on their heads, departed angrily, Mohanycom declaring, with a mysterious air, as he opened
his shark-like jaws in our presence for the last time,
that "when the mightiest of monarchs should behold such trash, his royal heart would be *very sore !*"

Without either guide, escort, or interpreter—in
the midst of an unknown wilderness, bordering on
the recent scene of bloody strife, and still scoured
by the contending parties—our little band was now
left in a highly unenviable position.   After providing us, as he supposed, with a guard to the
verge of his dominions, his Majesty had not, in all
probability, deemed it necessary to acquaint the
different frontier outposts of our approaching exit ;
and deprived as we now were of the means of holding
communication with his warriors, should we fall in
with them, the least evil that could be anticipated
in the present excited state of their feelings, would
be a journey back to Kapain.   Adding to the above
prospect, the probability of annoyance or misre-
presentation on the part of the recreant escort, we
plainly perceived that the sooner we were out of
Moselekatse's country, the better it was likely to
fare with ourselves.

The Matabili were fast receding in single file towards the northern horizon, when we commenced our retreat to the southward; and crossing the river by a natural causeway which formed a small bubbling cascade, shaped our course along the bank. A verdant meadow, on which numerous elands were grazing in herds like tame cattle, stretched away before us, and was traversed, throughout its length, by the silver stream of the tortuous Chonapas, winding in rainbow brightness between fringes of waving bulrushes. The direction it assumed convincing us that it must be a tributary of the river to which we were journeying, we determined, by hugging the bank, to avoid the chance of passing the night without water; and to guard as far as possible against other misfortunes, a new order of march was ordained—the oxen, horses, and sheep, being driven close to the waggons, *en masse*, and not suffered to straggle as of yore.

We had proceeded some ten miles in this fashion, when two human figures were descried at a distance, accompanied by several dogs. Immediately on perceiving us, they concealed themselves beneath a bush; and on our approach, fled in the greatest consternation, sitting gloomily down as " men without hope" when our horses were actually at their heels. Expecting nothing at our hands but instant death, these miserable savages were not a little surprised at receiving a liberal supply of tobacco, and an invitation to the waggons, where they feasted so heartily, that although anxious to

N 5

accompany our party, they were utterly unable to
keep pace. Before losing sight of them we discovered that they were members of the Barapootsa
tribe, acknowledging an independent king named
Bapootsa, and occupying the hills at the head of
the Likwa; which river, they assured us, we could
not possibly reach before the next night. In accordance with African caprice, which assigns a
parasol to the male instead of to the female sex,
these sons of the desert were each provided with a
long staff decorated with the black body feathers
of the ostrich. Besides affording protection from
the sun's rays, these implements not unfrequently
prove serviceable in the chase; and being stuck
into the ground at the proper moment, divert the
attention of a charging lion from the object of his
vengeance, and thus enable the rest of the party
to rush in and dispatch him with their assagais.

By sunset, having abandoned two of the sick
oxen, and accomplished twenty-five miles, our farther
advance was prevented by the pack-waggon sticking
fast in a morass. It was at length extricated at the
expense of a *trek-touw*, to repair which a tax was
levied on the hides of two elands that were grazing
in the neighbourhood, and we then drew up in a
strong position, before an old stone enclosure, which
served as a cattle pound, the rear being fortified by
an isolated tumulus. Andries having confidently
predicted some unpleasant occurrence, Cœur de
Lion perched himself upon the summit of this eminence, and maintained another weary vigil through-

out the night, the early half of which was illumined by a brilliant moon.

We commenced another forced march before daylight on the 19th, still taking the course of the Chonapas for our guide. Several long strings of wild buffaloes passed ahead of us on their way up from the river, and a lion, with tail erect, was observed in full career after a troop of scouring gnoos. The capricious distribution of animal forms is no where more remarkable than in Africa, and to solve the mysterious causes by which it is influenced, has long been reckoned among the most puzzling problems in the great scheme of the creation. As if by magic, the brindled gnoo had suddenly given place during the last three days, to the common, or white-tailed species, and not another specimen occurred during the remainder of our journey. Whilst hunting the *wilde beest*,* as the latter species is termed by the Cape Colonists, the abstraction already recorded of my shoes by his Amazooloo Majesty, had nearly been the cause of a serious disaster. In order to avoid the disagreeable alternative of walking barefooted, I had been compelled to adopt a pair rudely manufactured of untanned hide; and the sole becoming entangled in the stirrup, while, with both hands encumbered, I was in the act of jumping off to administer the *coup de grace*, I fell on my back; and the wounded animal bellowing and struggling at the same instant, my horse started off, and before I could extricate myself, had kicked me

* *Anglice*, Wild Ox.

severely on the knee and ankle, besides dragging
me a sufficient distance over the loose stones, to
remove the whole of my clothes, and a large portion
of the skin from my back.

Merciless and repeated applications of the whip-
cord and double thong, enabled us, with the loss of
another ox, to achieve twenty-five miles more by
four o'clock in the afternoon.   The blue mountain
range, now on our left, had gradually assumed a
deeper and deeper tint, and as we advanced over
the broad bosom of the trackless plain, like a ship
through the ocean, was fast developing its rugged
character.   At length, lifting up our eyes, we beheld
before us afar off, a long dark streak of bushes,
stretching parallel to the horizon, and marking the
course of the stream of which we were in search.
Shouts of exultation burst from the mouths of the
Hottentots, as they sprang from the waggon boxes
from which they had been gazing, and cracking
their long whips with increased energy.   The patient
oxen broke into a trot—the object upon which all
eyes were riveted became better and better defined,
our friendly pilot stream rapidly increased in breadth,
and as the sun disappeared below the horizon, we
were standing on the banks of the river Vaal.

This remote arm of the Gareep, or Great Orange
River, forms the southern limit of the territory to
which Moselekatse lays claim.   Rising nearly opposite to Delagoa Bay, about three degrees to the
westward of that port, and joining the parent stream
some two hundred and fifty geographical miles

below the confluence of the Chonapas, it traverses the South African continent from east to west,; like a great artery, and discharges its waters into the Atlantic ocean. At the spot where we reached it, the breadth did not exceed one hundred and fifty yards, but the fresh deposition of rubbish on the bank, showed that the water had very lately risen at least ten feet above its present level—and from the strength and muddiness of the current, we were not a little apprehensive it might be again flooded during the night, and obstruct our progress for many days. The absence, nevertheless, of anything approaching to a practicable ford, obliged us to take our chance.

The river was literally teeming with hippopotami, about forty of those amphibious monsters protruding their laughable countenances at the same time, and grampus-like, blowing a spout of muddy water as if in honour of our arrival. Although two lions had been seen the moment before, the Hottentots, to a man, without unyoking the oxen, left the waggons standing on the brink of the high bank, and rushed like school-boys to the water's edge. A gigantic hippopotamus was making directly for the shore by a succession of plunges, his broad snout appearing nearer and nearer every time he rose, puffing to the surface, sending a thousand bubbling circlets eddying round it. I was in the act of firing in at his garret window, when I perceived the tail of a couchant lioness knocking angrily within a few yards of my foot. So completely was her attention engrossed by the waggons, that although close behind her, she did not perceive either Piet or myself, and was retiring, when one of the followers foolishly firing at her, she galloped back through the middle of our party, and being joined by a lion, disappeared among the bushes.

The savage loneliness of this wild spot might well have constituted it the metropolis of *Feræ*; but in spite of all the warnings we had received, it was with the greatest difficulty, and not before we had set the example in person, that the perverse Hottentots could be induced to suspend hostilities against the *Zeekoes*, and construct a thorn fence for the security of the cattle. Scarcely was it completed before there set in a drenching and dismal night, which has left behind it, on my mind, an indelible impression. If the panorama that presented itself on our first arrival, had agreeably recalled to recollection the inconsistent medleys of a dream, the gloomy terrors of the night that now succeeded, might fitly be likened to an incubus. " Darkness that could be felt," and torrents of rain, accompanied by vivid flashes of lightning, and peals of deafening thunder, were rendered trebly terrible by the howling of the wind, the incessant snorting of hippopotami in the river, and the prowling of lions around our slender fortification. About midnight the affrighted oxen contrived to effect their escape, and after fruitless attempts to recover them, we were left in no very enviable plight, to muse, while we counted the tedious hours until morning, upon the improbability of our ever finding them again.

CHAPTER XXXII.

EXIT FROM MOSELEKATSE'S DOMINIONS, AND PASSAGE ACROSS THE NAMA-HARI.

THE 20th of December, though it placed us
beyond the Matabili territories, was a day of excessive toil, and but little progress.   As soon as it was
light enough to see, Andries started on horseback in
quest of a ford ; and all but one of the oxen having
by the most unlooked-for good fortune, been recovered, we shortly afterwards moved down the
river, the waters of which had risen upwards of a
foot during the night.   After crossing many perilous
ravines, we at length became alarmed at the protracted non-appearance of our scout, and had just
resolved to send back in search of him when he rejoined us, triumphantly bearing the teeth of a seacow—whilst extracting which for his own private
advantage, he had unfortunately suffered his masters
to overshoot, by several miles, what he termed an
admirable ford.   Retracing our steps to this spot,
we found the current waist deep, the bank acclivitous,
and the bed strewed with large blocks of granite ;
but having first taken the precaution of sending a
horseman repeatedly across, we determined to attempt the passage.   After much violent bumping,
the leading waggon reached the opposite side with-

out any difficulty, but not so its consort. Owing to
some mismanagement on the part of the driver, the
luckless "omnibus," when about half way over,
became firmly wedged between two masses of rock;
and although every one stripped to the skin, and
"applied his shoulders to the wheel," three provoking hours were passed in abortive attempts to
extricate it. Whips, shin-bones, and *trek-touws*,
were alike fruitlessly broken, and fresh oxen repeatedly applied without the smallest advantage;
and the river rising rapidly, we had almost despaired
of saving our property, when cracks and yells,
followed by the simultaneous struggling of twenty-
four of our sturdiest beasts, were answered by the
grating of a wheel. An interval of intense anxiety
succeeded. One after another, the fore and hind
nave on the same side, rose slowly above the
surface of the water, and the fall of the slanting
vehicle appeared inevitable. To our joy, a sudden
jerk restored it, tottering, to the perpendicular—pair
after pair of the long string of oxen obtained their
footing on the bank—once again the whips resounded in the hollow, and the dripping van emerged
in safety from the flood.

Another hour had passed away before our little
flock of sheep could be reclaimed. These stubborn
animals, having in the first instance been forced into
the stream by dint of much pelting and persecution,
had been carried down a considerable distance;
and, as a matter of course, whilst all hands were
engaged in extricating the waggon, had strayed

into the thicket.   At length every thing was ready.
Little dreaming of the distance that still divided
them from their beloved gin-shop, the Hottentots
cheered and fired a salute, as they turned their
backs upon the " yellow river," and upon the execrated dominions of his beer-drinking Majesty.

We had not advanced more than three miles
before our progress was opposed by a furious storm
of hail and thunder.   Many of the stones were half
an inch in diameter, and the oxen being unable to
face them, turned their backs to the pitiless shower,
and stood in the yokes.   With some difficulty we at
last gained the shelter of a neighbouring hill, in an
amphitheatre enclosed by which we passed the night.
To Andries in particular this friendly spot wore an
aspect of charmed interest, it having been described
by 'Lingap, with what truth I know not, as the scene
of Truëy's enslavement.   To me it is remarkable
from the circumstance of my having there, for the
last time, seen and destroyed the rhinoceros.

Thus far on our pilgrimage we had been directed
in some measure by the course of rivers and mountains, but during the remainder of our journey we
were to be guided by the compass alone.   A perfectly unexplored country intervened betwixt us and
the colony, and the distance that we had travelled
south of the known latitude of Mosega, convinced
me that we were still much farther from it than the
maps would indicate.   It was believed by the Hottentots that a southerly course would have led us to
Lishuani, the residence of Peter David, conjectured

to be about one hundred and fifty miles from the present position. In order to reach the missionary station of Phillipolis, therefore, which was supposed to be rather less than double that distance, it was determined to adopt a south-westerly route. Day after day, as I pricked off on the chart the progress that we had made, was I strengthened in the opinion I had formed, and the sequel fully confirmed its correctness.

The first day we travelled over an uninterrupted plain strewed with small land-tortoises, and covered with a profusion of gay flowers, red, yellow, purple, and crimson. Amongst these the gaudy marigold was predominant—growing sometimes singly, and at others spreading out into beds of several acres in extent. A sultry and tedious march of nine hours brought us at length to a bog, with a scanty pool of excessively fetid mineral water, which nothing but the direst necessity could have induced us to taste. The number of animals collected in the vicinity first drew our attention to this treasure, which was surrounded by a clump of bulrushes, with a strong calcareous incrustation at their roots. So exhausted were the oxen, after their three hours' cold bath the preceding day, that they would hardly have reached this oasis, had not the fresh scent of a lion recruited their vigour. However tired the poor beasts might be, a sniff of one of their feline enemies never failed to put them in the highest spirits. Several gnoos rushed with them to the water's edge, as if to dispute their share, and I

shot one from the waggon; but in the total absence
of fuel, we were driven to the necessity of burning
one of the spare waggon-poles, in order to cook a
portion of the flesh.

A heavy dew fell during the night, and was followed by a dense fog, in spite of which we were
fain to decamp from this inhospitable bivouac at
an early hour.   The face of the country here, so
beautifully clothed with herbage and flowers, would
appear to be kept fresh and verdant by these nightly
dews and humid mists, rather than by the partial
showers which, few and far between, are wont to
visit it.   The being able to sleep in the open air
with perfect impunity is a convincing proof that in
Africa these vapours are little prejudicial to health.
As the fog dispersed, long files of quaggas were
observed moving across the distant profile of the
plain, like a rival caravan on its march; a range of
mountains could shortly afterwards be distinguished
to the westward, and about noon the hawk-eyed
Hottentots, who possessed an extraordinary facility
of detecting objects at a distance, descried a troop
of savages.   Of the two parties it is difficult to say
which was thrown into the greatest consternation by
the mutual discovery; but I can only aver, that
while every preparation was making on our side for
a gallant defence, the enemy was observed in igno-
minious retreat.

After we had advanced twenty-five miles, a long
line of karree trees darkening the horizon proclaimed
our approach to some hidden stream; and late in

the afternoon, to our surprise, we struck upon a sudden bend of the Vaal River, which here winds abruptly between willowed banks, round a narrow peninsula, the neck of which is not more than six hundred yards across. The cavalcade was in the act of drawing up near some deserted bushman wigwams, when three lionesses leaped out of a bush immediately on our flank; and Piet, who declared that he could discern the head of a fourth, having cracked his long whip, forth there stalked also a venerable lion, evidently subdued and enfeebled by years. A bullet discharged at him from the waggon-box, having penetrated the patriarch's shoulder, he thrust his hoary head into a bush and was gathered unto his fathers. It was not, however, until Richardson, with a party on horseback, had tested his demise by repeated volleys, that his remains were dragged out for inspection.

My knee was still so painful from the effect of the kick I had received, that I was unable to mount a horse. The task of providing food for the followers had therefore devolved principally upon my fellow *voyageur*. Elands were still abundant, and as a *dernier resort*, we had upwards of twenty sheep left, notwithstanding the ravages committed on our herd by wild beasts. The hardiness evinced by our little flock became daily more the theme of admiration, an instance of foot soreness rarely occurring during the longest march. When it did, the cripple either rode in the omnibus, or was placed at the disposal of the fire-worshipper, at whose hands it had little

mercy to expect. The prevailing scarcity of fuel
in this part of the country, induced us to take in a
good supply before again leaving the river; and in
order to make room for it, and relieve the oxen as
much as possible, nearly all their necks having
become raw by drawing in wet yokes, we threw
out every article that could possibly be dispensed
with, amongst the most bulky of which was a large
supply of *Zeekoe fat*, commissioned by our friends
in the colony.

On the 23rd, having skirted the river about five
miles, we unexpectedly found ourselves at the embouchure of one of its principal tributaries, the Nama
Hari, or Donkin, a river which takes its source one
hundred and fifty miles to the eastward, midway
between Port Natal and Delagoa Bay, in the great
mountain range that divides Caffraria from the
Bechuana country. The point of confluence of these
streams is situated at the very apex of the bend
already described; and the meeting of their troubled
waters, rolling towards each other from opposite
points of the compass, was an imposing and unusual
spectacle. As we were witnessing it from the brink
of the precipitous and well-rounded scarp, which
forms the salient angle, *Behemoth* at intervals thrust
out his broad snout for a moment to gaze at us, or
suddenly emerging, with a snort and splash, from
beneath the belt of Chaldean willows * which graced
the opposite shore, plunged his shapeless bulk into
the flood. About sunset, having advanced ten

* Salix Babylonica.

miles up the right bank of the Nama-Hari without
discovering a ford, we halted at a spot where the
banks might with some labour have been pared
down sufficiently to admit of our waggons crossing;
but our scouts discovering a practicable road two
miles higher up, we were fortunately spared the
trouble.

Two hours' toil the following morning placed us
safely on the southern bank of the Nama-Hari; and
after filling up our water-casks, and endeavouring to
persuade the cattle to drink their fill, which at so
early an hour they refused to do, we resumed a
south-westerly course, and again made sail over the
interminable plain. Our attention was presently
arrested by the fresh *spoor* of several horsemen in
pursuit of elands; and, after a hundred sapient
conjectures had been offered on the subject, some
of the Hottentots, feeling convinced that the hunters would prove to be a band of Bastards from
Lishuani, determined to follow them, and inquire
the news. A few hours afterwards, however, they
returned in dismay, with the intelligence that they
had unexpectedly come upon a spot near the river,
where the ground was spread with human skeletons
as with a table-cloth, under which circumstances
they had thought it prudent to return.

The day was distressingly sultry, and by the time
we had advanced twenty-five miles, three more of our
invalid oxen had been left to perish. Hour after
hour the prospect was still the same. Tantalized
by the dancing mirage, we had scoured the country

in every direction, without being able to discover a drop of water, although the thirsty earth was seamed with dry tanks and gullies. Late in the afternoon, still plodding our weary way over the cheerless expanse, we were vainly listening for the melodious croaking of some friendly frog, which alone was likely to be the index to the element we required, when our eyes were unexpectedly greeted by a waggon-road. The appearance of the deeply ploughed ruts, the first that we had seen since leaving Tolaan, showed that upwards of twenty laden vehicles had passed about twelve months before, during a fall of rain. Trusting that they might lead us to water, we followed them as long as daylight lasted. Then the sky became overcast, and flashes of lightning, at short intervals, showing us something on the verge of the horizon which looked like a thick bush, we persevered towards it. Alas! like the delusive lakes in the morning, it was metamorphosed, on our approach, into a few dwarf shrubs barely a foot in height. Unable to proceed further, we halted in the middle of the bleak and exposed heath, without either fuel or water beyond the scanty supply in the waggons. The sheep were placed in a circle formed by haltering the horses together; and to prevent the oxen from straying, we were compelled to secure them to the waggon-wheels, although the unfortunate beasts had passed twelve hours in the yoke, without tasting a morsel of food.

CHAPTER XXXIII.

THREE DAYS' SOLITARY WANDERING IN THE WILDERNESS.

CHRISTMAS-DAY was pregnant with an event which for some time cast a dismal gloom over the party, and had nearly caused my separation from it during the remainder of the journey. Three hours before that festive morn had dawned upon us, our search for water was renewed—the moon enabling us to trace the waggon road, although at every step it was becoming less and less distinct. Arriving as the day broke, at the summit of a gentle ascent, which here disturbing the monotony of the otherwise uniformly level flat, had obstructed our view to the southward, another vast landscape presented itself to our gaze. Endless meads, clad in a vernal and variegated robe of gay but scentless flowers, in whose presence the desert seemed to smile, spreading away before us, exhibited the motley confusion of a Turkey carpet. One isolated tumulus stood like a pine-apple in the centre, and in the distance, three rectangular table-topped mountains, of singularly uniform appearance, reminded the spectator of terraced barrack-rooms—shooting-boxes perhaps, erected by the giants of olden times. Hair-brained gnoos, careering over the plain, hailed our advance

—now stopping inquisitively to scrutinize the waggons—then lashing their dark sides with their snowy tails, as they hastily retreated. Large troops of bles-bucks,* or white-faced antelopes, a pied species that we had rarely met with before, likewise chequered the scene ; and with herds of spring-bucks, quaggas and ostriches, announced the proximity of water. Presently, to our delight, we descried a " reed encircled fountain," at which, after twenty-eight hours of total abstinence, the dying oxen were enabled to slake their terrible thirst. A strong calcareous deposit adhering to the vegetation, rendered the water extremely bitter to the taste, and it was by the exercise of the long whips alone that the cattle were prevented from plunging into the pool before our casks had been filled.

The accidental, but important discovery of portions of a broken yoke key, here enabled the Hottentots to decide the knotty and long-argued question, whether the outward bound tracks upon which we were proceeding, were those of Dutch, or of Griqua waggons. Opinion being now unanimous in favour of the former, it was determined to follow them as long as they should preserve a south-westerly direction. The total absence of fuel obliged us, after an hour's halt, to continue our march over numerous salt-pans, upon which herds of bles-bucks were busily licking the crystallized efflorescence. Alarmed at our approach, vast troops of them were continually sweeping past against the wind, carrying their

* *Gazella Albifrons.* Delineated in the African Views.

O

broad white noses close to the ground like a pack of
harriers in full cry.   Never having killed any of
these antelopes, and our stock of provisions requiring to be recruited, I mounted *Breslar*, my favourite
Rozinante, and never heeding whither I sped, dashed
into the thick of them.   The pine-apple hill bore
east about five miles, and I fancied was a never-failing land-mark to direct my return to the road, which,
although faint, could readily be distinguished by a
practised eye.   Dealing death around, I continued
to scour the plain, the herd before me increasing from
hundreds to thousands, and reinforcements still pouring in from all directions, when crying " Hold,
enough !" I stayed my hand from slaughter.   Having divested some of the slain of their brilliant
parti-coloured robes, and packed the *spolia* on my
horse, I set out to rejoin the waggons, but ah! how
vainly did I seek for them.   Again and again I
strained my eyes for the road, and cantered to and
fro between the string of frosted salt-pans and the
little hill, which, floating in the sea of mirage that
environed me, seemed as if poised in the sky.   The
monotony of the landscape baffled all my attempts
at recognition, and my search was utterly fruitless.
Every feature of the cone was precisely the same—
the table mountains were completely obscured by the
vapour—and in the constant recurrence of similar
forms, I lost the points of the compass, and at last
became totally bewildered.

   To retrace my steps over plains so trampled by
innumerable herds was clearly impossible.   At one

moment, as if in mockery, a solitary quagga, magnified ten thousand times by the treacherous mirage, loomed like the white tilt of a waggon ; but my joy at the supposed discovery was invariably followed by the bitterest disappointment. Again a group of pigmy Bushwomen, walking unnoticed among a herd of bles-bucks, and seen through the same deceptive medium, personated our followers with the cattle. Alas! these too fled at my approach, and jabbered like baboons when I had overtaken them. Several hours had thus passed in idle search. Spent by fatigue and anxiety, my parched tongue rattling like a board against the palate of my mouth, I wandered on over flowery wastes, still lengthening as I advanced. Dry tanks, surrounded by a garden of pinks and marigolds, served only to increase my sufferings, but neither fount, nor pool, nor running stream, greeted my straining gaze. At length the refraction dissipating with the declining day, the three table-topped mountains became again visible in the horizon. With the consoling reflection that at all events I was now advancing in the same direction as the caravan, I hastened forward, and before dusk, found myself not a little revived by a draught of the clearest water from a serpentine river flowing to the westward; the banks of which were trimmed with reeds and dwarf willows, while portions of its sandy bed were imprinted with the heavy foot-steps of a troop of lions.

The mind becomes even more readily habituated to hardship and suffering than the body. Every

thing around me was vague and conjectural, and
wore an aspect calculated to inspire despondency;
yet my heart was light and my spirit buoyant; and
I no sooner became convinced that I was actually lost
in the heart of a howling wilderness, inhabited, if at
all, by barbarous and hostile tribes, than I felt myself
fully prepared to meet the emergency.   The setting
sun having given me the bearing of the table
mountains, considerably to the westward of south,
it was evident that, without being aware of it, I had
crossed the road, and ridden too far to the eastward.
In the hope of yet retrieving my error, I hurried
down the river as fast as possible, but, night closing
in, I was fain to prepare for a bivouac among the
bushes.   The stars were completely concealed
behind a clouded sky, and repeated flashes of
lightning were accompanied by distant thunder.
Having completed all my preparations, I was listening, with breathless attention, for the cracking
of a whip, or the signal guns, which I knew would
be fired from the waggons, when, to my inexpressible delight, a joyous beacon-fire shone suddenly forth on the river.   Upon consideration, I
felt puzzled to account for its appearance in a spot
which I had so recently passed, but, concluding
that the waggons had subsequently arrived there,
I laid the flattering unction to my soul, and groped
my way towards it.   My disappointment and disgust
may better be imagined than described when,
flitting round the unfriendly blaze, I discovered a
gang of Bushmen, with their imp-like squaws,

carousing over a carcass. I slunk silently back to my den, fully impressed with the necessity of remaining perfectly quiet, but scarcely hoping that my horse would be so fortunate as to escape the observation of these lynx-eyed vagabonds.

The uneasy snorting of my unfortunate steed, and his constant efforts to get loose, soon apprized me of the presence of lions at no great distance to windward, but the fear of attracting my two-legged enemies to the spot prevented my kindling a fire for his protection, or even for dressing a *koorhaan*,* with which I had taken care to provide myself. Dying of hunger, and my " girdle of famine "† tightened to the last hole, I felt strangely tempted to devour my Christmas repast uncooked. About midnight, however, having prepared a deep oven, I ventured to light a fire, and the fowl being duly baked and disposed of, I presently betook myself to sleep.

The following morning set in with tremendous rain. Drenched, cold, and cramped, I arose from my aquatic bed, and at once perceived that all hope of finding the trail of our waggons was at an end. The soil consisting chiefly of a red loamy earth, from which the faintly marked tracks were easily obliterated, I resolved to follow the course of the river several miles farther to the westward; and then, should I fail in finding the waggons, to cross the country in a direct line to the conical hill, which

---

* Florican.

† The leathern strap worn round the waist is called by the savages a *lambele* strap, or hunger-girdle.

was still a conspicuous land-mark—thus certainly
intersecting the road, if, indeed, any traces of it remained, of which I began to be doubtful. To this
programme I rigorously adhered, walking the
greater part of the way to save my harassed steed,
upon whose back I now contemplated the probability
of having to seek my way to the colony—a probability which was mightily increased about sunset, when
I found myself preparing to perfect my acquaintance with the cone, by roosting on its summit,

"In a deep cave, dug by no mortal hand."

During this second day's weary pilgrimage,
scorched by the ardent and reflected rays of a summer sun, I arrived at an extensive pond covered with
water-lilies, and bordered by a broad belt of flags
and rushes. Hastily approaching the margin, I became suddenly ingulfed in a pit-fall, six feet in depth,
filled with mire and water, from which I extricated
myself with inconceivable difficulty. On recovering
my shoes out of the stiff blue clay at the bottom, I
perceived that the whole tank was closely invested
by a chain of these traps, which had been carefully
covered over by my friends the Bushmen. Having
shot a spring-buck, I here scorched enough of the
flesh to satisfy the cravings of hunger, and slinging
a fine fat leg on either side of the saddle, took up
my night's lodging as already described, without
having been able to discover the smallest traces of
the road.

The night was serene and starlight. From the
top of my strong-hold I looked out upon the tran-

quil expanse beneath me, and listened for hours to
catch some friendly melody that might direct my
bewildered footsteps.   Where, alas! was the "busy
hum of men?"   The shrill neighing of the wild
ass, the bleat of the timid spring-buck, or the
bellow of the gnoo, with the deep-drawn distant
sighing of a prowling lion, occasionally borne along
upon the breeze, alone disturbed the grave-like stillness of the wilderness!   Seriously did I now debate
with myself upon the propriety of making for the
Colony, instead of prolonging my search.   It is true
that every thing betwixt me and it was wrapped in
uncertainty, and that to arrive there I should have
to pass alone through an unknown and inhospitable
region; but on the other hand, I had already done
all that human ingenuity could devise, without the
smallest success.   I estimated my distance from the
New Hantam to be about two hundred miles; and
being well provided with ammunition, there was a
fair prospect of my being able to reach that district
in six or seven days, unless the scarcity of game
should oblige me to sacrifice my steed.   Taking
into consideration, however, the long and dismal
state of uncertainty that the measure would entail
upon my companion, I finally determined to make
one more huntsman-like cast, before giving up the
search in despair.

Another day dawned, and again I saddled my
trusty beast, and struck into the pathless waste, intending to make a wide sweep to the northward and
westward, where it was possible that rain might

not have fallen.   About noon, lifting up my eyes
from the ground, on which they had vainly sought
for any indication of the party having passed, to
my unutterable joy and delight I recognised the
sedge-grown fountain at which we had breakfasted
on Christmas morning !   Vaulting into the saddle,
I eagerly dashed towards the spot, and instantly
hit upon the trail of our waggons, steadily following
up which, I shortly fell in with a party of Bechuana
of both sexes, who proved to be members of the
remnant of a tribe called Lihoya, and were engaged
in eating up a bles-buck that had been caught in one
of their pit-falls.   Having, through the agency of
a broken cigar, negociated a treaty of alliance with
these terrified savages, who as usual had fled on
perceiving me, I pointed to the wheel-tracks, and
gave them by signs to understand that I was in
search of my waggons.   They instantly understood
my meaning, and holding up both hands, pointed
to the western horizon.   The ladies, although very
nervous at first, had in the mean time conceived a
violent attachment for the brass buttons of my
jacket—pointing to them, and repeatedly exclaiming
with dry mouths, " *Tullana, Tullana !*"* Upon
my presenting these, together with a knife with
which their amputation had been performed, they
became perfectly insane, and declared their intention
of accompanying me in person for the purpose of
receiving further presents.   Placing myself under
the willing guidance of this savage party, I struck

* *Anglice*, Buttons, buttons !

across the plain, and in the course of another hour
was within sight of the waggons. Jaded and way-
worn, it was with profound gratitude to a protecting
Providence, that I thus found myself restored to the
cafila, after three days of anxious wandering over
an unexplored and inhospitable wilderness.

Great was the anxiety, and many were the dismal
forebodings to which my mysterious absence had
given birth. A general gloom had pervaded the
camp, and it was conjectured that I had reached
"that bourne whence no traveller returns." There
being no fuel with which to kindle a beacon fire,
whips had been cracked, and muskets discharged at
intervals, both during the day and night; and my
horse's *spoor* having been completely effaced by the
rain, three separate parties had gone out in search
of me, in different directions. Those only who
have experienced the warm cordiality which grows
up between partners in so wild and adventurous an
expedition as that in which my companion and myself had embarked, are capable of fully understanding the nature of the welcome I received—the
sensations created by my safe and unhoped-for return even extending themselves to the disaffected of
our followers. On comparing notes with my fellow-
traveller, I was concerned to find that in some respects he had scarcely fared better than myself; the
knuckle-bone of a tainted ham having supplied the
place of a smoking sirloin and richly-dotted plum-
pudding—and, with a cupful of dirty water,
constituted, alas! his Christmas dinner.

CHAPTER XXXIV.

JOURNEY RESUMED, TO THE 'GY KOUP, OR VET RIVIERE OF THE EMIGRANTS.

MISFORTUNES, according to the old adage, never come singly; and I have assuredly no grounds for recording a special exception to the rule in our favour.   Shortly after my restoration on the 27th, the sudden brewing of a whirlwind, or more properly speaking, of a *simoon* in miniature, whilst it caused the partial destruction of one of the waggon awnings, led also to the temporary loss of our live stock ; the natural consequence of the latter calamity being, that one of the best oxen fell into a pit, and two of the sheep into the maw of the hyæna.   This extraordinary squall of dust and gravel, which raged as if all inanimate nature had been stirred into commotion, was the forerunner of a thunder-storm, that lasted the greater part of the night, and ultimately gave place to a drenching and steady rain during the whole of the following day.   Towards evening, our allies, the Lihoya, honestly brought in the remaining sheep, and our position being very exposed, we made an attempt to reach the river; but after travelling five miles, were compelled to halt at a puddle of rain-water, where we passed the dreary wet night of the 28th, as we had spent its predecessor, without either fuel or shelter.

The next morning brought us to the scene of my bivouac on Christmas night, and according to my prediction, we experienced no little difficulty in discovering a spot where the capriciously winding river might be crossed. The interval was turned to account by Cœur de Lion in cooking provisions, a man having been sent in advance to collect fuel, which, however, proved to be abundant. At length the exploring parties returned—one of them having discovered a practical ford two miles higher up the stream, whilst the other had fallen in, to the westward, with the skeletons of several horses, together with some fresh human remains, which, from the dimensions of the *crania*, they declared to be those of Dutch Boors. A favourite wheel-ox, that had fallen sick the preceding day, being now unable to proceed farther, Claas, at his own request, was permitted to put the unfortunate beast out of its misery—a task which he accomplished in five clumsy shots.

The perpendicular character of the bank rendered a *skid*, or as it is termed by the Colonists, a *remscoan*, necessary upon each hind wheel, in addition to the drag-chain; but even after this precaution, the weight of the vehicles caused them to descend with frightful velocity. Safely arrived at the bottom, the long waggon presently settled down to the axle in a quicksand, the team also sinking to their bellies; and it was not until our remaining supply

of flour and sugar had been spoiled in the water,
during an attempt which was made to drag the van
out backwards, that the latter was at length un-
loaded, and towed on shore by the application of a
twenty-four ox power.   In commemoration of this
disaster, the treacherous stream was christened by
the Hottentots *Sant Riviére*, or Sand River, by
which homely designation it will be recognised in
the map as a tributary of the Likwa.

We had not advanced above ten miles, before a
violent storm of hail and rain obliged us again to
halt on the open heath. Piet, who had gone in advance to reconnoitre, lost his way, and did not
rejoin the party until midnight, having at length
been attracted by the signals made, and by Cœur
de Lion's kitchen fire, which, on account of the
weather, had with considerable difficulty been kindled
in an ant-hill. The country over which we passed
was usually covered with dome-shaped mounds of
clay, thrown up by the pismire, and invariably
scooped out either by the long nails of the ant-
eater, or by Bushmen, so as to resemble a baker's
oven. In wet weather especially, or during a
dearth of fuel, these mounds were our stoutest allies;
but on the other hand, the Hottentots not unfrequently put the strength of our waggons to the test
by driving carelessly over them.

Two distinct animals are found in this part of the
country, that alike burrow in the ground, and appear
to subsist entirely upon ants and termites, leaving
upon every habitation thrown up by those minute

insects, unequivocal marks of their desolating visits. Of these the Ant-bear, or *Aard-vark** of the colonists, is the more common; it is from six to seven feet in extreme length, covered with coarse brown hair, and furnished with a slimy, flexible tongue, capable of being protruded to the extent of eighteen or twenty inches beyond the attenuated snout. It possesses the singular peculiarity of walking, or rather hobbling, upon the sides instead of upon the soles, of its fore-feet. The latter are provided with four robust nails, which form a complete rake, and with which the animal digs into the bowels of the mound, its taper tongue being always in readiness to seize the swarming inmates as fast as they issue from their beleaguered abode.

Although differing greatly in external appearance, the equipments, as well as the habits, of the second species, are essentially the same. Seen from a distance, the *Pangolin*, or Manis,† might easily be mistaken for a small alligator. The upper parts of the body are clad in a complete suit of flexible armour; consisting of numerous stout horny scales, overlapping each other like the tiles of a house, and presenting an appearance precisely similar to the bark of the brab tree. Possessing also, the power of rolling itself into a ball like a hedgehog, this otherwise defenceless animal is at once rendered perfectly invulnerable to the attacks of its foes.

The soil in this neighbourhood was black; and

* *Orycteropus Capensis.*   † *Manis Temminckii.*

owing to the great quantity of rain that had fallen
during the night, we found ourselves fairly water-
logged in the morning.   This was considered a rare
opportunity for breaking in some of the oxen that
had never yet bowed their stiff necks to the yoke,
and their rebellious spirits once subdued by the
unsparing administration of the whip, they presently
dragged us out of our difficulties.   Ascending
gradually to the base of the three table mountains,
which like natural buttresses protruded their bold
outlines into the monotonous landscape, an extensive
and stirring prospect burst upon · our astonished
gaze.   Gone were the level plains, over which the
lingering eye had wandered for days without once
finding an object upon which to repose.   Hill and
dale, mountain and valley, stretched away at our
feet in fair variety, terminated in the remote horison
by the craggy summits of the well-known *Witte-*
bergen—those

> "Sterile mountains, rough and steep,
> That bound abrupt the valley deep,
> Heaving to the clear, blue, sky
> Their ribs of granite, bare and dry."

Half crazy with delight, and never dreaming of
the distance that still intervened, or the troubles
that were yet in store, every one instantly affected
to recognize some landmark with which he was
familiar ; and whilst many actually talked themselves into a belief that they could distinguish the
smoke from the missionary's chimney at Phillipolis,
still one hundred and fifty miles distant, Andries

positively asserted that a line of bushes, which
skirted the remaining proportion of level land, was
the *Modder Rivière.*

As we gradually descended towards this stream
of promise, which ultimately proved to be the 'Gy
Koup, or Vet Rivière of the emigrants—rising near
the missionary station of Umpukani, and also a
tributary to the Likwa—we passed over a low tract
about eight or ten miles in extent, strongly impregnated with salt, and abounding in lakes and pools.
The number of wild animals congregated on this
swampy flat almost realized fable; the roads made
by their incessant tramp resembling so many well-
travelled highways.   At every step incredible herds
of bonte-bucks,* bles-bucks, and spring-bucks, with
troops of gnoos, and squadrons of the common, or
stripeless quagga, were performing their com-
plicated evolutions; and not unfrequently, a knot
of ostriches, decked in their white plumes, played
the part of general officer and staff, with such strict
propriety, as still further to remind the spectator of
a cavalry review.   Late in the afternoon, we struck
into a waggon-track, and crossed the river, by a
made road, to a deserted camp of the emigrant
farmers, whose temporary reed huts formed so
inviting a shelter, that it was resolved to halt for a
day—as well for the purpose of recruiting the
oxen, three more of which were unable to proceed
from the effects of distemper, as to manufacture a
new *trek-touw,* wash our linen, eject the host of

* *Gazella Pygarga.* Delineated in the African Views.

ticks which had taken possession of the waggons, and give the Hottentots an opportunity of dancing in the new year.

Together with the old year, we had fairly bidden adieu to the great plains of the Vaal River, which to the traveller appear to be completely taken possession of by wild animals, and may with strict propriety be termed the domain of savage nature. A region, to the perception as vast and trackless as the ocean, and like it presenting an undisturbed horizon, is spread out, from the Cashan Mountains, into one level and treeless expanse of serene and sunny plain. In vain we seek for the bewitching variety of hill or dale, forest or glade, which constitutes the charm of landscape—the eye wanders on without the smallest check over endless flats, which are utterly wearisome from their extent and monotony. Yet nature has endeavoured in some measure to supply the deficiency by decking them out in her gayest flowers, and in some of the most eccentric and attractive forms that exist in the vegetable world. The chandelier plant, and purple amaryllis, with many other splendid bulbs, grow wild in profusion; and being interspersed with geraniums, several species of the cactus, and an endless variety of the succulent green-house plant called the Hottentot fig, literally impart to the waste the appearance of a flower-garden.

The monotony of this extraordinary wilderness is at length broken in upon by the Wittebergen, or Quathlamba Mountains, a broad basaltic belt that skirts the eastern coast at a distance varying from sixty to ninety miles from the shore, and divides Caffraria from Bechuana land. This wild chaos of rocks and cliffs—of barren ridges and towering peaks, worn by time into castellated fortresses, and other fantastic shapes, resembles the ruins of a world; and being intersected by yawning chasms, offers an impassable barrier. Both the Caledon, and the Nu-Gareep, take their source in this vast chain, and its wild fastnesses not only afford shelter to the *Mantatees*, under King Sikonyela, and to many other broken tribes who have been driven from their native homes by " war's alarms"—but they have lately been discovered by adventurous French missionaries, to be the haunts of two cannibal tribes, called the *Barimo* and *Ba-Mahakana.*

December and January constituting the hottest season, we crossed the plains of the Vaal River at the proper time for suffering all the inconvenience of rain, without enjoying any of its advantages. In common with other countries remote from the sea-coast, this portion of the continent receives its rain in thunder showers during the summer months; and there being none during the rest of the year, the climate, notwithstanding frequent nocturnal dews, is characterized by extreme aridity. The sun shines with matchless splendour through a sky of delicious blue, which is rarely visited by a cloud; and during his meridian blaze over a level expanse in many parts strongly impregnated with salt, the delusion of mirage is nowhere more perfect. Optical lakes impart to the wanderer fevered with thirst, the torments of Tantalus; yet even on these naked plains he will experience none of the debilitating fervour of an Indian sun.

Although thinly populated by skulking broods of Bushmen, and by the starving remnants of nomadic pastoral tribes, which have been broken up by war and violence, this is a land in which no man permanently dwells—neither is the soil any man's property, being abandoned as water or fuel fails. Nearly all the rivers by which it is traversed are periodical, and the few pools that exist, being dried up at certain seasons, the miserable wretches, whose existence depends upon the wild animals, migrate with them to distant parts, keeping within the verge of expiring verdure. Owing to the devastation occasioned in the countries north-east of the colony by the hordes called Mantatees and Ficani especially, as well as by marauding bands of *Bergenaar-Griquas* —a race of mixed European and African lineage— many hundred famishing survivors of the Bechuana tribes took refuge, during the years 1824 and 1825, in the frontier districts of Graaff Reinet and Somerset. Indeed, amongst the savage nations of South Africa, as elsewhere, a principle of extinction has for ages past been in active operation. Regions now silent and deserted, once contained their busy throng, whose numbers and strength have been gradually brought down by war and want. Whole tribes have been rooted out from their hereditary homes, and have either disappeared from the face of the earth, or, pursued by the "gaunt and bony arm" of famine, still wander with fluctuating fortunes over these measureless tracts. For hundreds of miles, therefore, the eye is not greeted by the smallest trace of human industry, or by any vestige of human habitation—the wild and interminable expanse ever presenting the same appearance—that of one vast uninhabited solitude.

CHAPTER XXXV.

PLUNDERED BY BUSHMAN HORDES, AND LEFT A WRECK IN THE DESERT.

Resuming our pilgrimage on the morning of the 1st January, 1837, our road wound among singular groups of detached hills, which wore the appearance of having accidentally fallen there after the formation of the plain; blue peaks and mountain ridges stretching along the horizon, and deepening their tints as we advanced. Again, the valleys were spread, as with flocks of sheep, with countless herds of graceful spring-bucks, displaying the snow-white folds on their haunches while they vaulted over each other's heads; and for the first time since quitting the Colony, several secretary birds were now observed strutting about the plain, in search of snakes, upon which reptiles they principally subsist. In many places the ground was strewed with the blanched skeletons of gnoos and other wild animals, which had evidently been slaughtered by Bushmen, and the traces of these *Troglodytes* waxed hourly more apparent, as the country became more inhabitable; the base of one hill in particular, in which some of their caves were discovered, presenting the appearance of a Golgotha—several hundred gnoos' and bonte-bucks' skulls being collected in a single heap.

The bonte-buck is the twentieth and last known species of the antelope tribe * that is to be met with in Southern Africa, remote from the sea-coast. It was formerly common in the Cape Colony, and a few are even still preserved in the district of Swellendam, a fine of five hundred rix dollars being attached to their destruction, unless by special license from Government. In point of shape and size, the bonte-buck bears a close resemblance to the bles-buck, being equally robust, hump-backed, and broad-nosed; but it is more remarkably piebald, the legs being perfectly white, and the horns black, instead of being light-coloured. The two animals have in common, a broad blaze down the face, a *glazed* bluish-white back, wearing the appearance of a saddle, and fiery red eyes. The horns are placed vertically on the summit of the head, and both species alike invariably scour against the wind, with their noses close to the ground. Numbers of these antelopes had fallen to our rifles during the last few days, and several of the common quagga also. That quadruped had now entirely supplanted Burchell's zebra, and its flesh, although infinitely more yellow, rank, and oily than that of a horse, was greatly esteemed by the Hottentots.

During this part of our journey, I again met with the oryx, or gemsbok, which splendid antelope

---

* I have retained the term *antelope* as applied to the eland, gnoo, koodoo, and others, with the view of avoiding confusion. The modern classification of these animals will be found in the Appendix.

has been described in an early chapter of my narrative, as the animal that in all probability gave birth to the figure of the fabulous unicorn. When seen *en profile*, the long straight horns so exactly cover each other, that the existence of two might almost be doubted; and whilst rude delineations in this posture have been discovered in many of the Bushmen caves, the algazel, a corresponding species in North Africa, is to be found similarly represented on the sculptured monuments of ancient Egypt and Nubia. The oryx is a powerful and dangerous antagonist, charging viciously, and defending itself, when hard pressed, with wonderful intrepidity and address. Its skeleton has not unfrequently been found locked in that of a lion—the latter having been transfixed by its formidable horns, in a conflict which has proved fatal to both the combatants.

With the ostrich,* a bird famous from the most remote antiquity, and which was usually common during our journey, I conclude my notice of objects that especially interest the sportsman. Miserably mounted as we were, any attempt to overtake this most gigantic of the feathered race would have been vain, but a shot could always be obtained at arm's length by galloping to a point in the course it had selected, and from which it rarely swerved. The food of the ostrich is exclusively of a vegetable nature; it pastures in large troops, and evidently constitutes the link between the birds and the mam-

---

* *Struthio Camelus.* Delineated in the African Views.

malia. The male bird often measures nine feet at
the crown of the head, and exceeds three hundred
pounds in weight—the thigh being equal in size to
the largest leg of mutton. Excepting the costly
white plumes, so prized by the fair sex, and which
are chiefly obtained from the wing, instead of from
the tail, as generally imagined, the colour of the
body is the deepest black in the male bird, and in
the female a dingy brown. While running, the
wings are raised above the back, and the clatter of
the feet, which are only provided with two toes,
resembles that made by a horse in trotting, pebbles
of considerable size being cast behind them. The
usual cry of the ostrich is a short roar, but when
brought to bay, it hisses like the gander. The
Bechuana, with what truth I know not, are said
occasionally to domesticate this stately bird for equestrian purposes; and the puny Bushman avails himself
of the disguise afforded by its skin, to mix with a
troop of wild animals, and select his victim. At
the twang of his tiny bow, away scours the herd in
dire consternation, and more alarmed than all, off
scuds the impostor with them, again propelling a
shaft as soon as the panic has subsided. The
destruction committed in this manner is incredible
—a slender reed, only slightly barbed with bone or
iron, but imbued with a subtile poison, and launched
with unerring dexterity, being sufficient to destroy
the most powerful animal.

The principal ingredient of this deadly bane is
said by Pringle to consist of the venom of the most

dangerous serpents that infest the desert. In seizing and extracting the poison from beneath the fangs of the fatal puff-adder, or the cobra-di-capello, the despised African displays the most wonderful dexterity and boldness; simply placing his naked foot on the neck of the writhing reptile, and not unfrequently closing the exhibition of his intrepidity by fearlessly swallowing the contents of the bag he has extracted, as a supposed antidote, or rather as an effectual charm, against the deleterious consequence of the venom, should it ever be accidentally brought into contact with his blood. Being of itself too thin and volatile to retain its powers long unimpaired, this animal poison is skilfully concocted into a black glutinous substance, by the due admixture of powerful vegetable and mineral poisons; the former being generally obtained from the root of a species of amaryllis, called by the colonists the *gift-bol*, whilst the latter is an unctuous or bituminous substance, which is said to exude from certain rocks and caverns that exist in particular parts of the Bushman country.

Late in the afternoon, as we were journeying, several imp-like figures of human form were observed through a telescope, making with all dispatch for a neighbouring hill, the summit of which was crowded with them. Anxious to obtain information regarding our position, we halted the caravan, and made friendly signs to induce the wild beings to approach. After warily reconnoitring us from their

* Poison Bulb.

fastnesses, nine of them at length ventured down, and having replied to our questions in fear and trembling, received some tobacco and retreated. Their intercourse being conducted with such circumspection, the sum total of intelligence gained was, that Piet Whitefoot, the Coranna captain, resided about three days' journey to the westward. At sunset, having advanced twenty miles, we crossed a small stream and drew up on the bank, making the whole of the cattle fast to the waggons, lest they should fall into the hands of the Lilliputians, several of whose watch-fires were visible on the surrounding hills.

The following morning we unyoked for half an hour at a small river, near a nest which contained upwards of thirty women. These gipsies, as usual, approached the waggons with great familiarity, pointing to the flatness of their stomachs, and suing for tobacco, which luxury was doled out to them by the inch. Twenty miles more brought us to another deserted camp of the emigrant farmers, in which, amongst other interesting marks of human labour, stood a lofty scaffolding, used in the manufacture of *riems*, or leathern halters. Hence, a made road led us across a stream of considerable size, pronounced by the followers, with their usual sagacity, to be the *Reit* river, although subsequently it was discovered to be the *Modder*, rising near the missionary station of Thaba Uncha, and joining the Likwa a little above the *embouchure* of the Nu Gareep. The sheep having been placed in a deep

P

pit to prevent them from straying, were visited during
the night by a party of hyænas, which slaughtered
three, and drove the residue to the summit of a high
hill, where they were found the following morning.

Having travelled until dark on the 3rd without
being able to discover any water, we halted in a wide
plain under an isolated hill, which, it will be seen,
was destined to be the scene of sad disaster and
anxiety. A party of Bushwomen, who had their
den among the rocks at its base, presently arrived,
bringing fuel and eatable wild roots for barter. One
of them, whose foot measured barely four inches in
length, was a most bewitching creature, and completely turned the heads of the Hottentots. Besides
being far more elaborately embellished with red
clay and ornaments of fat—and perhaps even more
redolent of villanous smells than any lady we had
hitherto seen, this Venus carried a jackal's tail by
way of a pocket-handkerchief, and spoke the melli-
fluous Dutch language with surprising fluency. It
appeared that she had effected her escape from a
boor residing in the Sneuwbergen, whose slave she
had been from infancy; but we could elicit little
information of value, beyond the existence of a dirty
pool about two miles distant, whither the cattle
were immediately driven.

Since leaving the Cashan Mountains, one or two
of our oxen had been almost daily abandoned; but
including *Mutlee*, the old cow, and a dwarf bull—
neither of which royal gifts could be worked in the
teams—we were still the proprietors of thirty-eight

of all sorts. They had fasted the preceding night, and the plain being very open, we left them to graze in a verdant hollow, from which it did not appear probable that they would stray. About midnight, however, the roar of a lion being followed by a general rush towards the waggons, Andries was appointed to keep watch; but spent with fatigue, and possessing withal a most gentlemanly abhorrence of trouble, he did not preserve his vigil long, and the consequence was, that at daybreak not an ox was to be seen. This being an event of every day occurrence, created so little uneasiness at first, that Andries, whose business it also was to look for them, instead of atoning for his carelessness by a suitable display of activity, took his leisure to indulge in a little more gossip with the pretty Bush-girl, who very knowingly persuaded him that she had seen the cattle not a quarter of a mile off only a minute before. In the course of an hour, however, the Hottentots, who had gone out to look for them, returned for horses—the appearance of the trail leading them to believe that the oxen had been chased by lions. Owing to some intestine feuds and jealousies, difficult to be explained, Piet alone obtained a steed, but Andries and Cobus were also mounted the moment we discovered the real state of affairs; and although much valuable time had been unnecessarily thrown away, still no doubt was entertained that the oxen would eventually be recovered. All that day, however, and part of the next, were passed in a state of anxiety and suspense.

P 2

During the night it rained a deluge, and about 2
P.M. on the 5th, Piet returned empty-handed for
ammunition, or rather for no reason at all, having
left the other two men upon the tracks, which, still
indicating a chase, led in the direction of some
distant hills.   Owing to the hardness of the ground,
he had been unable to discover the cause of the
panic.

In this posture of affairs, I determined to proceed
in person without another moment's delay, and
whilst mounting my horse, faithfully promised my
comrade not to show my face again until I had
recovered our cattle.   Alas! it was destined that
I should not redeem my pledge.   I had cantered
about eight miles, less than half way to the hills,
when Andries and Cobus were descried plying the
lash, and approaching at speed, with the dismal
intelligence that the oxen were in the hands of a
troop of Bushmen, occupying the summit of the
nearest hill, whence one of the pigmies, in broken
Dutch, had challenged the gallant equestrians to
do them battle.   Cobus, who the morning before,
when he dreamt not of the real state of the case,
had ridden forth gasconading of his prowess in
arms, now repeated several times emphatically that
the contemptible spokesman had actually defied him
in terms derogating from his valour.   "Here," said
he, " Here stand your oxen; come up if you're a
man! Take them, ye poltroons, if ye dare!"   Yet
although mounted, and abundantly supplied with
munition, these hulking white-livered villains did

not blush to acknowledge that their personal fears had induced them to decline the invitation. Neither was it possible now to persuade them to turn back with me; the enemy, they declared, being so exceedingly numerous, and ensconced in so strong a position, that nothing could be attempted with so small a force.

Here then, like sailors who have foundered upon a rock when within sight of their destined haven, were we—after weathering many a storm, and accomplishing the most hazardous portion of our journey—left at last, a wreck in the desert. The spirit of Ethaldur groaned within him, when he thus saw his prediction on the eve of being verified, and the lower jaw of Cœur de Lion dropped until his beard was dangling at his girdle. To add to *his* misfortunes, the scanty pool upon which our supply of water depended, being drained to the dregs, it had become necessary to perform a journey of *six miles* over an enemy's country, in order to replenish the tea-kettle.

The vindictive and improvident character of the Bushman hordes, rendered it extremely probable that the whole of our unfortunate oxen had already been wantonly sacrificed to their malice; but at all events, the day was too far spent to admit of our reaching the scene of action before dark, and the night being moonless, it was necessary that our attack should be delayed until the following morning. The hateful squaws had abandoned their kraal the preceding day, and it was not unlikely

that a party of the marauders might be lurking in
the hill, ready to fall upon the waggons during our
temporary absence.   After much consultation, therefore, it was resolved to leave Claas and Frederick,
who confessed their inability to fight, together with
the two domestics, whose black beards were calculated to instil terror into the stoutest heart—starting
ourselves with the other five Hottentots in the dead
of night, in order if possible to avoid creating suspicion of our departure.   All the preliminaries of
a surprise thus skilfully arranged, the best horses
were selected and fastened to the waggons, and one
hundred rounds of ammunition having been served
out to each of the little band, we retired to rest,
leaving the watch in charge of Cœur de Lion, with
instructions to keep his eye steadily fixed upon the
hands, and not fail to arouse us when they pointed
to the hour of twelve.

CHAPTER XXXVI.

NIGHT ATTACK ON THE MARAUDERS.

I WAS still broad awake, conjecturing the success of our projected commando, when the watchful valet thrust his well-furnished chin under the canvas curtains of the waggon, and in a tremulous voice proclaimed the midnight hour. A dram of spirits having been issued to each Hottentot knight, with the design of inspiring chivalrous sentiments, the skeleton steeds were silently saddled; and not a word having been spoken above a whisper, we commenced our march towards the enemy's position. The night was cold and clear, and withal gloriously starlight; and it was in truth a goodly sight to behold the motley band of gay cavaliers, girded about with their furniture of war, and carrying their heavy carbines on their shoulders, jauntily pricking over the plain. The distance of the Bushman castle not being less than eighteen miles, it was necessary, in order to arrive in proper time, that we should move as briskly as possible. Ever and anon, as we cantered blindly along, in momentary apprehension of losing each other, some one of the party was to be seen floundering among the meerkat burrows, with which the soil was completely undermined. Herds of timid spring-bucks, upon whose

repose we had unceremoniously obtruded, bounded,
panic-stricken, across our path; and spectral gnoos,
cantering inquisitively up at intervals, stood within
pistol shot, whisking their streaming tails, and
bellowing defiance.   After three hours' journeying,
we arrived on the bank of a narrow stream, completely choked with bulrushes and tangled sedge;
shortly after forcing our way through which, with
incredible difficulty and many casualties, we descried the Lilliputian fortress rising before us in dim
perspective.   There being yet no glimmering of
dawn, we halted for a few minutes behind a group of
rocks to reconnoitre; and a council of war being
held, it was decided that we should ascend the hill
on the opposite side, and having carried the enemy's
position in reverse, by a *coup de main*, should shoot
all who made any show of resistance.   Dismounting,
therefore, and leading our steeds, we noiselessly
groped our way among crags and brushwood to the
summit of the hill, which, although rather abrupt
in front, was spread out into undulations behind.
Here the horses, having been fastened together by
the bridles, were left in charge of one of the Hottentots—the rest, with us, creeping on all-fours
towards the table-land occupied by the enemy, of
whose increasing proximity our noses began now to
apprize us. Cautiously peeping with uncovered
heads over a natural parapet, we could presently
perceive their fires burning about two hundred yards
in advance; and thus securely ambushed, scarcely
daring even to breathe, we awaited the approach of

dawn with a degree of nervous impatience which may be estimated by those who recollect that upon its successful issue, the salvation of our waggons and property almost entirely depended.

While thus watching the cold darkness of night, which seemed as though it would have lasted for ever, the bright morning star—that joyous herald whose appearance I had never hailed with greater delight, suddenly shot like a rocket above the horizon. A faint light immediately pervaded the eastern sky, before which, as it gradually increased, the stars appeared to fade away, while the earth still continued in night. Imperceptibly, almost, this light had presently given place to a ruddy tint, which speedily extended itself over the whole vault of heaven; but though the outline of objects in the extreme distance could now be indistinctly traced, those immediately about us were yet shrouded in darkness. Around, all was silent as the grave, not a zephyr disturbing the death-like stillness that was reigning. As objects became gradually plainer, the forms of several conical huts could be distinguished, and, lastly, by a still less dubious light, the prostrate carcases of many of our oxen became visible. Alas! it was then, as we had feared; but, if indeed we were irretrievably ruined, our moment for taking vengeance had arrived. Stealing over the parapet, every rifle was noiselessly cocked, and a finger flew to every trigger, as, with palpitating hearts and wary tread, we approached the wretched wigwams. Woe unto that luckless wight who had there been found

sleeping—he would never have woke again.   But,
though smouldering fires were smoking in various
directions, every cabin was deserted; and having
visited each in succession, and diligently searched
every nook and corner, without being able to discover
a solitary human being, we turned for a moment to
contemplate the tragic scene before us.   Nineteen
of our gallant oxen, swollen and disfigured with
many a wanton wound, were stretched in the wild
enclosure, from which arose the most sickening of
savage odours.   Lean dogs,

"Gorging and growling o'er carcass and limb,"

held their carnival over the dead, but were too busy
even to bark at our intrusion; while torpid vultures,
distended to such a size that they could with
difficulty hop out of our way, were perched like
harpies upon the surrounding rocks.   It was by
this time broad daylight, and a few of our oxen
being, to our great delight, perceived standing at
the foot of the hill, a party was immediately detached
to take possession of them, while we glanced over
the field of slaughter, to ascertain the extent of our
loss.   Side by side at our feet, and swollen almost
to bursting, from the effects of a subtile poison, were
Holland and Olifant, the two sturdy wheelers of our
choice Naudè *span*,* which had never failed to
extricate us from every difficulty.   Near them, and
weltering in a pool of blood, lay Lanceman and
England, the steadiest and staunchest of our leaders.

* Ten oxen usually compose a *span* or team.

Passing onwards, our attention was next attracted to
a headless trunk, and at no great distance from it—
the white eyes glaring upon us as if still alive—was
the hornless cranium of *Mutlee*.   Every eye turned
upon the caitiff Andries, and peals of ill-timed
merriment burst from every Hottentot mouth.   The
arm of retribution had for once descended on a right
worthy victim.   Maddened with rage at the heart-
rending prospect before us, again and again did we
search every chink and cranny, and unweariedly did
we cast about for the trail of the marauders.   "Grim
satyr-faced baboons" railed hoarsely at us from
their rocky clefts, and, to whichever side we turned,
the slope of the hill was besprinkled with mouldering
human bones; but, after the closest scrutiny, no
object could be discovered upon which to wreak our
vengeance.   A rhee-buck, that our early approach
had disturbed, having bounded through the encampment, and given the alarm, the "dwellers with owls
and bats," although doubtless spectators of all that
we were doing, had effectually concealed themselves
from observation, and, after the strictest search, nine
tracks only could be discovered.   Of these, six were
females, and one was that of our bewitching acquaintance.   Barely four inches in length, but yet fully
developed, there could be no mistaking *her* foot-
mark; and it now became evident that, whilst she
and her elfin colleagues had been aiding and
abetting to our ruin from the very commencement,
our luckless followers had fled—not from the over-

whelming host, which their heated imaginations
had conjured into existence—but from the empty
challenge of a woman, given from a position to
which, either on horseback or on foot, they could
have ascended without the smallest difficulty!

Completely frustrated in our endeavours to chas-
tise the authors of our heavy misfortunes, we at
length descended the hill in order to muster the
remnant of our ill-fated teams; and little less
melancholy was the prospect that there awaited us.
Exclusive of the old cow, and the equally useless
black bull, neither of which were touched, seventeen
drooping wounded wretches, with glazed eyes, and
fallen crest, were huddled together—some shivering
in the last agonies of death—and many others
barely able to rise. In addition to sundry wounds
which had been inflicted by our merciless and ma-
licious foes whilst urging them across the plain,
the unfortunate animals had recently received many
cold-blooded gashes, bestowed, apparently, with
the design of rendering them unserviceable to us;
and, thus crippled, it was not without infinite labour
and difficulty that we eventually succeeded in
driving them to the camp, which we reached long
after the sun had sunk in the west. On our way
thither, visiting the demon kraal, we found a filthy
area, inclosed by masses of rock heaped together
by the hand of nature, and overgrown with wild
olives; but inhabited only by meagre curs, which
had been left, by the vindictive sprites, to guard,

during their absence, from the assaults of vultures, the garbage and putrid skins with which the trees were festooned.

Taking a review of the whole of this unfortunate affair, it was poor consolation to reflect that the catastrophe had been brought about by a tissue of the grossest neglect, pusillanimity, and mismanagement on the part of our followers. Next to the inexcusable want of vigilance, and subsequent credulity of Andries, in which the whole mischief had originated, came the needless and provoking loss of time on the morning of the 4th, followed by an extraordinary lack of energy and zeal, on the part of the Hottentots who were sent in quest of the truants. The retreat of the marauders, whose adroitness in driving off cattle has already been noticed, was doubtless greatly favoured by the undulating character of the ground; but if instead of plodding on the trail, the mounted men had galloped in advance, and reconnoitred the country, there can be no doubt that the event would have been widely different. An examination of the footmarks showed that Piet, in the first instance, without any reason whatever, had turned back when. actually within a quarter of a mile of the plunderers, whom he must have seen had he ridden to the brow of the next eminence. And even after the golden opportunity of retaking the greater portion of our oxen had been thrown away through the cowardice of Andries and Cobus—still the day might have been retrieved, had those doughty characters been persuaded to accompany me to the hill, as I repeatedly urged them to do. In the end, it appeared that the former of these worthies had some days before sold his ox to the latter for a stipulated sum, which was to be paid on arrival at Graaff Reinet; and never was their apathy and indifference to the interest of their masters more perfectly illustrated than on the present occasion—the irreparable loss which we, through their agency, had sustained, being totally merged in a dispute which had arisen between the two principal delinquents as to which was to be considered the owner and loser of the one-eyed *Mutlee*.

It rained pitilessly during the night, and in the morning three of our oxen were stiff and cold, four others being quite unable to rise. The accursed women, who had in a great measure been instrumental to this disastrous state of affairs, had nevertheless in some degree assisted us in finding the remedy—the pretty Bush-girl having informed us that there was a boor's habitation about two days' journey to the westward of our camp. To that quarter every eye had been anxiously turned; and as another cheerless evening closed upon us, unusual columns of dust which arose in the distant horizon, appeared to be indicative of flocks returning from pasture. It was therefore resolved that I should set forth immediately in that direction in search of assistance, leaving Richardson to proceed to a point agreed upon, at whatever pace six suffering oxen could transport our heavy vans; and that failing to discover the farmer's residence, of which even the existence was extremely uncertain, I should make the best of my way to the Colony, now probably less than one hundred miles distant, whence, having procured fresh teams, I could return to the relief of the wreck with all practicable expedition.

CHAPTER XXXVII.

EXCURSION ON HORSEBACK IN QUEST OF ASSIST-ANCE, AND MEETING WITH THE EMIGRANT FARMERS.

So dreadfully had our horses suffered during the late campaign, that it was with considerable difficulty I succeeded in selecting from the whole drove, three that appeared fit for service. With these, and a good supply of ammunition, I set out on the morning of the 8th of January, attended by Andries, and joyfully turned my back upon the disastrous hill, near which we had been so long spell-bound. Proceeding several miles to the westward, we ascended a high barren range, overlooking an extensive valley, and soon discovered that the columns of dust which had been greeted as the harbingers of relief from our misfortunes, were occasioned by the mad careering of troops of gnoos. Thus disappointed, we swept round to the southward, and night closing in after we had ridden about forty miles, we lay down to sleep in an olive brake, on the bank of a small stream. It rained very heavily for some hours, and the bushes not keeping out the water, rather added to than diminished the discomfort, so that I had sufficient reason to rejoice at the return of daylight. Continuing our search in

parallel lines along the heights, I reconnoitered the
whole country through a telescope, and after
having been twice deceived by herds of spring-bucks,
at length discovered a *veritable* flock of sheep,
grazing in a distant valley. Overjoyed at the discovery, I hastened towards the spot, and turning
the flank of a detached range, a most cheering
prospect was suddenly opened to my view. Forty
Dutch colonists, with their kith and kin, were encamped on the banks of the Calf river, where it
wound between two ranges of hills; the assemblage
of snow-white waggon-tilts, around which herds of
oxen and droves of horses were grazing, imparting
to the animating scene the appearance of a country
fair. Several women, attended by their husbands,
were washing linen in the river, but as both sexes
declined holding any communication with me, I
rode up to the nearest tent, and learnt from a slave
boy that it belonged to Christian Breck. Pipe in
mouth, the portly *Baas*, or master, presently sallied
forth, and after the customary salutation, I inquired
how many days' journey it was to the Great river.
Instead of receiving any reply to this question, however, I was elaborately catechised as to my age,
name, residence, calling, destination, and domestic
history. The mention of " Sillekat's land," while
it elicited an oath, and an exclamation of surprise,
procured me also an invitation to " saddle off;" and
walking with mine host into the pall, I was minutely
scrutinized through a pair of spectales by the
good *vrouw*, who was seated, agreeably to colonial

custom, with her feet over a warming-pan. Neither
my ragged and weather-beaten appearance, nor my
patriarchal beard, were pleasing to the old lady
on first acquaintance, but as I was now an accomplished Dutch scholar, we speedily became better
friends; and after I had patiently satisfied *her*
curiosity also, on all points connected with my
private biography, a Hottentot girl was directed to
set before me a plateful of mutton bones drowned
in Chili vinegar; to which savory dish the mistress
added an apology for the absence of bread. Over
this frugal meal, I detailed my misfortunes, which
provoked but little sympathy, although the offer of
a bribe in tea and snuff readily induced Mynheer
Breck to desire his son and nephew to accompany
me with two *spans* of oxen, for the purpose of
bringing up the waggons. Several other boors
joining the party whilst the preparations were
being made, I fortunately succeeded in hiring a
couple of horses from them, my own three being
completely exhausted.

Escorted by my young Dutch friends, with two
frisky teams, which had been selected from their numerous well-conditioned herds, I again set forth at
two o'clock, to rejoin my wrecked fellow-traveller,
who, advancing at a snail's pace, was not a little
rejoiced at my speedy return. We encamped, from
necessity, about eight miles south of the execrated
hill, upon which the Hottentots, with a design of
perpetuating their chivalrous exploits, had conferred
the appellation of *Bushman's Kop*. It again brought

us evil fortune. The timidity of our little flock of sheep had increased in the ratio of their reduction in numerical strength; and during this night, all efforts to keep them near the waggons proving abortive, they dashed for the last time into the wilderness, and we saw them no more. Leaving Frederick to hunt for his truant charge, we pursued our journey at a merry pace in the morning, and after experiencing much difficulty in crossing the Calf river, the bottom of which is extremely muddy, we reached the *trek-boor's* encampment. Like most of the Cape colonists, our juvenile allies held English men and English rifles in equal contempt; and until I had shot two gnoos for their edification, at four hundred yards, were not to be persuaded that a barrel under four feet in length, or of smaller calibre than their own clumsy *roers*, could be of the slightest avail. The gnoo and spring-buck, although still abundant, had become now so exceedingly wild from constant persecution, that during the rest of our journey I found it requisite to display a red handkerchief on the muzzle of my rifle, in order to inveigle the former within shot. This exhibition invariably produced the most violent excitement, and caused the herd to charge past in single file, with mane erect and blazing eye —following their leader—flinging out their heels, lashing their tails, and butting with their horns in so menacing a manner, that I was not unfrequently compelled to strike my colours.

Our object now being to recruit our teams and lighten the waggons of all redundant stores, we lost

not a moment in opening a *winkel*, or shop—propos-
ing to exchange, for oxen, either tea, sugar, snuff,
meal, lead, or gunpowder.   But although these articles were all in especial demand, we found it impossible to negociate by barter—that being a mode of
dealing which, strange to say, they appeared quite
unable to comprehend.   After repeatedly shaking
the wheels of our admirable waggons, in order to
ascertain whether they " ran lightly," we received
many generous offers of shattered rickety vehicles,
with a few indifferent oxen, in exchange for them;
but ultimately we found ourselves obliged to refer to
our treasury, which fortunately still containing two
hundred and fifty rix dollars, we were enabled to
purchase a few head of cattle to begin with—receiving back the cash in payment for our wares, and
again disbursing it for more oxen—until, having realized the requisite number, we had still ten shillings
left in our pockets to carry us to Graaff Reinet.

In the course of conversation at a tea-party given
to the ladies and gossips of the Dutch camp, we
learnt that they had left Colesberg three months before, and were on their way to join the emigrants,
who were assembled at the head of the Modder river,
near the Rev. Mr. Archbell's missionary station at
Thaba Uncha, lying about two days' journey eastward of the scene of our catastrophe.   The men
spoke in the most contemptuous terms of Moselekatse, regarding whom, nevertheless, they were very
inquisitive; informing us that they were awaiting the
return of a commando under *Gert Maritz*, our

Graaff Reinet acquaintance, who had marched some time before to invade the Matabili territories and crush the despot. I must add also, that the circumstance of *our* having been well received by his Majesty, and suffered to escape with our lives—while it elicited every one's astonishment, appeared also to create a general feeling of jealousy and dissatisfaction.

Again there was a drenching rain all night, and two more of our finest oxen being completely powerless from their wounds, we presented them to young Breck, in part acknowledgment for his father's assistance, and pursued our journey on the morning of the 11th. Even to the colonial boundary, we had still a weary distance before us, and grass was represented to be extremely scarce; but we now travelled with fresh oxen along a beaten waggon road, an accommodation to which we had been stangers for several months. In the course of the forenoon, we were met by a farmer from Beaufort, on the Karroo, with a Hottentot *achter ryder*, or footman, going to *kek*, as he called it, or in other words, to see how the emigrants were likely to thrive, before selling his own farm. On learning that we were from Sillekat's land, his first question was, " How the Kafirs had happened to let us come out in a sound skin?" And this, in fact, wherever we went, was the theme of wonder and astonishment— few being able to understand the difference between conciliating a savage with presents, and entering his territories uninvited.

In the course of this day's journey, which occupied nine hours, we crossed the Reit river, and
were rejoined by Frederick, who reported that he
had seen the remnant of our flock safe in the hands
of a party of Bushmen, whom, although mounted
and armed himself, he durst not approach.   It was
waxing late, when volumes of dust attracted our
attention to countless flocks of sheep that were being
driven from pasture; following which, and entering
a gorge in the hills, an astounding panorama burst
upon the sight.   A lone green valley, which stretched
between two ranges of rocky hills, lay extended before us, and, covered in every direction with white
waggon-tilts, canvas-palls, bell-tents, oxen, horses,
sheep, and human beings, literally presented the
appearance of the encampment of a goodly army.
Having obtained permission from a Dutchman
named *Humans* to unyoke in an unoccupied spot,
we again opened our *negotie winkel;* but, coming
from Moselekatse's country by the forbidden route,
every one appeared suspicious of our object, and
declined to barter their oxen.   The next morning,
however (the 12th), being on our journey some
miles, we were overtaken by a youth with pack-
horses, who came from the emigrant camp provided with monies for the purchase of leaden balls,
of which munition, notwithstanding the lavish expenditure during the campaign, we had still a
plentiful supply.

Advancing, we passed several filthy kraals of
Griquas, under *Dam Kok,* a hybrid chieftain re-

siding at Phillipolis; and halting for an hour at one of them, the fellows clamorously demanded to see the portrait of their arch enemy, which they understood from the Hottentots I had brought. The Napoleon of Southern Africa having been accordingly exhibited at the end of the waggon, they spit at, and offered him every indignity—their captain, a diabolical looking ruffian, whose head had been turned by "the schoolmaster" at his elbow, logically inquiring, in reply to our remonstrances, " whether he had not as good a right to put us to death for shooting ducks on his tank, without paying for the same, as Moselekatse to destroy the Griquas who hunted *zeekoes* in the Likwa?" They at last became so exceedingly insolent and overbearing, that we were fain to decamp ; and Cobus and April, who had contrived to obtain some brandy from their countrywomen, attempting to desert at the same time, we narrowly escaped adding the whole of our horses to the catalogue of our losses.

Great had been the pointing of fingers, and long and loud the discussions touching the geographical position of Phillipolis—one declaring his conviction that it still bore to the south-east, and another to the south-west. About sunset, however, having now achieved upwards of three hundred and fifty miles, in a straight line from the Cashan mountains, a peak rose to view, which, being unanimously recognized, and acknowledged to mark the position of the missionary station, was hailed, as a beacon on the sea-shore is hailed by mariners after a long and danger-

ous voyage.   Our followers were now as bold as
lions; and an unusually diminutive Bushman in-
judiciously presenting himself with the humble salutation of " *Goen-dakha, tabakka*," ("Good morrow,
gentlemen, some tobacco if you please,") Piet un-
corked his indignation—let off the superfluous foam
in a volley of oaths and anathemas, levelled against
the whole race—and finally chastised the luckless
individual of it with the long waggon-whip within
an inch of his life.   Twenty-five miles the following
day brought us to an extensive lodge of Griquas,
under Captain Abraham Barend, where we passed
the night, and in exchange for tea and snuff, obtained
from the civil old man the luxuries of fowls and
milk, to which we had so long been entire strangers.

CHAPTER XXXVIII.

RETURN TO CIVILIZATION, AND ARRIVAL IN THE CAPE COLONY.

On the afternoon of the 14th, having advanced some sixteen miles through a dreadful storm of dust, which literally darkened the atmosphere, the rushing of mighty waters suddenly announced our approach to the Great River. Hastening to the bank, our mortification may be imagined at perceiving, from the agitated and muddy tide, and the drift-wood which was borne past by the impetuosity of the current, that it had only just become swollen. A farmer had brought over his light horse waggon with some difficulty a quarter of an hour before, but to cross now was impossible. Two tedious days were passed in watching the willowed banks—the troubled waters now subsiding sufficiently to tantalize us with the prospect of being shortly able to pass over, and again receiving a fresh accession of the turbid element. Andries, who was in the bosom of his family, bore the calamity without a murmur, until certain misdeeds, committed when sent from Bok's Fontein in pursuit of the truant horses, accidentally transpiring—even he was unable longer to bear the detention, and he then obligingly informed us of the existence of a

Q

raft, a few miles higher up the river, of which he
had hitherto carefully kept us in ignorance.   Proceeding thither, we found the river straightened,
between rocky sides, to one-third of its usual breadth;
and after we had bribed a man to swim across in
order to summon the proprietor of the *float*, whose
house was some miles distant, our waggons were
at length taken to pieces, and transported wheel
by wheel, into the colony.   This tedious operation
occupied an entire day, and so frightfully · strong
was the current, that in bringing the oxen across,
poor *Whitefoot*, the only survivor of our *Naudé*
team, that till now had escaped unscathed, and had
never once failed us during our long pilgrimage,
was clumsily forced under the raft, and drowned.
Some consolation, however, was to be derived from
the information that our loss was comparatively
trifling, a loaded waggon having a short time before
slipped off the raft, and gone bodily to the bottom.

At length then, we were fairly standing upon
the civilized ground of the Hantam.   Loud was
the shouting and huzzaing, and many were the
discharges of musketry, that proclaimed the fact,
of which, however, the inhospitable conduct of an
insolent boor, named Pienaar, at whose farm we
passed the night, might almost have rendered us
sceptical.   Not a blade of grass met the eye from
this moment; and as we were penniless, we could
only obtain, with difficulty, provisions in exchange
for tea, sugar, and tar; which last, being used in the
composition for greasing the wheels (an operation

which it was found necessary to perform every other day), was fortunately in great demand amongst the boors. Every Hottentot now tricked himself out in ostrich plumes, and dragged to light some hidden article of finery which had been reserved against his return amongst his clansmen, for whose especial edification he had also prepared right wondrous tales of his deeds in arms, and his perils by field and flood. The town of Colesberg being known to possess a licensed retailer of ardent spirits, we preferred passing the night of the 18th without water, to visiting it; but after all, it was only by frequent pointed allusions to field cornets, and clerks of the peace, that the impatient and thirsty souls were prevented from absconding thither.

Blending their craggy summits with the passing clouds, the lofty Sneuwbergen next rose to view; and on the 21st we struck into the high road near Dassies' Fontein, where we had the happiness of finding our ancient Kafir acquaintance inhaling his *dacca* with unabated industry. Our followers, more fantastically arrayed than a band of banditti, were here unexpectedly met by a party of their cronies with waggons from Graaff Reinet, who greeted them as men risen from the dead, with the astounding intelligence that a report had gone forth in the colony of our whole party having been put to death by the king. It was known that we were in the neighbourhood of the emigrants at the time of their massacre, and so long a time having elapsed without any tidings being received of our safety, the

Q 2

tongue of rumour had not been idle. Our colonial
friends, who had entertained so contemptuous an
idea of our travelling capabilities, were by no means
unprepared for this dismal intelligence, which had
spread far and wide, and was even credited at the
Cape. Unimportant though it may appear, it had
nevertheless proved the death-blow to the domestic
happiness of most of our followers—their faithless
consorts having soon forgotten their plighted vows,
and embraced the earliest opportunity of casting
aside their widow's weeds. The report was subsequently traced to a Lothario from the frontier,
who had actually backed the offer of his hand and
heart to Ethaldur's relict, with the assurance that
he had himself performed the last melancholy offices
for her husband, to whose corpse the infidels had
offered indignities too barbarous to be here recorded.

Sixty-nine casualties had already occurred
amongst our oxen; and on the 24th another
victim being left in the Sneuwbergen, we had
barely a sufficient number remaining to drag our
waggons into the village of Graaff Reinet. This
dreadful mortality, although partly attributable to
the rapidity of our march, which will have been
estimated from the extent of ground we passed over
—was owing in a still greater measure to the neglect and cowardice of the Hottentots, and eventually
swelled the expenses of the expedition to £800
sterling. But it is proper to state, for the information of those of my Indian friends who may resolve
upon such a campaign, that by entertaining a suffi-

cient number of Europeans to keep the Hottentots
in awe, and employing also a third waggon to
carry out grain for the best horses, as well as to
bring back ivory and rare quadrupeds to the colony,
the expedition might be made to cover its own
expenses. In addition to the sable antelope,
which had travelled the whole way on my cot, and
was—besides being a most unenviable bed-fellow—a
source of constant anxiety, my collection consisted
of two perfect crania of every species of game quadruped to be found in Southern Africa, together with
skins of the lion, quagga, zebra, ostrich, &c., tails
of the cameleopard, and tusks of elephants and
hippopotami, besides elaborate drawings of every
animal that interests the sportsman, from the tall
giraffe to the minutest antelope.

The unlooked for return of the "two Indian
gentlemen" from the interior, together with the exhibition of these creditable trophies, most of which
were novelties to the oldest resident, created a considerable revolution of sentiment in our favour;
hundreds who twelve months before had shaken
their heads at our projected expedition, now declaring that had they only been aware of our intention
of visiting "the terror of the interior," (whose
portrait was not considered the least attractive of
our curiosities,) nothing on earth should have deterred them from taking part in so interesting an
adventure. There is doubtless a wide difference
betwixt setting out and returning, but I can assure
these enterprising travellers, that unless the track-

less desert hath charms for me, which it would not
possess in the eyes of the less enthusiastic, they would
have found no cause to repent of their rashness.
To all others I prefer a life of adventure—its very
privations, when coupled with scenes such as I have
attempted to describe, constituting an excitement
peculiarly adapted to my humour.   The tracts
through which we travelled extending into the tem-
perate zone, and being surrounded also on three
sides by the ocean, while they possess the advantage
of a moderate climate, are the nursery of the noblest
quadrupeds.   There was something truly soul-
stirring and romantic in wandering among these
free-born denizens of the desert—realizing as it
were a new creation, in regions hitherto seldom, if
ever, trodden by white man's foot.   During the
whole period that we were absent from the colony,
I never once omitted to take the field at break of
day, or as soon after as the weather would permit,
frequently preparing my own breakfast, and never
returning unladen with spoils.   Firmly determined
to bring back correct delineations of the whole of
the feræ naturæ inhabiting Africa, south of the
tropic, I never moved without drawing materials
in my hunting-cap, and during brief cessations from
hostilities, found ample employment for the pencil
instead of the rifle.

Although the Indian traveller, who has been accustomed to the accommodation afforded by tents
and retinue, can form little conception of the ten
thousand difficulties, distresses, and drawbacks,

that beset the wanderer in the African desert, he is nevertheless, from his locomotive habits, and experience in oriental travelling, far more capable of overcoming them than the lethargic and home-loving natives of the colony, or those less skilled in the art. Nearly all my sketches were made under a bush in the open air, and completed on my knees in the waggon amid rain and wind—the zoological specimens, which I had in the first instance realized and brought home myself, being subsequently prepared with my own hand. Nothing could exceed the annoyance given by the Hottentots, whose indolence and indifference throughout the journey, obliged us frequently to rise during the night—the rain, which pursued us whithersoever we went, heightening in no small degree the discomforts we experienced. Nor shall I deny that we sometimes sighed for the luxuries to which we had been accustomed; bread and meat, with simple tea or coffee, forming for many months our monotonous diet. But in spite of all these hardships and privations, toilsome and tedious as our journey frequently was, across deserts of utterly hopeless sterility, we were more than amply repaid by the unparalleled magnificence of the sport that we enjoyed; and I can safely aver, that some of the happiest days of my existence have been passed in the wilds of Africa. They form a passage in my life which time can never efface from the tablet of my recollection—a green spot in memory's waste, to which, in after years, I shall revert with intense and unabating pleasure.

CHAPTER XXXIX.

SKETCH OF THE EMIGRATION OF THE BORDER COLONISTS.

THE abandonment of the Cape Colony by the old Dutch inhabitants, to which I have so frequently had occasion to allude, and which has in fact become completely interwoven with the thread of my narrative, has no parallel in the history of British colonial possessions. Partial emigrations are by no means uncommon, as the existence of the colony itself sufficiently proves, but here is an instance of a body of between *five and six thousand* souls, who have with one accord abandoned the land of their nativity, and the homes of their forefathers—endeared to them by every interesting association—and have recklessly plunged into the pathless wilds of the interior; braving the perils and hardships of the wilderness, and, many of them already in the vale of years, seeking out for themselves another dwelling-place in a strange and inhospitable soil.

The first question that presents itself must naturally be, what has led to so extraordinary an expatriation? The losses to which they have been subjected by the emancipation of their slaves; the absence of laws for their protection from the evils of uncontrolled vagrancy, and from the depredations of the swarm of vagabonds by which the colony is infested; but, above all, the insecure state of the eastern frontier, and the inadequate protection afforded by the English Government against the aggressions of their wily and restless Kafir neighbours, by whose repeated predatory incursions the fairest spots have been laid desolate, and many hundreds of the border colonists reduced to ruin, are the inciting causes assigned by the emigrants for the unprecedented and hazardous step they have taken.

If it be impossible to view the violent remedy sought by these oppressed but misguided men in other than a criminal light, yet no unprejudiced person, who has visited the more remote districts of this unhappy colony, will hesitate to acknowledge that the evils they complain of actually exist. Long subjected to the pilferings of a host of Hottentot vagrants, whose lives are passed in one perpetual round of idleness, delinquency, and brutish intoxication on the threshold of the gin-shop, the South African settler has lately, in too many instances, been reduced from comparative affluence to want, by being unseasonably, and without adequate compensation, bereft of the services of his slaves—who, prone to villany, and no longer compelled to labour, have only served to swell the swarm of drones by which it is his destiny to be persecuted. Far greater than these, however, are the evils that have arisen out of the perverse misrepresentations of canting and designing men, to whose mischievous and gratuitous interference, veiled under the cloak of philanthropy, is principally to be attributed the desolated condition of the eastern frontier; bounded, as it is, by a dense and almost impenetrable jungle, to defend which nine times the military force now employed would barely be adequate; and flanked by a population of eighty thousand dire, irreclaimable savages, naturally inimical, warlike, and predatory, by whom the hearths of the Cape border colonists have for years past been deluged with the blood of their nearest and dearest relatives. And whilst, during the unprovoked inroads of these ruthless barbarians, their wives and helpless offspring have been mercilessly butchered before their eyes; whilst their corn-fields have been laid waste, their flocks swept off, and their houses reduced to ruins, to add bitterness to gall, they have been taunted as the authors of their own misfortunes, by those who, strangely biassed by *ex parte* statements, have judged them unheard, at the distance of several thousand miles from the scene of pillage, bloodshed, and devastation.

It does indeed furnish matter of amazement to every thinking person, how such a state of things should so long have been suffered to exist; how those who have legislated for the affairs of the Colony should not long ago have seen the imperious necessity, dictated alike by reason, justice, and humanity, of exterminating from off the face of the earth, a race of monsters, who, being the unprovoked destroyers, and implacable foes of Her

Majesty's Christian subjects, have forfeited every claim to mercy or consideration. Denied redress, however, and deprived of the power of avenging themselves of the wrong under which they have writhed, in utter hopelessness of recovering their property, or even enjoying future tranquillity, the border colonists have at length thrown off the yoke of their allegiance; and whilst seeking out for themselves an asylum in other lands, are now retorting upon our allies the injuries they have so long sustained at home.

My visit to Moselekatse, and subsequent return by the hitherto unexplored route of the Vaal River, afforded me opportunities of observing the proceedings beyond the boundary, of these voluntary exiles, and of making myself acquainted with their position in relation to the numerous native tribes, by which they are surrounded. Neither being correctly understood, I shall endeavour, as briefly as possible, to trace their steps from the commencement of the emigration.

Weary of the insecurity of their homes, several of the frontier farmers, who had heard much of the soil and capabilities of Port Natal, resolved to decide for themselves on the accuracy of these reports, and forming a large party, with ten or twelve waggons, proceeded to explore the country. So well pleased were they with what they saw, that they formed a determination of locating themselves in that neighbourhood, and returned forthwith for their families, when the breaking out of the last

Kafir war obliged them to postpone the execution of their design.

Shortly after the conclusion of hostilities, the first party of actual emigrants, consisting of about thirty families, left the colony under the guidance of an Albany farmer, named Louis Triechard. Being desirous of eluding the Kafir tribes, they proceeded across the Great River in a north-easterly direction, skirting the mountain chain which divides Caffraria from Bechuana Land; with the intention, when they had cleared it, of turning to the eastward, and gaining the neighbourhood of Port Natal. The features presented by this barrier are rugged and forbidding in the extreme; they have the appearance of innumerable pyramidical hills thrown together in the most grotesque and disorderly manner: one peak jutting beyond, or soaring above the other, as though precluding the possibility of any human foot, much less any wheeled vehicle, from passing over; and, from the imperfect knowledge possessed by the wanderers, of that section of Southern Africa, the geography of which is still veiled in considerable obscurity, they were led by the course of the mountains far beyond the latitude of Port Natal, and found themselves, about the end of May 1836, in a fertile but uninhabited waste, lying between the 26th and 27th parallels of south latitude, on the eastern banks of the large and beautiful river, noticed in a former part of this Narrative, which flows sluggishly through a level tract in a north-easterly direction, and is said to join the Oori, or

Limpopo, and discharge its water into the Bay of
Delagoa.

From this point, in order to reach the unoccupied
country about Natal, it would have been necessary
to traverse the whole length of Dingaan's dominions,
a journey fraught with difficulties of the most formidable kind, and opposed by a climate of the most
destructive character.   And, as the newly discovered
country was abundantly watered, abounding in game,
and affording all the materials requisite for building,
the further progress of the emigrants was for the
present discontinued.

The example thus set by Louis Triechard was
speedily followed by many of his countrymen.   Numerous parties were formed on the frontier by the
border colonists, who, with their families and flocks,
crossed the Great River, and dived into the very
depths of the wilderness, with no very clear idea
perhaps of what their ultimate destination was to
be, but yet firmly determined to abandon their
native hearths for ever, and to fix their future residence in some distant land.   For the sake of obtaining pasturage for their numerous herds, and in
opposition to the advice of the Missionaries through
whose stations they passed, by whom they were
warned of the imminent risk that they would incur
from the native tribes, they scattered themselves
heedlessly along the luxuriant banks of the Likwa
or Vaal river, with the design of remaining until
the country in advance should be explored, and their
plans digested and arranged.

About the end of May, two parties, headed by
J. S. Bronkhorst, and H. Potgeiter, left the emigrant camp for the purpose of exploring the country
to the north-eastward. They visited Louis Triechard
at the Zout-pans-berg, or Salt-pan-hill, and penetrated sixteen days' journey beyond, through a lovely,
fertile, and unoccupied country, until they arrived
within six day's journey of Delagoa Bay, where
they met with two sons of the notorious Conrad
Buys, living amongst a friendly tribe of natives,
whom, from a peculiarity in the nasal prominence,
they dignified with the appellation of "knob-nosed
Kafirs." Returning hence by a nearer route with
the account of their success, and of the discovery of
a land flowing with milk and honey, they found
their camp totally deserted, and the ground strewed
with the mutilated bodies of their friends and rela-
tions! The migratory farmers had been attacked
three days before, by Moselekatse, and twenty-eight
of their number had been butchered.

It will have been seen, from the foregoing pages,
that the country over which this powerful and despotic prince claims sovereignty, is of great extent,
and is bounded on the south by the Likwa, or Vaal
river, one of the two principal branches of the Gareep. From that direction he had been repeatedly
attacked by Jan Bloem, a notorious and often successful freebooter, and by other leaders of predatory
bands of Griquas, who had scoured his territories,
and swept away his cattle. In 1831, it has been
shown, he was last attacked by a strong commando

of Barend Barend's Griquas, who succeeded in obtaining possession of the whole of the Matabili herds; and, all the regular warriors of Moselekatse being absent at the time on an expedition to the northward, the ruin of the tribe had nearly been accomplished. Owing, however, to a want of proper precaution on the part of the invaders, they were signally defeated by a mere handful of irregulars, who attacked them during the night, and ere the day dawned, had slaughtered the greater part of them.

Since that occurrence, Moselekatse had publicly and positively prohibited any trader or traveller from visiting him, or entering his territories from that quarter: whilst, to guard against the inroads of his enemies, strong armed parties were frequently sent to scour the country watered by the Likwa. But, on the other hand, he declared his willingness to receive as friends, those visiters who might find it convenient to approach him by way of Kuruman, or New Litakoo, having the most implicit confidence in Mr. Moffat, the enlightened Missionary at that station, through whose assistance only they could effect an entrance.

Can it be wondered at, under these circumstances, that Moselekatse should have viewed with a jealous and suspicious eye, the sudden advance of so formidable a body of strangers from the forbidden quarter, to the very borders, if not actually within, the confines of his territories? Without so fair a pretext as their open defiance of his commands afforded him, would it have been surprising that the

temptation afforded by the fat flocks and herds of
his new, opulent, and very unceremonious neighbours, should have induced the despot to impart a
lesson which might inculcate the necessity of at least
propitiating him with presents, which are known
to be the only sure road to the friendship or good
offices of a savage?   Towards the close of August,
a commando, consisting of about five hundred Matabili warriors, was despatched from Mosega *for this
very purpose.*   On their way to plunder the emigrants, who were encamped in scattered detachments
along the Vaal River, they accidentally fell in with
Stephanus Erasmus, who had been on a hunting
expedition still farther to the northward, and was
then on his return to the colony by the forbidden
route.   Arriving at his waggons in the evening with
one of his sons, and finding them surrounded by a
host of armed savages, he precipitately fled to the
nearest emigrant camp, about five hours' ride on
horseback from his own, where, having succeeded
in persuading a party of eleven farmers to accompany
him, he returned towards the spot.   On the way
thither they were met by the barbarians, whose impetuous onsets obliged them to seek refuge within
the encampment.   A severe struggle ensued, but the
enemy were finally repulsed with great slaughter,
and the loss, on the part of the farmers, of only one
man named Bronkhorst.

This was, however, but the prelude to a more
bloody tragedy.   A party of the Matabili soldiers
had in the mean time detached itself from the main

body, and fallen upon nine other waggons that were assembled at a distance from the principal camp. The waggons were saved, but the greater part of the flocks and herds were carried off, and twenty-four persons massacred—viz., Barend Liebenberg, sen. Stephanus, Hendrick, and Barend Liebenberg, jun. Johannes de Toit, an English schoolmaster named M'Donald, Mrs. H. Liebenberg, Mrs. de Toit, four children, and twelve black servants.

Six days after this catastrophe, Erasmus's curiosity prompted him to ascertain the fate of his family and property. Proceeding to the spot, he found the bodies of his five black slaves, and could distinguish the wheel-tracks of his five waggons going in a northerly direction. Two of his sons, and a youth named Carel Kruger, had been taken prisoners, and it was afterwards ascertained, that having attempted to effect their escape, they were mercilessly put to death on their way to the king.

CHAPTER XL.

EMIGRATION OF THE BORDER COLONISTS, CONCLUDED.

ALMOST immediately after this disastrous occurrence, being rejoined by the parties that had proceeded to explore the north-east country, the migratory farmers fell back about four days' journey from their first position to the south side of the Vaal river; and encamped near the embouchure of the Donkin—one of its principal tributaries, called by the natives the Nama-Hari. Here they remained in blind and fancied security, without taking any steps towards an amicable understanding with the king, until the end of October. They had scarcely recovered from the confusion into which they had been thrown by the first attack, when, to their great consternation, they received intimation of the near approach of another and far more formidable body of Moselekatse's warriors. Retreat being impossible, they sedulously applied themselves to fortifying their position. They drew up their fifty waggons in a compact circle, closing the apertures between and beneath them with thorn-bushes, which they firmly lashed with leathern thongs to the wheels and *dissel-booms* ;* and constructing within the enclosure so formed, a smaller one for the protec-

* Waggon-poles.

tion of the women and children. These arrangements
hastily completed, they rode forth to confront the
enemy, whom they presently met in number about
five thousand on their march towards the camp,
when some skirmishing took place, in which several
of the Matabili were slain. It has already been
remarked that their principal weapon is a short
spear, or assagai, termed *unkonto,* which is not
thrown, as with the Kafir tribes, but used for stabbing, for which purpose they rush in at once upon
their opponents. Terrible as is this mode of fighting
to unwarlike nations, it is calculated to effect little
against muskets in the hands of cavalry. Their
numbers and impetuosity, however, rendering it
impossible to keep them from the waggons, the
farmers retired within the enclosure; where, by the
time their guns were cleansed, they were furiously
assailed by the barbarian horde, who, with savage
yells and hideous war-cries, poured down like locusts
upon the encampment. Closing around the circle,
and charging the *abattis* with determined resolution,
again and again did they endeavour to break through
the line, or clamber over the awnings of the waggons.
Dealing however, with men whose lives were the
stake, their attacks were as constantly repelled.
Repeated volleys of slugs and buck-shot, discharged
at arm's length from the heavy bores of the besieged,
ploughed through their crowded ranks;

> " Even as they fell, in files they lay,
>   Like the mower's grass at the close of day,
>   When his work is done on the levell'd plain;
> Such was the fall of the foremost slain."

A desperate struggle of fifteen minutes terminated in their discomfiture. Hurling their javelins into the enclosure, they retired in confusion over the heaps of slain, leaving upwards of one hundred and fifty of their number dead or disabled on the field.

In this affair, which took place on the 29th October, Nicholaas Potgeiter and Piet Botha were killed behind the stockade, and twelve other farmers were severely wounded. The assault was led in person by Kalipi, Moselekatse's principal captain, and most confidential counsellor. Although shot through the knee, he contrived to make good his retreat, nor did he retire empty-handed; the whole of the flocks and herds of the emigrants, amounting to six thousand head of cattle, and forty-one thousand sheep and goats, being swept away by the barbarians, and safely conducted to Kapain. Remounting their horses, the farmers took advantage of the retreat of their savage foes, to add a few more to the list of slain, until the sun descending below the horizon, let drop the curtain upon the scene of carnage.

This second gentle hint on the part of his Majesty had the desired effect. A portion of the farmers remained with the wreck of the late flourishing camp, whilst others, with all possible haste, conveyed the women and children to the Rev. Mr. Archbell's missionary station at Thaba Uncha; whence, having procured fresh oxen, the whole party fell back, and encamped near the sources of the Modder river. Here their numbers were shortly reinforced by a strong detachment of emigrants under the guidance of Gert Maritz, a wealthy and ambitious burgher, from Graaff Reinet, who soon contrived to cause himself to be elected governor-general. At this period the number of waggons assembled near the populous Barolong village of Thaba Uncha, amounted to about two hundred and fifty, and the number of souls may be estimated at above eighteen hundred.

Maritz's first step, after assuming the reins of government, was to assemble a force for the purpose of retaliating upon the Amazooloo monarch the injuries that the emigrants had received at his hands; but for which, in truth, they had alone to thank their own obstinacy and imprudence. On the 3rd of January, 1837, a commando, consisting of one hundred and seven Dutch farmers, forty of Peter David's mounted Griquas, and sixty armed savages on foot, left Thaba Uncha on their march to invade Moselekatse's country, under the guidance of a warrior, who, having been taken prisoner in the affair of the 29th October, durst never again present himself before his royal master. Keeping considerably to the westward of north, they crossed the head of the Hart river, and struck into the Kuruman road—by this masterly manœuvre approaching the Matabili from the very quarter whence they were least prepared to expect an attack. A lovely and fertile valley, bounded on the north and north-east by the Kurrichane mountains, and in form resembling a basin of ten or twelve miles in circumference, contained the military town of Mosega, and fifteen

other of Moselekatse's principal kraals, in which
resided Kalipi, and a large portion of the fighting
men.   To this spot were the steps of the emigrant
farmers directed.   As the first streaks of light
ushered in the eventful morning of the 17th of January, Maritz's little band suddenly and silently
emerged from a pass in the hills behind the houses
of the American missionaries ; and ere the sun had
reached the zenith, the bodies of four hundred
chosen Matabili warriors, the flower of barbarian
chivalry, garnished the blood-stained valley of Mosega.   Not a creature was aware of the approach of
danger, and the entrance of a rifle-ball by one of the
bed-room windows, was the first intimation received
by the missionaries of the impending onslaught.
One of their domestics, Baba, the converted Bechuana, who, it will be remembered, accompanied the
author to the king's residence in capacity of interpreter, being mistaken for a Zooloo, was hotly
pursued to the river, into which he plunged, hippo-
potamus-like, and narrowly escaped annihilation by
counterfeiting death, after three bullets had whistled
past his protruded head.   So perfect were the military dispositions which the information afforded by
the captive had suggested, that the valley was
completely invested, and no avenue of escape remained.   The Matabili flew to arms at the first
alarm, and bravely defended themselves, but were
shot like sparrows as fast as they appeared outside
of the inclosure, nor did they succeed in perforating
the leathern doublet of a single Dutchman.   But

the star of Moselekatse was still in the ascendant.
At the time of this successful attack he was residing
at Kapain, fifty miles farther to the northward;
and Kalipi, having singularly enough been sum-
moned thither only the day before, escaped the fate
of a large proportion of his brave but unfortunate
followers.

Had Maritz followed up the advantage thus
gained, and marched at once upon Kapain, Moselekatse could not possibly have effected his escape.
Inflated by the recent success of his arms, the
despot was basking in the sunshine of security, little
dreaming of so sudden an invasion. Struck at
that moment, another blow would have completed
the work of destruction, and left the emigrants to
pursue their pilgrimage in safety. Blind, however,
to the obvious course they should have pursued,
and content for the present with what they had
achieved, the boors secured seven thousand head of
cattle, and the waggons that had been taken from
Erasmus, with which they immediately set out on
their return, by forced marches; and, accompanied
by the American missionaries, who, whilst they
reasonably dreaded the summary vengeance of the
exasperated savage, had now no further field for
their labours—arrived in a few days at Thaba
Uncha, without molestation or pursuit on the part
of the Matabili.

Magical indeed was the effect which the news of
this victory produced upon the Dutch colonists. It
fanned the smouldering embers of the epidemic

into a flame, and caused the rage for emigration to
burst forth and spread like wild-fire.   The promise
of land unlimited, and of relief from taxation, tempted
hundreds whose remoteness from the border had
smothered the incentives which actuated the original
projectors of the scheme.   Another class, who, like
the bat in the fable, had been prudently watching
the turn that affairs would take, now openly avowed
their abhorrence of the English rule, and freed
themselves from its trammels.   Some having yielded
to the claims of relationship, went because their
kinsmen had gone; others to gratify their ambition,
their love of adventure, or passion for a nomadic
life; and not a few from a natural desire to participate in the loaves and fishes.   For several weeks
the whole of the frontier line was in a state of
ferment and commotion, and large caravans were
daily to be seen hurrying across the border, and
flocking to the standard of their expatriated countrymen.   In the month of April, Piet Retief, a
gallant and distinguished Field-cornet of the Winter-
berg, who, with a very large cavalcade was encamped
at a distance from Maritz, was induced, after much
entreaty and persuasion, to accept the office of
Governor and Commander-in-chief—a post which
he was eminently qualified to fill, and to which he
was elected by the unanimous voice of the united
emigrants.   He appointed subordinate officers,
enacted wholesome laws, and ratified treaties which
had already been concluded with the neighbouring
native chiefs, the principal of whom are Sikonyela,

king of the Mantatees; Moshesh, chief of the
Basuto; Moroko, chief of the Barolongs at Thaba
Uncha; Tauani, chief of the remnant of the Baharootzi; and Peter David, captain of the Lishuani
Bastards.   This last, it will be remembered, is the
father of Truëy the Griqua maid, and the successor
of Barend Barends, whose exploits have already
been sung.   One and all are the deadly enemies of
Moselekatse, ready to take up arms against him on
the slightest reverse of his fortune.

These arrangements completed, the emigrants
once more advanced towards the scene of their former misfortunes, and in May last (1837), upwards
of one thousand waggons, and sixteen hundred
efficient fighting men, with their wives, families, and
followers, were assembled near the confluence of the
branches of the Vet Rivière.   A commando, consisting of five hundred farmers, was preparing to march
on the 1st June, for the purpose either of arranging
matters with the king, or completely subverting his
power.   This done, their march towards Louis
Triechard's camp will be resumed—there the corner
stone of their city is to be laid, and a NEW AMSTER-
DAM will rear its head in the very heart of the
wilderness.

Such, in a few words, is the history of the emigration of the border colonists—an event which,
while it has materially weakened the north-eastern
frontier, has kindled a flame in the interior which
can be only quenched with blood.   The place
vacated by every Dutch farmer will doubtless be

R

speedily filled by an industrious peasant; and
when the colony shall have recovered from the
first shock, it will probably be found not to have
suffered from the change. Yet, taking a political
view of this important feature in the colonial history,
it cannot but appear extraordinary that so large a
body of disaffected subjects, from what cause soever
their discontent may have arisen, should have been
permitted to detach themselves from their allegiance, and cross the frontier in open defiance of
existing laws—taking with them their slaves, and
forcibly entering the territories of an ally, for the
avowed purpose of establishing themselves in a
position where they might shortly become the
most formidable of our enemies. Fortunately, however, many and insuperable obstacles are arrayed
against the success of their scheme. The golden
opportunity of crushing the formidable viper in
their path is gone; and Moselekatse, having gained
wisdom from the past, is not likely to be assailed
a second time with success. No sooner had the
tidings of his disastrous defeat at Mosega reached
the ears of his hereditary foe Dingaan, than the
Zooloo tyrant despatched an army with orders to
complete what the emigrant farmers had, in his
eyes, so laudably begun. Already harassed by a
long march, in the course of which they had suffered
the severest privations, the invaders were promptly
met by the Matabili, and routed with terrible
slaughter. Taking advantage of the confusion, a
band of vagabond Griquas and Korannas slunk,

jackal-like, into the Amazooloo territories from the westward, and were actually in full retreat with a considerable booty in cattle, when* they too were overtaken by a party of the Matabili warriors, and utterly destroyed. Thus badgered and worried on all sides, the Lion of the North will not again be found sleeping; and granting that the superior strength of the emigrants enables them eventually to despise his opposition, their situation will still be far from enviable. Shut out from Natal, as a sea-port, by their remote location from the coast; and excluded from the advantages of Delagoa Bay by the jealousy of the Portuguese, their supplies, more especially of ammunition, must necessarily be extremely limited. By an old colonial law, the transit of gunpowder across the border is contraband, and by a late Act of Parliament, offences committed within the 25th parallel of south latitude have been rendered capitally cognizable. Their horses must speedily perish by the epidemic already described, and thus precluded from hunting they will become solely dependent for support upon domestic resources. Admitting that intestine dissensions have not already caused a division, the necessity of obtaining pasturage for their numerous herds will shortly compel them to break up into small parties; and want of water, the curse of unhappy Africa, will couple a similar contingency with any attempt at cultivation. Thus situated, the isolated, ammunitionless emigrant will fall an easy prey to the lurking and predatory savage—

repenting, when it is too late, of the folly that induced him to resign himself to the hazards of so wild an adventure.

Much then, as these deluded exiles have already suffered, and deluged as their path has already been with blood, even they can form at present but a very inadequate conception of the dangers and difficulties with which their undertaking is fraught. Hemmed in on one side by Moselekatse, who will never lose sight of the past, but, tiger-like, will watch his opportunity of revenge, with unceasing and savage vigilance; and on the other hand by Dingaan, who cannot fail to regard their obtrusion with more than his wonted jealousy and suspicion; surrounded, too, by a whole host of marauders, who, whatever they may pretend to the contrary, are ever on the alert to enrich themselves at the expense of their more opulent neighbours, the position of the migratory farmers can hardly be said to be improved by the step they have taken. They have cast off the yoke of a government which they felt burthensome, and whilst they flourish, are the judges and the avengers of their own cause. But to an unprejudiced observer, their path would seem strewed with difficulties, and beset with perils. Thus far their course has been marked with blood, and with blood must it be traced to its termination, either in their own destruction, or in that of thousands of the native population of Southern Africa.

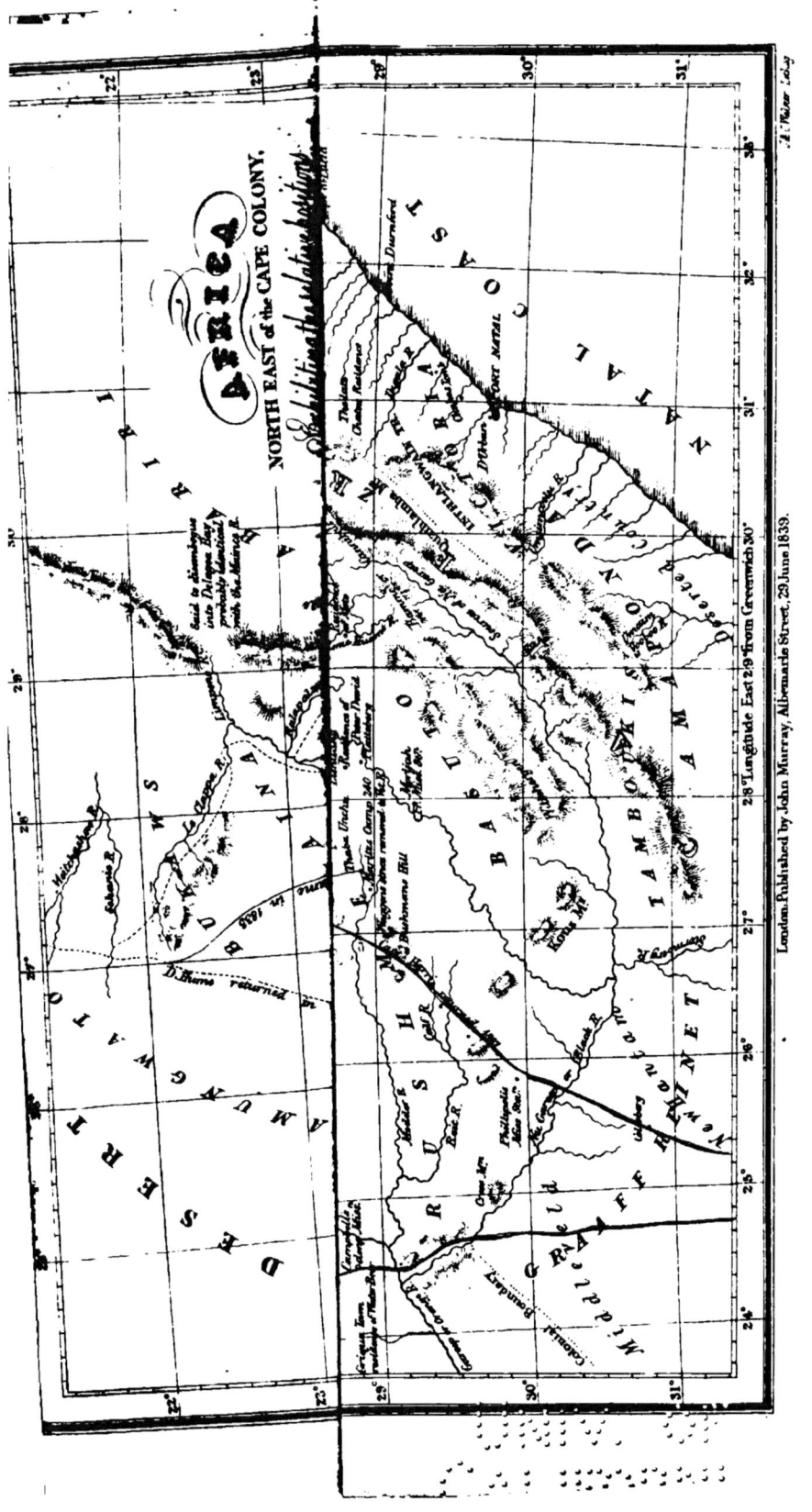

AFRICA

NORTH EAST of the CAPE COLONY.

London, Published by John Murray, Albemarle Street, 29 June 1839.

2.8 Longitude East 2.9 from Greenwich 30°

APPENDIX.

DESCRIPTION OF THE FERÆ NATURÆ THAT INHABIT SOUTHERN AFRICA.

APPENDIX.

.

Order. FERÆ.*

Genus. FELIS.

1. *Felis Leo.* The Lion. Leuew *of the Cape Colonists.* Tao *of the Matabili and Bechuana.*

Adult male about three feet eight inches high at the shoulder, and less at the rump. Extreme length usually about ten feet six inches. Tail three feet long, tufted with black hair at the extremity. Ears round and black. Five toes on the fore feet, four on the hind. Claws retractile, each concealed by a tuft of blackish hair. Hair on the body and extremities short, of a tawny yellow colour, darker on the back, and lighter on the belly. The upper parts of the head, the chin, neck, shoulders, and belly, covered with long shaggy hairs forming a copious mane. The colour varying between tawny, brown, and black, according to the age of the animal. A black spot at each corner of the mouth. Whiskers strong and white. Eyes yellow. Lioness smaller, and without any appearance of a mane.

Inhabits variously; usually found amongst reeds in open plains. Gregarious, and very common.

2. *Felis Leopardus.* The Leopard. Tiger *of the Cape Colonists.*

Adult male about two feet seven inches high at the shoulder, and seven feet six inches in extreme length. Claws retractile. Chin, neck, breast, belly, and insides of extremities, white. The rest varying in different specimens between tawny, fulvous, and reddish brown, irregularly marked with spots of black, which vary greatly in number, size, and appearance, at different ages

* With few deviations, I have followed the classification adopted by Dr. Smith, in his copious "*African Zoology.*" The descriptions have all been drawn up from numerous specimens killed by myself.

S 2

or seasons. Tail about three feet eight inches long, ringed with black. Whiskers strong and white. Eyes yellow.

Female similar, but smaller.

Inhabits thick coverts. Monogamous, or solitary.

3. *Felis Jubata.* The Hunting Leopard. Luipaard *of the Cape Colonists.* 'Nquane *of the Bechuana.*

Size of both sexes about that of a greyhound. Body slender; legs very long; claws semi-retractile. Belly and insides of extremities white; the rest pale yellow, studded with small round black spots, larger on the back and outside of thighs. Hair of the upper part of the neck and withers rather long, forming a small mane. A black stripe on the ears, and another from the corners of the eyes to the angle of the mouth. Tail annulated with black and white bars, and tipped with white.

Inhabits open places. Not common.

Genus. HYÆNA.

4. *Hyæna Crocuta.* The Spotted Hyæna. Wolf *of the Cape Colonists.* Impeese *of the Matabili.*

Height at the shoulder of both sexes about two feet six or eight inches; much less at the rump. Extreme length about five feet ten inches. Feet with four toes; nails not retractile. Head short, and very broad; muzzle and nose black. Lower part of the head, throat, belly, and inner surfaces of the extremities, dingy white. General colour of the other parts fulvous brown, irregularly blotched with circular black spots. Tail sixteen inches; the lower two-thirds of its length furnished with long black hairs, forming a tassel. Hair on the back of the neck and withers long, forming a reversed mane. Both sexes furnished with a glandular pouch below the tail.

Very common everywhere.

5. *Hyæna Fusca.* The Fuscous Hyæna. Strand Wolf *of the Cape Colonists.*

Usual height at the shoulder about two feet four inches; much lower behind. Extreme length about four feet ten inches. Hair very long and shaggy on the upper parts of the neck, back, and tail. General colour reddish grey, brindled with brown and black stripes and spots. Extremities yellowish, with deep black, transverse bands. Tail twelve inches; black, with red hairs towards the tip.

Female similar.

Less abundant than the preceding, but common.

6. *Hyæna Venatica.* The Wild Dog. Wilde Hond *of the Cape Colonists.*

Height at the shoulder under two feet; rather lower behind. Length about four feet three inches. Form slight; muzzle pointed. Ground colour of the hair sandy bay, or ochreous yellow, irregularly blotched and brindled with black and variegated spots of exceedingly irregular shape. Face, nose, and muzzle black. Tail bushy like that of a fox, divided about the middle by a black ring, above which the colour is sandy, and below white.

Hunts in large organized packs.

Order. PACHYDERMATA.

Genus. ELEPHAS.

7. *Elephas Africanus.* The African Elephant. Oliphant *of the Dutch Colonists.* Maclou *of the Matabili.*

Male attains the height of twelve feet at the shoulder; droops behind. Extreme length between eighteen and nineteen feet. Skin black, rough, and nearly destitute of hair. Tail short, tufted at the end. Head rounder, forehead more convex, and ears much larger than in the Asiatic Elephant. The latter extremely flat, reaching to the legs, and overlapping each other on the top of the neck. Five toes on all the feet. Tusks arched; between eight and nine feet in legth, and weighing one hundred pounds. Female upwards of eight feet; usually provided with tusks about four feet in length. Mammæ two, placed between the fore legs.

Solitary or gregarious in large troops. Common in the extensive plains and forests of the interior.

Genus. HIPPOPOTAMUS.

8. *Hippopotamus Amphibius.* The Hippopotamus. Sea Cow, or Zeekoe *of the Cape Colonists.* Imfooboo *of the Matabili and Kafirs.*

Between four and five feet high at the shoulder, and from ten to eleven feet long. Body ponderous and shapeless; legs very short, terminating with four toes. Head thick and square, muzzle broad; eye very small, placed in a prominence; ears small, round, and approximated. The upper incisors and canine teeth greatly developed; the latter forming tusks. Skin rough, hard, and very thick : entirely destitute of hairs, a few scattered bristles on the lips, ears, and tail, excepted. General colour pinkish brown, with freckles on the flanks and belly. Tail twelve inches.

Female smaller. Mammæ two.

Amphibious. Inhabits the rivers and lakes of the interior.

Genus. Sus.

9. *Sus Larvatus.* The Wild Hog. Bosch Vark *of the Cape Colonists.*

Height at the shoulder about two feet four or five inches. Extreme length between five and six feet. Four toes on all the feet, the two middle ones only touching the ground. Nose elongated, and cartilaginous. Canine teeth very strong; those of the upper jaw projecting horizontally, those of the lower, upwards. A tuburculous excrescence, covered with coarse hair, upon the chaffron. Colour dirty brown. Bristles very long, especially on the neck and back. Tail slightly tufted, and upwards of a foot in length. Mammæ twelve.

Gregarious. Inhabits the plains and forests.

Genus. Phascochærus.

10. *Phascochærus Africanus.* The African Boar. Vlacke Vark *of the Cape Colonists.* Ingooloob *of the Matabili.*

Height at the shoulder about two feet six inches. Extreme length, six feet two inches. Colour reddish brown. The top of the head, upper part of the neck, shoulders, and back, covered with long rigid bristles; those on the top of the head diverging like the radii of a circle. Canine teeth very large and long, and directed upwards. Head extremely large, and muzzle very broad. A large fleshy wen behind each eye, and a prominent warty excrescence on each side of the muzzle, between the eye and tusks. Eyes small and sinister. Tail tufted with bristles; twenty inches in length, straight and thin.

Gregarious. Inhabits the plains and forests.

Genus. RHINOCEROS.

11. *Rhinoceros Africanus.* The African Rhinoceros. Rhinaster *of the Cape Colonists.* Chukuroo *of the Matabili.*

Upwards of six feet high at the shoulder, and above thirteen feet in extreme length. Body very robust and clumsy. Legs short and small, each with three toes. Head long and large. Eyes small and lateral. Snout hooked, and resembling that of a tortoise: armed with two horns* on the muzzle, placed one behind the other; the anterior usually from one to two feet long; the posterior generally small, but capricious—in some specimens attaining the same, or nearly the same length. Ears pointed and approximated, placed on the neck. Skin naked; very thick, rugous, and knotty, but without plaits or folds. Colour brownish black. Tail about two feet long, laterally compressed at the end, and furnished with a few bristles.

Female similar, but smaller. Mammæ two. Very common in the interior.

12. *Rhinoceros Sinusus.* The White Rhinoceros. Witte Rhinaster *of the Cape Colonists.* Chicore *of the Mat-l*'w *und Bechuana.*

Six feet six or eight inches high at the shoulder, and above fourteen in extreme length. Head four feet long. Muzzle truncated, upwards of eighteen inches in breadth; furnished with two horns placed one behind the other as in the last species; the anterior robust at the base, tapering, and about three feet in length; the posterior a mere excrescence, five or six inches long. Ears pointed and approximated, placed on the neck. A square hump immediately behind them. Eyes very diminutive and lateral. Legs short and straight, terminating in three toes. Tail about two feet long, compressed and bristled at the extremity. Hide very rough and knotty, extremely thick, with folds and plaits about the neck. Colour varying; usually dirty brownish white.

Female similar, but smaller. Mammæ two. Very common in the interior, after passing Kurrichane.

* The horns of no two specimens of this animal that came under my observation were exactly the same. Disease or accident not unfrequently renders the anterior horn the shorter of the two.

Genus. Equus.

13. *Equus Zebra.*   The Zebra.   Wilde Paard *of the Cape Colonists.*

About four feet high at the shoulder, and eight feet two inches in extreme length. Shape light and symmetrical. Legs very slender. Feet small, terminating in a solid hoof. Head light and bony. Ears and tail asinine; the latter blackish, about sixteen inches long, and tufted at the extremity. Ground colour of the hair white. The whole of the body, neck, head, and legs, covered with narrow black bands, placed wider or closer together; the upper ones connected with the dorsal line, but not extending over the belly, or inside of thighs. Mane erect and bushy, alternately banded white and black. Two transverse black bands on the ears. Brown stripes on the face terminating in a bay nose. A bare spot a little above the knee on all four of the legs.

Female with two inguinal mammæ.

Gregarious. Found within the Cape Colony. Inhabits mountainous regions only.

14. *Equus Burchellii.*   Burchell's Zebra. Bonti Quagga *of the Cape Colonists.*   Peechey *of the Bechuana and Matabili.*

Four feet six inches high at the shoulder, and eight feet six inches in extreme length. Body round. Legs robust. Crest arched and surmounted by a standing mane, two inches high, banded, black and white. Ears and tail equine; the latter thirty-five inches long, flowing and white. Muzzle black. General ground colour of the head, neck, and body, sienna, capriciously banded with black and deep brown transverse stripes forming various figures, and unconnected with the dorsal line, which widens towards the croup. Belly and legs pure white. Bare spots above the knees on the inside.

Female an udder with four mammæ.

Inhabits the plains of the interior beyond the Gareep in immense herds.

15. *Equus Quagga.*   The Quagga.   Quagga *of the Cape Colonists.*

About the height of Burchell's Zebra, but of a more robust form. Ears and tail equine, as in the preceding; the former

marked with two irregular black bands. Crest very high, surmounted by a standing mane banded alternately brown and
white. Colour of the head, neck, and upper parts of the body,
reddish brown, irregularly banded and marked with dark brown
stripes, stronger on the head and neck, and gradually becoming
fainter until lost behind the shoulder. Dorsal line broad; belly,
legs, and tail, white.

Still found within the Cape Colony. Inhabits the open plains
south of the Vaal River in immense herds.

Order. RUMINANTIA.

Genus. CAMELOPARDALIS.

16. *Camelopardalis Giraffa.* The Giraffe. Kameel *of the Cape
Colonists.* Intootla *of the Matabili.*

In stature the tallest of mammiferous animals. Adult male
twelve feet high at the shoulder, and eighteen at the crown of
the head. Legs slender, seven feet in length. Feet terminating
in a divided hoof. No succentorial hoofs. Body short. Withers
elevated, a scanty, upright, rufous mane extending along the
whole neck. Back oblique. Tail thirty-four inches long, terminating in a tuft of bristly black hair about the same length,
which reaches to the hocks. Head light and tapering, thirty-
four inches long; provided with osseous penduncles (common
to both sexes) covered with a hairy skin, and terminating in a
tuft of black hair. A tuberculum on the chaffron. No muzzle.
Upper lip entire. Eyes large and melting. No lachrymary
sinus. Ears pure white, and ample. Callosity on the breast.
Tongue very long, pointed, and flexible. General colour deep
sienna, with large angular ferruginous spots, variously disposed
over the whole; each spot darker in the centre. Belly and
cheeks white, with dark blotches.

Female sixteen or seventeen feet in height at the crown, of a
dirty white colour, with pale ferruginous spots as in the male.
Mammæ four.

Gregarious in small troops. Inhabits the great plains of the
interior.

Genus. Bos.

17. *Bubulus Caffer.* The Cape Buffalo. Buffel *of the Cape Colonists.* 'Neast *of the Matabili.* Bokolokolo *of the Bechuana.*

Adult male about five feet six inches high at the shoulder, and upwards of twelve feet in extreme length. Structure very powerful. Body ponderous. Neck short. Breast and shoulder deep, and slightly dewlapped. Back straight and hunchless. Limbs short and solid, terminating in a divided hoof, which is nearly circular. Succentorial hoofs very long. Tail three feet long, terminating in a tuft of coarse black hair, which reaches below the hocks. Head short, and small in proportion to the animal's bulk. Eyes small and sinister, overshadowed by rough and ponderous dark coloured horns, nearly in contact at the base, spreading horizontally, and turned upwards and inwards at the tips, which measure about four feet between. Hide bluish black, and naked, with exception of a few distichous bristles. No lachrymary sinus. Muzzle bovine, square, and naked.

Female similar, but smaller, with smaller and more vertically disposed horns. An udder with four mammæ.

Still found within the Colony. Inhabits the plains and forests of the interior in large herds.

Genus. CATOBLEPAS.

18. *Catoblepas Gnoo.* The Gnoo. Wilde Beest *of the Cape Colonists.* Gnoo *of the Hottentots.* Impatoomo *of the Matabili.*

Adult male upwards of four feet high at the shoulder, nine feet in extreme length. General contour very muscular, and exhibiting great energy. Head large and square. Muzzle large, spread out, and flattened, with narrow linear nostrils. Above the muzzle is situated a conspicuous tuft of black bristling hairs, radiating laterally, and resembling a blacking brush. A tuft of similar hair beneath each eye, concealing a gland which distils a viscous humour. Eye wild and fiery. Ears short and pointed. White bristles surrounding the eye, like the radii of a circle. Numerous white bristles on the upper lip. Horns broad, and approximated at the base; furrowed upon the summit of the head; scarcely advancing from the skull, they taper out sideways over the eyes, and uncinate up into a pointed hook, sweeping with a regular curve, and producing a sinister and suspicious aspect. Shoulder deep. Neck thick, and much arched. Body round. A pillow of fat on either haunch. Legs slender and long. A full vertical mane on the neck, composed of wiry white hairs. A bushy black beard on the under jaw and throat; and a bush of full black hair between the fore legs, extending some distance along the belly. Tail equine, white, and reaching to the ground. General colour of the hair deep brown. Hoofs pointed, blue-black.

Female similar, but slighter. Base of horns less approximated. An udder with four mammæ.

Very gregarious. Abundant on the plains south of the Vaal River.

19. *Catoblepas Gorgon.* The Brindled Gnoo. Blauw Wilde Beest *of the Cape Colonists.* Kokoon *of the Bechuana and Matabili.*

Adult male about four feet six inches high at the shoulder, and nine feet eight inches in extreme length. Withers very elevated. Neck not arched. Nose aquiline, and covered with coarse black hair. Muzzle broad and square: bare, with large hanging nostrils. Horns black, placed horizontally on the head; the points turned upwards, and then acutely inwards; a few rugosities at the base. A long flowing mane on the neck, extending beyond the withers. Chin covered with a copious bristly black beard, descending down the dewlap to the breast. Tail black, flowing, and reaching to the heels. Ears small and pointed. Eyes very high in the head. A large glandulous naked spot, of an oblong form, below each eye, distilling a viscous humour. Legs slender. General colour dirty dun, or sepia grey, variegated with obscure streaks or brindles. Four or five cross streaks on each arm.

Female precisely similar, but on a smaller scale.

Gregarious. Inhabits the plains beyond the Orange River in vast herds.

Genus. DAMALIS.

20. *Boselaphus Oreas.** The Impoofo. Eland *of the Cape Colonists.* Impoofo, or Pooffo *of the Bechuana and Matabili.*

Adult male six feet six inches high at the shoulder, and about twelve in extreme length. Facial line straight. Muzzle broad. Forehead square, covered with a cluster of strong wiry brown hair, margined on either side by a yellow streak, commencing above the eyes, and nearly meeting half way down the face. Horns placed on the summits of the frontals; about two feet long, massy, and nearly straight, with a ponderous ridge ascending in a spiral direction nearly to the tips. Proportions of the body like those of a bull. Neck very thick. Shoulders very deep. Larynx very prominent. A broad deep dewlap, fringed with long wiry brown hair, descending to the knees. A crest of bristles from the forehead, passing upwards and recurrent along the edge of the neck. Legs short. Hind quarters very large. Tail two feet three or four inches long, with a large tuft of coarse brown hair. Hide black. Hair very short. General colour rufous dun, or ashy grey tinged with ochre. A muzzle. No suborbital sinus.

Female smaller and slighter, with longer and more slender horns. No dewlap, but a tuft of hair on the larynx. Colour redder. An udder with four mammæ.

Gregarious. Inhabits the open plains of the interior in vast herds.

21. *Strepsiceros Koodoo.* The Koodoo. Eechlongole *of the Matabili.*

Adult male upwards of five feet high at the shoulder; above nine feet in extreme length. Horns bulky and compressed, having an anterior ridge, which forms with them two complete spiral circles: the tips turned outwards and forwards; length about three feet; colour brown; the tips black with a white point. Chaffron straight. Muzzle very broad. Ears oblique, very broad, and pointed at the tips, of a light brown colour. Neck thick. Withers elevated. Dewlap anteriorly square. Forehead black. A white line passing over the orbits unites on

---

* The *Bastard Eland* of the Cape Colonists (*Boselaphus Canna*), is doubtless identical with *B. Oreas*, and cannot be considered a distinct species.

the chaffron.   Three white spots on either cheek below the eye. Chin white bearded.   A long fringe of variegated black and white hair on the dewlap, and a standing mane on the neck and withers.   General colour of the hair a buff-grey or sky-blue, marked with a white line along the spine, and intersected by five or six transverse lines running downwards to the belly, and four more over the croup.   Buttocks white.   Legs rufous below the knees.   Tail two feet long, rufous, edged with white, tapering to a point, and black at the tip.   No suborbital sinus.   An entire moist muzzle.

Female slighter, hornless, and with fewer and fainter white markings.   Has an udder with four mammæ.

Gregarious.   Still found within the Colony.   Inhabits thickets and wooded hills.

22.   *Acronotus Caama.*   The Caama.   Hartebeest *of the Cape Colonist.*   Intoosel *of the Matabili.*   Caama *of the Bechuana.*

Adult male about five feet high at the withers, and nine in extreme length.   Shoulders very elevated, and head very large and long.   The whole animal made up of triangles.   Horns placed upon a high ridge above the frontals, very close at the base; robust, divergent, and again approximating so as to form a lozenge, with double flexures strongly pronounced, turned forwards, and the points backwards, with several prominent knots on the anterior surface.   A black spot at their base, above the forehead, continued behind, and terminating in front of the ears. A black streak down the nose, commencing below the eyes, and terminating at the nostrils.   Chin black.   A narrow black stripe down the back of the neck.   A black streak on the fore leg commencing about mid shoulder; another down the hind leg commencing about the middle of the buttock.   A triangular spot of white immediately above on each buttock, and a white spot above each eye.   Tail reaching to the hocks, covered with posteriorly directed black hair.   General colour bright sienna, with a deep red cast.   A half muzzle.   No suborbital sinus, but a mucous discharge.   Eyes fiery red.

Female similar, but smaller, with more slender horns. Mammæ two.

Inhabits the plains of the interior beyond the Orange River, in immense herds.

23. *Acronotus Lunata.* The Sassayby. Bastard Hartebeest *of the Cape Colonists.* Sassabe *of the Matabili and Bechuana.*

Adult male four feet six inches high at the shoulder, four feet at the croup. Eight feet two inches in extreme length. Horns robust, about twelve inches long, placed on the summit of the frontals, turning outwards, and forming two crescents with the points inwards; marked with from twelve to fifteen incomplete annuli. Neck short. Body rather bulky. Legs slender. Withers very elevated. Head long, narrow, and shapeless. Facial line strait. A dark streak from between the horns to the nose. Ears fawn colour, nine inches long. General colour deep blackish purple-brown above, fulvous beneath. A dab of slate colour extends from the middle of the shoulder to the knee; and another from the middle of the flank to the hock, outside. A band of the same colour passes across the inside of both fore and hind legs, upon a fulvous ground. Lower part of the legs, deep fulvous. Tail twenty-two inches long, rufous, and covered with posteriorly directed black hair. Rump fawn colour. Eyes fiery red. A half muzzle, and very indistinct lachrymary perforation.

Female precisely similar, but smaller, with more slender horns. Mammæ two.

Gregarious. Inhabits the country of the Bechuana in considerable herds.

Genus. ANTILOPE.

24. *Aigocerus Harrisi.* The Sable Antelope. *Undescribed by Naturalists. Unknown to the Matabili.*

Adult male four feet six inches high at the shoulder; nearly nine feet in extreme length. Horns thirty-seven inches over the curve; placed immediately above the eyes; flat, slender, sub-erect, and then strongly bent back scimitarwise; at first gradually diverging, and then running parallel to each other; three-fourths annulated with about thirty strongly pronounced incomplete rings, more rigid on the edges, but chiefly lost on the outside of the horn; the remaining one-fourth, smooth, round, slender, and pointed. Head somewhat attenuated towards the muzzle, and compressed laterally. Carcase robust. Withers elevated. Neck broad and flat. Hoofs black, obtuse, and rather short. Hair close and smooth. General colour of the coat, intense glossy black, with an occasional cast of deep chesnut. A white streak commencing above each eye continued by a pencil of long hairs covering the place of the suborbital pouch (of which cavity no trace is to be found), and then running down the side of the nose to the muzzle, which is entirely white; the same colour pervading the throat and one-half of the cheek. Ears ten inches long; narrow, tapering, and pointed; white within, lively chesnut without, with black pencilled tips. A broad half-crescent of deeper chesnut at the base of each ear, behind. A small entire sharp black muzzle. A copious standing black mane, somewhat inclined forwards, five and a half inches high, extending from between the ears to the middle of the back. Hair of the throat and neck longer than that of the body Belly, buttocks, and inside of thighs, pure white. A longitudinal dusky white stripe behind each arm. Fore legs jet black inside and out, with a tinge of chesnut on and below the knees. Hind legs black, with a lively chesnut patch at and below the hock. Tail black; long hair skirting the posterior edge, terminating in a tuft which extends below the hocks.

Female smaller than the male, with smaller but similarly shaped horns. Colour deep chesnut brown, verging upon black.

Very rare. Gregarious in small families. Inhabits the great mountain range which threads the eastern portion of the Matabili country.

25. *Aigocerus Equina.*[*] The Roan Antelope. Bastard Gemsbok *of the Cape Colonists.* Etak *of the Matabili.*

Adult male about five feet high at the shoulder, and nine in extreme length. Horns very robust, about two feet in length, strongly bent back scimitarwise, and nearly parallel; with from twenty-five to thirty prominent rings, more remote from the orbits, and extending to within about four inches of the points. Face and head hoary black, with a large white streak before and behind each eye, formed of a pencil of long hairs. A white spot between the horns, and a white muzzle. Ears of

---

[*] If the *Blue Antelope* (*Aigocerus Leucophœa*) ever did exist, it is now extinct. I am disposed to regard it as a variety of the Roan Antelope, and Daniell's *Takhaitze* (*A. Barbata*) is probably so too.

asinine dimensions, fourteen inches long, pointed, and the tips bent back very eccentrically. Tail descending to the hocks, slender black, and tufted. Hair coarse, loose, and undulating; mixed red and white, forming a roan. Beneath the throat longer and whiter. Neck furnished with a stiff upright mane, terminating at the withers. A half-muzzle. No suborbital sinus.

Female similar, but hornless. Mammæ two. Gregarious in small families or herds, but rare. Inhabits the elevated ridges near the source of the Vaal River.

26. *Aigocerus Ellipsiprymnus.* The Water Buck. Phitomok *of the Matabili.*

Adult male four feet six inches high; nearly nine feet in extreme length. Horns upwards of thirty inches; upright, curved forwards and sometimes inwards, but always diverging; of a whitish green colour; the first third slightly compressed; the other two-thirds nearly cylindrical; very strongly annulated along the front and outside to within six inches of the points. Face deep brown. Forehead, base of horns, and behind the eyes, rufous. A white patch on the throat. Under lip and muzzle white. A white streak before each eye, and a white elliptical band encircling the tail. Ears round and large; white inside, brown without. General colour of the hair greyish brown; in texture coarse, and resembling split whalebone; shorter on the body, but on the neck long and reversed, having the semblance of a mane. Hide black. Legs dark brown. Tail brown and tufted, not quite reaching to the hocks. A muzzle. No suborbital indent.

Female precisely similar, but hornless. Mammæ two.

Gregarious. Found only on the banks of rivers near the Tropic, the Limpopo and Mariqua, especially.

27. *Oryx Capensis.* The South African Oryx. Gemsbok *of the Cape Colonists.* Kookaam *of the Matabili and Bechuana.*

Adult male three feet ten inches high at the shoulder; ten feet in extreme length. Horns upwards of three feet long; straight, or very slightly bent; horizontal, divergent, and tapering to the points; the lower part annulated with from twenty-five to thirty rings. Eyes high in the head. Black space between the base of the horns descending in a streak down the forehead; another passing through the eyes to the corner of the mouth, connected by a third which runs round the head over the nose; a fourth passes from the base of the ears under the throat completing the appearance of a head-stall; the rest of the head white. Ears round; white with black edging. General colour of the coat vinous buff. The breast, belly, and extremities, white. A tuft of bristly black hair on the larynx, and the latter edged with black. A mane reversed; and a black list stripe from the nape of the neck along the back, widening angularly over the croup, and terminating in a bushy black tail, three feet long, which sweeps the ground. A broad black bar across the elbow, passing along the flank, and ending in a wide angular space on the thigh above the hocks; and a black spot upon each leg between the knee and fetlock. Nose ovine. No suborbital sinus.

Female similar, with longer horns. An udder with two mammæ.

Gregarious. Principally found in the Karroo, or in the open plains of Namaqua land.

28. *Gazella Euchore.* The Spring Buck. Spring-bok *of the Cape Colonists.* Tsepe *of the Matabili and Bechuana.*

Adult male about two feet eight inches high at the shoulder, and two feet ten at the croup. Extreme length about four feet ten inches. Head and face white, resembling a lamb's. Horns black, lyrate, robust, with about twenty complete rings; the tips turned inwards, and generally either forward or backwards. General colour of the hair yellow dun, with a white croup consisting of long hairs which can be erected or depressed at pleasure. Belly, throat, and inside of limbs, white, separated from the dun by a broad rich chesnut band along the flanks; another along the edges of the folds of the croup; and a streak from the back of the horns through the eyes to the nose. A truly ovine nose. Small indistinct lachrymary sinus. Ears long, attenuated, and dirty white. Eyes very large, dark, and expressive. Tail eight inches long; white, with a tuft of posteriorly directed black hairs.

Female similar, but smaller, with very slender horns, and few indistinct annuli. Mammæ two.

Scattered over the plains in countless herds.

29. *Gazella Albifrons.* The White-faced Antelope. Bles-bok *of the Cape Colonists.* Nunni *of the Bechuana.*

Adult male three feet eight inches high at the shoulder, and six feet three inches in extreme length. Head long and narrow. Muzzle broad. Horns from twelve to fifteen inches in length, white, very robust at the base; divergent, with ten or twelve semi-annuli on the anterior side. A patch of chocolate-coloured hair at the base of the horns, divided by a narrow white streak, which suddenly widens between the eyes to the whole breadth of the face, down which it passes to the nose. Ears rather long and white. Sides of the head and neck deep purple chocolate. The back and shoulders hoary bluish-white, as if glazed. Flanks and loins brown. Belly white. Legs brown outside, white within. Croup and chest rufous. Tail reaching to the hocks; seventeen inches long, with much posteriorly directed brown and white hair. Linear nostrils. Very indistinct muzzle. Small circular lachrymary perforation.

Female precisely similar, but slighter, less vividly coloured, and with more slender horns. Mammæ two.

Very gregarious. Inhabits the plains south of the Vaal River in immense herds.

30. *Gazella Pygarga.* The Pied Antelope. Bonte-bok *of the Cape Colonists.*

Rather larger than the preceding. Head long, narrow, and shapeless, with a very broad muzzle. Horns fifteen inches long; black, divergent, erect, very robust at base, with ten or twelve incomplete annuli, broken in the middle and striated between. Forehead and face white, as in the Bles-bok. Ears long and reddish. Sides of the head, neck, and flanks, deep purple brown. Back bluish lilac, as if glazed. Legs perfectly white from the knees and hocks downwards. Belly and inside of thighs white, and a large white patch on the croup. Tail reaching to the hocks; white above, with a tuft of posteriorly directed black hairs. Small detached lachrymary perforation. Linear nostrils. Very indistinct muzzle.

Female precisely similar, but on a slighter scale, with more slender horns. Mammæ two.

Gregarious. Still found in Zoetendal's V'ley, near Cape L'Agulhas. Common in the interior.

31. *Antilope Melampus.* The Pallah. Rooye-bok *of the Cape Colonists.* Pallah *of the Matabili and Bechuana.*

Adult male about three feet three or four inches high at the shoulder, and six in extreme length. Very high on the legs. Horns about twenty inches in length, ascending obliquely upwards, outwards, and backwards; and midway at an obtuse angle, obliquely inwards and forwards; black, coarsely annulated and striated between for about two-thirds of their length; the tips smooth. Ears round, seven inches long, tipped with black. Tail thirteen inches long; pointed white, with a dark brown streak down the middle. Colour of the head, neck, and upper part of the body deep fulvous. Sides and hinder parts yellow dun. Belly white. A dark brown streak down each buttock. A dark spot in place of spurious hoofs, which do not occur in this species. A large cushion of brown hair between the hock and fetlock. A white spot before each eye. A dark spot between the horns. No trace of a suborbital sinus. Small bare space for a muzzle.

Female similar, but hornless. Eye very large, soft, and full. Mammæ two.

Gregarious in small families or herds. Inhabits the banks of rivers chiefly in the Bechuana country.

32. *Tragelaphus Sylvatica.* The Bush Buck. Bosch-bok *of the Cape Colonists.*

Adult male about two feet eight inches high, and five feet two inches long. Form elegant; somewhat receding from the typical structure of true Antelopes, and assuming that of the goat. Horns about twelve inches long; erect, spiral, and sublyrate; marked with an absolete ridge in front, and one in rear; black, and closely wrinkled at the base; points a little bent forward. General colour brilliant chesnut, black above, marked with a narrow white streak along the spine; two white spots on each cheek; several on the flanks, and two on each fetlock. Inside of thighs and chin white. Forehead deep sienna. A broad naked black band encircling the neck as if worn off by a collar. Tail nine inches long; brown above, white beneath. Ears large and round. Moist naked muzzle. No lachrymary opening.

Female similar, but without horns. Mammæ four.

Monogamous or solitary. Inhabits the forests on the sea coast.

33. *Redunca Eleotragus.* The Reit Buck. Reit-bok *of the Cape Colonists.* Inghalla *of the Matabili.*

Adult male about two feet ten inches high at the shoulder, and four feet ten inches long. Horns ten or twelve inches long; advanced beyond the plane of the face; divergent, and regularly curved with the points forward; wrinkled at the base, and annulated with obsolete rings in the middle. Ears six inches. Tail ten inches long. General colour of the coat ashy grey, tinged with ochre, beneath white; hair of the throat white and flowing. A small muzzle, and imperfect suborbital opening.

Female similar, but smaller, and hornless. Mammæ four.

Gregarious in small families, or solitary. Resides variously, principally among reeds.

34. *Redunca Lalandii.* The Nagor. Rooye Rhee-bok *of the Cape Colonists.*

Adult male two feet eight inches high at the shoulder, and five feet in length. Horns about six inches long, approximating at base, sub-erect, nearly parallel, and hooked forward at the point, with five or six semi-annuli striated between. Legs, head, and neck, tawny. Chin and lower parts white. Body fulvous brown, with a cast of purple. The hair long, loose, and whirling in various directions. Tail ten inches, grey, with long white hair along the edges. Muzzle small. Suborbital opening barely perceptible.

Female similar, but hornless. Mammæ four. Found amongst rocks in small troops.

35. *Redunca Capreolus.* The Rhee Buck. Rhee-bok *of the Cape Colonists.* Peeli *of the Bechuana and Matabili.*

Adult male two feet five inches at the shoulder, and about five feet in length. Body very slender. Neck long. Head small, and ears pointed. Horns about nine inches in length; straight, slender, vertical, and pointed, with from ten to fifteen rings at the base. Hair very soft and villous, resembling wool. General colour whitish grey, with a cast of buff; beneath white. Tail about five inches; grey, tipped with white.

Muzzle naked and moist. Suborbital perforation low down, but distinct.

Female similar, but smaller, without horns. Mammæ four.

Found within the Colony in small troops, amongst hills and rocks.

36. *Redunca Scoparia.* The Ourebi. Ditto *of the Cape Colonists.* Subokoo *of the Matabili.*

Less than two feet high at the shoulder, and about four in extreme length. Very slight. Horns four or five inches long; black, round, and nearly vertical: wrinkled at the base, with four or five annuli in the middle. A white arch above the eyes. Tail short and black. General colour pale tawny; beneath white; long white hair under the throat; fulvous tufts below the knees. A small muzzle. Lachrymal opening well developed.

Female similar, but smaller, and hornless. Mammæ four.

Found in grassy plains, usually in pairs.

37. *Oreotragus Saltatrix.* The Klipspringer. Ditto *of the Cape Colonists.*

Adult male about twenty-two inches high at the shoulder, and thirty-six in extreme length. Tail three inches long. Form square and robust. Head short and broad. Horns about four inches long; round, distant, vertical, but slightly inclined forwards; obscurely wrinkled at the base, and annulated in the middle. Legs robust. Pasterns very rigid. Each hoof subdivided into two segments, and jagged at the edges, so as to give it the power of adhering to the steep sides of smooth rocks. Fur very thick and long; hard, brittle, and spirally twisted; ashy at base, brown in the middle, yellow at the tips, forming an agreeable olive. Suborbital sinus conspicuous. Muzzle pointed and small.

Female hornless, in other respects resembling the male. Mammæ two.

Common in the Colony. Inhabits rocks and precipices, in pairs.

38. *Tragulus Rupestris.** The Steenbuck. Steenbok *of the Cape Colonists.* Eoolab *of the Matabili.*

About twenty inches high at the shoulder, twenty-two at the croup, and thirty-five in length. Head short and oval. Snout pointed. Muzzle black, ending in a point upon the ridge of the nose. Horns vertical, parallel, and nearly straight; four inches in length, slender, round, and pointed, with one or two rudiments of wrinkles at the base. Ears large, round, and open. Tail barely an inch long, having the appearance of a stump, beyond which the hair does not protrude. General colour rufous, with occasionally a cast of brown or crimson. Belly white. Groin naked and black. No accessory hoofs. Pasterns very rigid. A detached suborbital sinus.

Female similar, but without horns. Mammæ four.

Monogamous or solitary. Inhabits the bushes of high ground. Common in the Colony.

39. *Tragulus Melanotis.* The Grysbok. Ditto *of the Cape Colonists.*

Adult male from twenty to twenty-two inches high at the shoulder, and about thirty-six in length. Head very broad and short. Snout obtusely pointed. Horns about three and a half inches long; smooth, round, slender, and vertical, or slightly inclining forwards. Ears round, open, and broad. Colour deep chocolate red, intermixed with numerous single white hairs; beneath rufous. A black horse-shoe on the forehead. Detached suborbital sinus, and small muzzle.

Female similar, but hornless. Mammæ two.

Monogamous or solitary. Common in the Colony, among the wooded tracts along the sea-coast.

40. *Cephalopus Mergens.*† The Duïker. Duikerbok *of the Cape Colonists.* Impoon *of the Matabili.*

Adult male about two feet high at the shoulder, and three feet eight inches in extreme length. Horns four inches long,

* The *Vlachte Steenbok* (Tragulus Rufescens), and the *Bleekbok* (T. Pedio-tragus) appear to be merely varieties of this Antelope, and not distinct species.

† *Cephalopus Burchellii* would appear to be a variety only of this species, of which no two specimens are exactly alike.

approximated, somewhat reclining, bending outwards, with a longitudinal ridge on the front traversing four or five annuli on the middle, but not traversing the wrinkles of the base. Forehead covered with a patch of long bright fulvous hair. A dark streak on the chaffron. Three dark striæ on each ear inside. A dark streak down the front of the legs, terminating in a black fetlock, as if booted. Colour various; usually cinereous olive above, and white beneath. Tail eight inches long, black, tipped with white. Spurious hoofs scarcely developed. A long suborbital slit down the side of the face, and a small naked muzzle.

Female similar, with very small horns, completely concealed by long rufous hair. Mammæ four.

Solitary or Monogamous. Common in the Colony, especially along the coast, among bushes.

41. *Cephalopus Cærula.* The Slate-coloured Antelope. Blauw-bok and Kleenebok *of the Cape Colonists.*

Adult male about fifteen inches high, and twenty-eight inches long. Head very long and pointed, with a spacious muzzle, resembling a rat's both in shape and expression. A bare spot round the eyes. Ears short and round, like a rat's. Horns black, conical, reclined, slightly turned inwards and forwards, two inches in length, closely and strongly annulated. General colour dull brownish, buff, or mouse colour, above; beneath whitish. Legs and rump rufous. Tail two inches long, dark above, white beneath. No suborbital sinus, but a suborbital sack lower down, marked by a lengthened streak upon the cheek.

Female similar, but hornless, and more diminutive.

Solitary. Inhabits the forests along the sea-coast.

Lightning Source UK Ltd.
Milton Keynes UK
UKOW022055030613

211709UK00005B/74/P